EMPATHY

Empathy is one of the most talked about and widely studied concepts of recent years. Some argue it can help create a more just society, improve medical care, and even avert global catastrophe. Others object that it is morally problematic. Who is right? And what is empathy anyway? Is it a way of feeling with others, or is it simply feeling sorry for them? Is it a form of knowledge? What is its evolutionary origin?

In this thorough and clearly written introduction to the philosophy of empathy, Heidi Maibom explores these questions and more, examining the following topics:

- The nature of empathy and key themes in the literature
- Empathy as a way of understanding others, particularly 'simulation theory' and 'perspective taking'
- Empathy, emotional contagion, and sympathy
- Empathy's role in moral understanding or motivation
- Empathy and art appreciation, with examples from film, music, and fiction
- Empathy and mental disorder, such as psychopathy and autism.

Including chapter summaries, annotated further reading, and a glossary, *Empathy* is an excellent resource for students of philosophy of mind, psychology, and cognitive science, as well as for those studying related subjects such as art, literature, and politics.

Heidi L. Maibom is Professor of Philosophy at University of Cincinnati, USA. She is editor of *The Routledge Handbook of Philosophy of Empathy* (2017) and *Empathy and Morality* (2014), and co-editor of *Neurofeminism* with R. Bluhm and A.J. Jacobsen (2012). She is currently writing a book on perspective taking.

NEW PROBLEMS OF PHILOSOPHY
Series Editor: José Luis Bermúdez

"*New Problems of Philosophy* is developing a most impressive line-up of topical volumes aimed at graduate and upper-level undergraduate students in philosophy and at others with interests in cutting edge philosophical work. Series authors are players in their respective fields and notably adept at synthesizing and explaining intricate topics fairly and comprehensively."

— *John Heil, Monash University, Australia, and*
Washington University in St. Louis, USA

"This is an outstanding collection of volumes. The topics are well chosen and the authors are outstanding. They will be fine texts in a wide range of courses."
— *Stephen Stich, Rutgers University, USA*

The *New Problems of Philosophy* series provides accessible and engaging surveys of the most important problems in contemporary philosophy. Each book examines either a topic or theme that has emerged on the philosophical landscape in recent years, or a longstanding problem refreshed in light of recent work in philosophy and related disciplines. Clearly explaining the nature of the problem at hand and assessing attempts to answer it, books in the series are excellent starting points for undergraduate and graduate students wishing to study a single topic in depth. They will also be essential reading for professional philosophers. Additional features include chapter summaries, further reading and a glossary of technical terms.

Abstract Entities
Sam Cowling

Embodied Cognition, Second Edition
Lawrence Shapiro

Self-Deception
Eric Funkhouser

Relativism
Maria Baghramian and Annalisa Coliva

Empathy
Heidi Maibom

For more information about this series, please visit: https://www.routledge.com/New-Problems-of-Philosophy/book-series/NPOP

EMPATHY

Heidi L. Maibom

Routledge
Taylor & Francis Group

LONDON AND NEW YORK

First published
by Routledge
2 Park Square, Milton Park, Abingdon, Oxon OX14 4RN

and by Routledge
52 Vanderbilt Avenue, New York, NY 10017

Routledge is an imprint of the Taylor & Francis Group, an informa business

The right of Heidi Maibom to be identified as author of this work
has been asserted by them in accordance with sections 77 and 78
of the Copyright, Designs and Patents Act 1988.

First published 2020

© 2020 Heidi Maibom

British Library Cataloguing-in-Publication Data
A catalogue record for this book is available from the British Library

Library of Congress Cataloging-in-Publication Data
Names: Maibom, Heidi Lene, 1969- author.
Title: Empathy / Heidi Maibom.
Description: Abingdon, Oxon ; New York, NY : Routledge, 2020. |
Series: New problems of philosophy | Includes bibliographical
references and index.
Identifiers: LCCN 2019045076 (print) | LCCN 2019045077 (ebook) |
ISBN 9780415790215 (hbk) | ISBN 9780415790222 (pbk) |
ISBN 9781315213477 (ebk)
Subjects: LCSH: Empathy.
Classification: LCC BF575.E55 M34 2020 (print) |
LCC BF575.E55 (ebook) | DDC 152.4/1--dc23
LC record available at https://lccn.loc.gov/2019045076
LC ebook record available at https://lccn.loc.gov/2019045077

ISBN: 978-0-415-79021-5 (hbk)
ISBN: 978-0-415-79022-2 (pbk)
ISBN: 978-1-315-21347-7 (ebk)

Typeset in Joanna and Scala Sans
by Taylor & Francis Books

CONTENTS

ACKNOWLEDGMENTS

This book has traveled with me to Portugal, Denmark, and Croatia, even though it was initially conceived of in the United States. I am grateful to my hosts and the opportunities for work that they afforded me. In addition, Jenefer Robinson gave me much valued feedback on some of the ideas in Chapter 5, and my graduate student, Kyle Furlane, read through the whole manuscript and provided valuable comments. Thanks to both.

I would also like to thank the anonymous reviewers of this book, as well as Crosby, and Tony Bruce and Adam Johnson of Routledge, who patiently waited for me to complete the book.

INTRODUCTION

Empathy is a hot topic. People write books about its potential for social change, its moral importance, its moral irrelevance, how children can't do without it, how we can't have justice without it, and even about it being the only thing that stands between us and annihilation. Clearly, the power of empathy has captured the public imagination. Although rather extravagant claims are sometimes made about it, empathy clearly plays a pivotal social role. What is harder to pin down, however, is what, precisely, empathy is and what it does.

Philosophers and psychologists enjoy bemoaning the many different uses of the term 'empathy.' And they are not wrong to point out that the term is often used in quite different ways. But what they often fail to consider are the commonalities. Empathy is an attitude towards others of taking them in, of being open to their emotions and thoughts, and of being interested in understanding them. Empathy is essentially about the other but in a way that is closely entangled with the personal. It is therefore hardly surprising to find that people believe that it will help us overcome the many limits that an egocentric orientation towards the natural and social world has.

Nonetheless, many misunderstandings proliferate about empathy, and they often divide along political lines. Conservatives are more likely to be mistrustful of empathy, which they regard as being in potential conflict with justice, and liberals tend to think it is the bedrock of morality. Jonathan Haidt has played a significant role in revealing this underlying ideological difference. But it is clear in public debate as well. Take, for instance, the famous debacle that arose from former president Obama's statement that he was looking for empathy in his new Supreme Court justice. As he said, "[w]e need somebody who's got the heart, the empathy, to recognize what it's like to be a young teenage mom, the empathy to understand what it's like to be poor or African-American or gay or disabled or old" (*The Weekly Standard*, March 17, 2008).

Obama's statement was widely interpreted as suggesting that judges should bend the rule of law to fit their intuition in particular cases, or even circumvent justice altogether. In her confirmation hearing, Sotomayor found it necessary to stress that she believed judges had to decide cases on facts and the law and not on personal or subjective considerations. A *New York Times* article written a year later described the word 'empathy' as radioactive. In defense of Obama, Pamela Karlan of Stanford Law School said that people are confused about the meaning of the word 'empathy,' often confusing it with sympathy. Empathy, she said, is the ability to imagine oneself in the position of another, whereas sympathy is sharing the feelings of another to the point of compassion or pity. But Karlan's construal is itself debatable, as we shall see. She was right, however, that what Obama seemed to have in mind was not pity but the ability to take up the point of view of others so as to fully understand their position and the effects on their lives that particular judgments would have.

I should note, however, that my Lyft driver today gave me a perfect definition of affective empathy, as I describe it in this book, and then went on to contrast and compare empathy and sympathy. I found it rather poignant that he should be more discerning in his understanding than many politicians. But I digress.

A new skepticism about empathy is now flourishing in public life with Bloom's trenchant critique of the use of empathy in ethics. And there has been no shortage of people happy to line up and point fingers at the negative effects empathizing can have. Reading through the debate, it quickly becomes clear that these criticisms present a very partial picture. They often rely on data concerning a range of different interpersonal phenomena and not simply feeling what someone else is feeling. When one engages in this debate, therefore, it can be very hard to get one's bearings. The good news is that help is at hand! You have already taken the first step in picking up this book.

The first thing you will be presented with—in Chapter 1—is a brief discussion of the major senses in which 'empathy' is used. The point of the book is to provide an inclusive account of empathy, namely one that covers most of the things that people mean by the term. Having said that, I do use the term 'empathy' primarily for 'affective empathy'—i.e. feeling what another is feeling because that person is feeling it. Nonetheless, this is not the only reaction that will be discussed in the book. Confused? Read Chapter 1.

An overarching goal of the book is to be closely engaged with the empirical literature on empathy, primarily social psychology. Philosophers are great at conceptual analysis, at being precise, and at coming up with startling and provocative ideas. But reality is reality. Without an empirical basis for our claims, our philosophy can make little claim to the truth. And so I will often present psychological terminology and explain to what extent it overlaps with philosophical concepts, so you can orient yourself in the empirical literature also. More importantly, perhaps, I also give a broad overview of empathy research in psychology and explain how it affects philosophical theorizing.

Psychology itself depends to some degree on conceptual analysis, of course. And so we cannot simply assume that psychology carves nature at its joints, as philosophers like to say. Psychologists *decide* what the phenomenon they are going to study will be, and there is no real guarantee that what they are studying isn't a somewhat artificial construct. As we shall see, I think that talking about imagine-self versus imagine-other perspective taking as if they were two clearly delineated ways of taking another person's perspective is artificial and problematic. And so my use of psychological research is not entirely uncritical.

I also sometimes refer to neuroscience research. In the last decades, a fair number of empathy studies have appeared. Although it would be a mistake to think that they are particularly authoritative compared to what we can learn by engaging directly with others or by means of more systematic psychological research, they still provide valuable insight into empathic phenomena. For instance, the discovery of mirror neurons has been quite pivotal for understanding how we understand what others do. In other cases, neuroscience studies have provided further support for ideas that many have taken for granted, namely that when we empathize we *do* experience another's emotion in much the same way as we would experience our own.

In Chapter 6, we move beyond philosophy and psychology and into psychiatry. To get a good sense of what empathy does, we can look at people who lack, or have deficient, empathy. In what other ways do they differ from people without diagnosable mental disorders? Is it plausible to link some of those impairments to deficient empathy? As we shall see, this is indeed the case. Using deficits to teach us about abilities obviously requires us to have some idea already of what empathy does. We then use data from psychiatry to test our hypotheses. Again, it is not like we get unvarnished access to empathy through empirical research. Nonetheless, we stand to learn a lot by using this method. As we shall see, research from psychopathy and autism does throw considerable light on our understanding of what empathy is and what it does.

Two other major areas of study are relevant when we explore empathy: ethics and aesthetics. Empathy is often thought to play an important role in our caring about other people. Whether it affects our ability to pick up on when a situation is morally relevant (moral perception), or our ability to tell right from wrong or good from bad (moral judgment), or enhances our motivation to do good (moral motivation), empathy is often thought to be central to ethics. We explore this issue in Chapter 4. Empathy is also often thought to be important in our appreciation of art. 'Empathy,' it turns out, is a translation of the German Einfühlung, a concept that played an important role in aesthetic theory. Although its importance waned, the idea that empathy is pivotal for appreciating art is now seeing something of a renaissance. I discuss empathy and aesthetics in Chapter 5.

Chapters 1–3 are fairly interconnected and are mainly concerned with explicating what empathy is, although doing so cannot quite be separated from what empathy does. Chapter 2 focuses on cognitive empathy and Chapter 3 on affective empathy and related phenomena. It would be difficult to understand later parts of the book without having a good grasp of the basic ideas discussed in these chapters. But for the rest, it should be easy to skip around.

As you will see, the list of referring literature is extensive, so if you are hoping to use this book as a springboard for more research into empathy, you're in luck. You will also find a much shorter list of recommended further readings at the end of each chapter. I hope you find the book enjoyable and enlightening!

empathizing in the moment. Many theory of mind tests are also called perspective-taking tests. This is particularly true of second-order theory of mind tests—i.e. tests where one is to figure out what some person thinks another person thinks. But, as we shall see in Chapter 2, it is not clear that one needs to take another's perspective in order to pass such tasks. Because these tasks test for theory of mind or interpersonal understanding that does not require identification or perspective change, they are of peripheral importance to the empathy debate. Accordingly, I won't discuss theory of mind tests here.

Dispositional empathy is understood as a personality or character trait and is measured almost exclusively using self-report indices. The most encompassing and widely used dispositional empathy scale is The Interpersonal Reactivity Index, or IRI for short. The IRI measures empathy, sympathy, emotional contagion, perspective taking, and fantasy (Davis 1983). We have talked about the first three items but not the last one. Fantasy, or imagination as philosophers would be more likely to call it, is closely related to perspective taking because without it our new perspective will have little, or no, content. Mark Davis, designer of the IRI, assumes that highly empathic people are also people who find it easy to imagine being in situations other than the one that they are currently in, who are readily transported by fictional stories, and who tend to identify with the main characters of the fictions that they consume. The idea seems solid enough. If you have poor imaginative skills, you will not be able to take other people's perspectives well and may, as a result, fail to experience both empathy and sympathy for them.

The idea that imagination or fantasy is central to empathy relates to the roots of the term. Empathy is the English translation of the German Einfühlung, a term used by philosophers such as Friederich Theodor Vischer and Theodor Lipps to describe a central element in art appreciation, namely the ability to live oneself into the aesthetic object (Lipps 1903, Vischer 1873). We shall explore that more in Chapter 5. In the book as a whole, I mostly report on studies that use IRI. There are other dispositional empathy scales, of course, but they tend to be more limited in scope and are not as widely used as IRI (see below).

Most situational measures also rely on self-report. Batson, for instance, simply asks his subjects to rate, on a Likert scale, how much of certain emotions they feel after having been exposed to a person in need (e.g. Batson et al. 1981). He typically uses an index consisting of 28 emotion terms, 10 characteristic of sympathy (empathetic concern), 10 of personal distress, and 8 neutral ones. Subjects who report feeling "sympathetic, kind, compassionate, warm, softhearted, tender, empathetic, concerned,

§1.5 Sympathy or empathic concern

Sympathy is the fuzzy other-directed cousin of empathic distress described in (D4). In the psychology literature it is known as 'empathic concern.' For Batson, empathic concern involves "feelings of sympathy, compassion, soft-heartedness, tenderness, sorrow, sadness, upset, distress, concern, and grief" (Batson 2014, 42). By contrast to affective empathy, sympathy is responsive to the overall welfare of the other person. Typically, we talk of sympathy with someone in dire straits, but it can also denote an 'up' feeling, such as happiness for the good fortune of another. What is not required is emotional consonance with what the other person is feeling or can be expected to feel.

Sympathy reflects an overall attitude of 'caring' towards the other person. It shapes the sort of emotional reactions one will have to another, much like affective empathy does. What is special about sympathy is that it encompasses a robustly other-directed set of emotions. One is usually not confused about whether one feels sympathy or compassion for oneself or for another person, in the way one might be confused about whether the sadness one feels is personal or empathic. One can, of course, sympathize with oneself, but that is a different matter. According to Stephen Darwall (1998), sympathy is unique in making us care for someone for her own sake. Other types of empathic affect are more self-centered.

Developmental psychologists, such as Nancy Eisenberg and Martin Hoffman, suggest that empathic distress morphs into sympathy. At early developmental stages, the child's distress at another child's distress is primarily self-directed. As the child gets older, however, distress turns into concern for the other (hence: empathic concern). But if the child has been raised in less kind ways, shall we say, she may continue to experience a preponderance of empathic distress to others in need. Another exception to this developmental rule is that when others are in really terrible situations— bleeding on the side of the road, partly dismembered, and so on—empathic distress is likely to be the predominant emotion (Hoffman 2000).

§1.6 How empathy is measured

There is a wide range of tests of empathy in psychology. Some are intended to measure empathy as a relatively broad and inclusive phenomenon, whereas others are more specifically oriented towards theory of mind-related abilities. Sometimes they measure dispositional empathy—one's tendency to empathize—and sometimes they measure situational empathy—one's actual directed not at the target but at the person, situation, or event that caused the target's affect in the first place.

Most agree that empathic affect is not *only* caused by *perceiving* the other person's affect, as described in (D3). It can also be aroused simply by imagining being in her situation (e.g. Maibom 2007, Sober & Wilson 1998), or by *knowing* that the other person feels sad or that she is in a bad situation, (D3) notwithstanding. (D1)–(D3) all require emotion matching also. In other words, if you are angry, I am angry; if you are sad, I am sad; and so on. (D4) merely demands that empathy be *congruent* with the 'perceive welfare' of the target. (D4) is what philosophers tend to call 'sympathy,' and psychologists 'empathic concern.' We move on to this in Section 1.5.

§1.4 Cognitive empathy, or perspective taking

Cognitive empathy is sometimes used broadly so as to signify any kind of folk psychological understanding (theory of mind). However, there are a number of different ways we can go about understanding others. The type of under-standing that does not require much *personal* involvement is most commonly called 'theory of mind' (in psychology) or 'folk/common sense psychology' (in philosophy), and the one that *does* involve a personal element is more often called 'perspective taking' (in psychology) or 'simulation' (in philosophy). Perspective taking, or simulation, describes the action of imagining being in another person's situation. Once placed there, the perspective taker considers what that other person would think, feel, or do, and then, returning to her own perspective, ascribes these thoughts, feelings, or intentions to her.

(D2) says that perspective taking is an essential feature of affective empathy, although none of the other views suppose this is the case. This strong reading has the disadvantage of ruling out a number of instances of supposed empathy, such as when it arises as a result of emotional con-tagion. It also conflicts with the phenomenological take on empathy, according to which empathy describes our ability to *directly perceive* other people's mental states (e.g. Zahavi 2017)

Psychologists tend to divide perspective taking into imagine-self and imagine-other (e.g. Batson, Early, & Salvarini 1997). The first clearly involves an imaginative shift whereby one projects oneself into the position of the other. But it is less clear that imagine-other perspective taking must involve a shift of perspective at all. If it does not, it is hard to see why we should call it *perspective taking* and not simply cognitive empathy.

(Gelder et al. 2004), anger (de Greck et al. 2012), anxiety (Prehn-Kris-tensen et al. 2009), pleasure (Jabbi, Swart, & Keysers 2007), embarrass-ment (Krach et al. 2011), and sadness (Harrison et al. 2006). Most of this evidence comes from neuroscience studies. Technically speaking, all these studies show is that overlapping brain areas are activated when the person is feeling the emotion directly (or for themselves) and when they feel it as a result of others feeling it (for a review, see Bernhardt & Singer 2012).[1]

Although you need to be able to pay some attention to what others feel in order to catch their emotions—you can't do it while sleeping or high on drugs, for instance—you don't need to know that this is what you are doing. We may be aware that the person we are interacting with is cheerful and that we are cheerful but not of any causal connection between the two. Our attention is directed more or less automatically, and this process may not be under conscious control at all during the initial stages of emotional contagion. We can, of course, *become* aware of what is happening. When we do so, however, the resultant affect is more likely to fit (D1) or (D2) in addition to (D3), as we shall see in the next section.

§1.3 Affective empathy

One way of looking at affective empathy is simply as emotional contagion *plus*. It is emotional contagion with a robust self-other differentiation. Sup-pose your friend is angrily telling you about how she was snubbed by her boss. You feel your anger rising. You are angry with her boss too now. But you know you are angry because of what happened to your friend. Your anger is not *yours* in a deep sense. It is empathic. (D3) has become (D1). The self-differentiation demanded by (D1) and (D2) should therefore not be understood as merely involving knowing that you and your friend are two different people but knowing that *she* is the one who has been snubbed (in our example). You are angry *for* your friend, we might say, not for yourself. This is true despite the fact that you are actually angry yourself.

The easiest way to conceptualize this is to say that *the object* of your anger is your friend's anger, along with the content of *her* anger perhaps. For suppose you are angry that your friend is angry that her boss snubbed her. This may *sound* like empathic anger, but it needn't be. You might have been angered by her anger, not because of what her boss did but because her ranting and raving have made you mad too. You feel angry *with* her, how-ever, not *for* her. Empathic affect, then, needs to have as an object the other person's affect, or something like that (soon to be discussed), *and* be is required is that the empathizer attends to the target and she comes to feel the corresponding affect herself. She may or may not know that her emotion is empathic. In other words, she may not be aware that her emotion is about the other person. For instance, our empathizer may come to feel sad upon observing sadness in her friend but feel her sadness as her own. (D3) comes from people working on animal cognition. It is easy to see how well this account will fit some animal scenarios. By contrast, proposed by a philosopher, (D2) insists that empathy requires a robust self-other differentiation. According to this philosopher, (D3) would not describe empathy but what psychologists call *emotional contagion*. To get to empathy, we must ask: "Is one feeling sad, distressed, concerned for the other, or feeling this way as a result of what has befallen oneself—including the experience of seeing another suffer?" (Batson 2014, 42). Only in the former case is what we feel empathy, if we are to believe Dan Batson or Amy Coplan.

It should now be clear why many people complain about 'empathy' being an impossibly confused term. Different people mean different thing by it. But things are not as bad as they seem. Mainly, people have one of four slightly different things in mind when they talk about empathy. They are: 1) 'emotional contagion,' which is described in (D3), 2) 'affective empathy,' which is described in (D1) and (D2), 3) 'perspective taking,' sometimes called 'cognitive empathy,' which is central to (D2), and 'sympathy,' sometimes called 'empathic concern' (particularly in psychology), which is described in (D4). Let us briefly look at each.

§1.2 Emotional contagion

Imagine arriving at a party. The room is light and full of cheer. You immediately feel cheerful yourself. Or, walking down a path with a friend, she startles and you startle immediately as a result. If you have ever had an experience like these, you have experienced 'emotional contagion.' In emotional contagion, one person responds to another person's emotion with a very similar one. In my examples, it was cheer and startle, but most researchers assume it can be any emotion. We don't actually know that this is true, and there is some reason to be suspicious about that claim. Can we 'catch' someone's jealousy or surprise? It's not obvious.

The current evidence suggest that we can catch the following emotions from others: pain-related distress (Cheng et al. 2007, Singer et al. 2004), disgust (Jabbi, Bastiaansen, & Keysers 2008, Wicker et al. 2003), fear

At first blush, it may seem that these definitions are not really that different. And in a way they are not. They all describe emotions that are singularly sensitive to others. Empathy, it is clear, is an *other-oriented state or activity*. However, they differ in *the ways* they take these emotions to be other-oriented, as we shall see below.

The cause of empathy. (D1) and (D3) specify that the other person's affective state is the cause of empathy. (D3) focuses on perception. In a typical instance, you express that you experience some emotion, and upon observing your expression, I come to experience an emotion of the same general type. For instance, I see you cry, and I come to feel sad. (D2) states that it is not enough that we *see* someone be sad; we must also *take her perspective*. That is, I must imagine that I am (her) in her situation. *Perspective taking* is often seen to be empathic in the psychological literature but is nonetheless different from feeling with and for others. (D1) has a slightly wider scope, for it takes into consideration that there are many different ways I can acquire information about your being sad, only one of which is seeing it for myself. For instance, I am told by a friend that you are sad. This makes me feel sad in turn. (D1) and (D2), as it turns out, also include as *empathic* my feeling sad when considering the *situation* you are in. In this case, I might actually not know what you feel, and there is the possibility that you do not feel sad at all. But, the thinking goes, it is fair to *assume* that the situation would make you feel sad, and so my sadness still counts as empathic. For example, I know that your spouse has left you for another person and that makes me feel sad for you.

Emotion matching. But not everybody has this focus on *affect*. (D4) is pretty clear that it is the overall *welfare* of the other person that is at issue, not what they happen to feel. In some ways, the thinking here is similar to the one above, where we assume that we can infer someone's feelings from the situation they are in. The situation in this instance, though, is general welfare. Put simply, has something *good* or *bad* happened to the person? When our affective quality matches their welfare, we feel *empathic concern*. Suppose you have just been turned down for a long-awaited promotion. For me to empathize with you, I must experience a negative emotion in response to this information. As we shall see later, Daniel Batson, who is the proponent of this definition, has pretty precise ideas about the affective quality of empathic concern.

Self-other differentiation. Another important factor in distinguishing these accounts is the degree to which the empathizer is aware that she is empathizing. What does this mean? Well, if you look at (D3) you see that all that

There are two types of attitudes to empathy. There is the narrow attitude according to which there is one right way to look at what *real* empathic phenomena are (Coplan 2011). And then there is the broader, more encompassing view, which allows many different ideas in under the rubric 'empathy,' not because adherents are wishy-washy but because they maintain that these ideas are all intimately connected (Maibom 2017). If we explore one in isolation, the thought goes, we risk missing something very important about each phenomenon. You may now suspect that I belong in the second camp. You would be right. This book, therefore, offers a somewhat ecumenical account of empathic phenomena. It covers the phenomena often called empathy, sympathy, emotional contagion, and perspective taking.

This chapter starts out with an illustration of the problems facing a person trying to understand what empathy is by comparing and contrasting four different definitions in the literature. I then briefly explain each aspect of empathic responding in turn: emotional contagion, affective empathy, sympathy, and perspective taking. I end by saying a little about how empathy is measured in the psychology literature.

§1.1 Empathic phenomena

To give you a flavor of the diverse interpretations of the term 'empathy,' have a look at the definitions below. They are not cherry picked, I promise. Instead, they are regularly quoted and used in the literature in both philosophy and psychology.

(D1) "We define *empathy* as an affective response that stems from the apprehension or comprehension of another's emotional state or condition and is similar to what the other person is feeling or would be expected to feel in a given situation." (Eisenberg 2005, 75)

(D2) "[...] the three essential features of empathy: affective matching, other-oriented perspective taking, and self-other differentiation." (Coplan 2011, 6)

(D3) "A perception-action model of empathy specifically states that attended perception of the object's state automatically activates the subject's representations of the state, situation, and object, and that activation of these representations automatically primes or generates the associated autonomic and somatic responses, unless inhibited." (Preston & de Waal 2002, 4)

(D4) "Empathic concern refers to other-oriented emotion elicited by and congruent with the perceived welfare of a person in need." (Batson 2014, 41)

1

WHAT IS EMPATHY?

Empathy has come to prominence as a worthy subject for study over the last decades. Up until quite recently, it has not been a serious topic of philosophical research, with the notable exceptions of the Scottish sentimentalists and German phenomenologists. There is now a thriving philosophical literature on this affective reaction, in addition to a huge popular one extolling its many virtues. Although there are some detractors, empathy seems to be on the up and up. But what is empathy? Is it a feeling, or a way of understanding others? Does it involve feeling what the other person is feeling, or is it a form of compassion? Any reader who first immerses herself in this literature is likely to be confused. 'Empathy' is used in so many different senses that it is hard to form an overall view of what it is and what it does. The aim of this chapter is provide an account of the main phenomena that go under this heading.

moved, and touched" are taken to feel sympathy (empathic concern), whereas those who feel "alarmed, bothered, disturbed, upset, troubled, worried, anxious, uneasy, grieved, and distressed" are thought to experience personal distress (Batson 2011, 103).

There are good reasons to be skeptical about how accurate self-report measures are. Empathy self-reporting has been found to be influenced by social desirability, desire for positive self-evaluation, and stereotyping (e.g. Cialdini et al. 1987, Eisenberg & Lennon 1983). Moreover, violent sex offenders have been found to score high on sympathy (empathic concern) on the IRI (Curwen 2003), as have psychopaths (Shamay-Tsoori et al. 2010). For reasons such as these, some researchers have looked elsewhere for more reliable ways of testing empathy.

Physiological measures are an attractive alternative. Someone like Eisenberg, for instance, has used heart rate, skin conductance, startle reflex, and facial expressivity to measure empathic reactions. Skin conductance and startle reflex both measure increased arousal. Increased arousal can be many things, but in the particular situation, it is thought to be a stress response, such as anxiety or fear. Previous studies have found that ordinary people have increased skin conductance to images of people in distress and to directly threatening images (Anieskiewicz 1979, Blair et al. 1997). Eisenberg (2005) interprets increased skin conductance to others in distress as personal distress (and to a lesser extent sympathy), but it is unclear why it could not be interpreted as empathic distress.

Something similar is true of the startle response. People startle more easily if they are fearful, anxious, or generally on high alert. Normal people, but not psychopaths for instance, exhibit this response when exposed to pictures of people in distress (Patrick, Cuthbert, & Lang 1994). Startle most likely measures contagious, personal, or empathic distress. Heart rate deceleration is taken to signify sympathetic arousal because physiological studies have associated it with an intake of information and an outward focus of attention (Cacioppo & Sandman 1978) and because it is a very common response to sad or sympathy-inducing films or clips (Eisenberg & Fabes 1990, Eisenberg et al. 1988). Heart rate acceleration, on the other hand, is typically interpreted as personal distress (Eisenberg et al. 1988), but it also correlates with: responses to pictures of others' distress (Liew et al. 2003), reactions to others who are in fearful situations (Eisenberg et al. 1988), and concern for others (Hastings et al. 2000). Physiological measures, therefore, are good indicators of emotional reactions to others in distress. But they are not very precise indicators of what emotion is experienced.

When it comes to facial expressions, Eisenberg and colleagues have had more success with children than with adults. They found that facial expressions of sadness and sympathy are more common for sympathy inductions (someone in need) than for distress inductions (someone hurt or highly distressed). Facial expressions of distress, however, were equally common for either sympathy or distress inductions (Eisenberg & Fabes 1990, Eisenberg et al. 1988). This suggests that sympathy and personal distress are often felt together in response to others' sad situations, just like the self-report data from Batson indicate (Batson, Early, & Salvarini 1997, Eisenberg, Spinrad, & Sadovsky 2006).

Empathy measures are quite diverse. *Hogan's Empathy Scale* (1969) measures mainly cognitive empathy. It has items that tap into perspective taking, such as "As a rule, I have little difficulty in 'putting myself into other people's shoes'" (Hogan 1969, 310), but also items that are hard to associate with any current view of empathy such as "I frequently undertake more than I can accomplish" and "It is the duty of a citizen to support his country, right or wrong" (reverse scored). IRI (Davis 1983) and the *Basic Empathy Scale* (Jolliffe & Farrington 2006) measure both cognitive and affective empathy. The Empathic Concern subscale of the IRI seems to measure only sympathy, but the *Basic Empathy Scale* and *Bryant's Index of Empathy* (Bryant 1982) do not include sympathetic items and do not distinguish between empathy, emotional contagion, or personal distress (e.g. 'I usually feel calm when other people are scared' (reverse scored), Jolliffe & Farrington 2006, 593). The *Questionnaire Measure of Emotional Empathy* (Mehrabian & Epstein 1972) is even less precise. This is particularly true of reverse scored items. If I score high on 'I become more irritated than concerned when I see someone in tears' and 'I don't get upset just because a friend is acting upset,' am I lacking in empathy, sympathy, emotional contagion, or personal distress (Mehrabian & Epstein 1972, 528)? Simon Baron-Cohen has thrown the *Empathy Quotient* (Baron-Cohen & Wheelwright 2004) into the mix, but it has been criticized for being gender skewed (Grossi & Fine 2012), perhaps in part because it often concerns social ability more than empathy ('When I talk to other people, I tend to talk about their experiences rather than my own' or 'If anyone asked me if I liked their haircut, I would reply truthfully, even if I didn't like it'). To evaluate the research on empathy, then, it is crucial to know which measure is being used.

§1.7 Take-home message

The discussion so far will hopefully have made the reader appreciate the similarities and differences between the different aspects of what is commonly called 'empathy.' Philosophers often focus on the dissociability of these different aspects of empathy. One can take another person's perspective without experiencing affect, for instance. One can empathize with someone without sympathizing with them and vice versa, and empathize or sympathize with someone without taking their perspective. And so the empathy literature is often messy because people are not exercising the right kind of conceptual hygiene in their treatments of intersubjective phenomena.

The upshot is that people define empathy in a variety of ways. Empathy is always about what is happening to someone else, but whether the other is merely a cause or also the object of the emotion is debatable. Moreover, people disagree about the roles of perspective taking and emotional contagion in empathy. Some seem to define empathy as a reaction in the situation to the experience of another; others think we can empathize with literary characters and with people we are not in the presence of. So there is a fair degree of variation.

Keeping these differences in mind, here is a guide to each of the aspects of empathy we have discussed in this chapter. The terms are those I will use in what follows. To describe 'empathy' broadly conceived to include all these various aspects, I suggest we use the term 'Empathy' capitalized. For what is 1. below, we can talk of 'empathy' with a small 'e.'

1. **Affective empathy** is an emotion experienced by a person A that is caused by A perceptually experiencing, being aware of, or imagining person B's feelings, affective expressions, or situation and has as its object B's feelings about her situation. The emotion is the same as, or very similar to, the emotion experienced by B, or the ones that it would be appropriate for B to experience in her situation. Affective empathy is experienced partly for the other and partly for the self. I am sad that you are sad. Some psychologists seem to talk of this emotion only as 'personal distress,' which is a version of this emotion where the other-focus has either disappeared or is largely superseded by self-focus.

2. **Emotional contagion** is an emotion experienced by a person A that is caused by perceiving affect in another person B. This emotion is the same as, or very similar to, the one perceived in B. It is relatively neutral between being experienced for self or other, even though A clearly experiences it. It may only describe a transitory state between empathy, personal distress and/or sympathy, at least for adult human beings.

3. **Perspective taking** is the activity of imagining being in someone else's situation. When person A takes person B's perspective, A imagines that she is the subject of whatever experiences B is having, making allowances for differences between A and B.

4. **Sympathy** is an emotion experienced by a person A for the wellbeing or plight of another person B. This emotion is rarely like the emotion(s) experienced by B, since sympathy is almost uniquely other-directed. By contrast to affective empathy, there is usually not the possibility of confusing whom the emotion is experienced for: self or other.

In this chapter, we have explored:

- how different the definitions of empathy can be,
- what is meant by emotional contagion,
- what affective empathy is,
- what sympathy is,
- what perspective taking is, and
- how empathy is measured in social psychology.

Note

1 There are other findings of overlap but in phenomena that may less straightforwardly be called empathic emotions, such as in touch (Blakemore et al. 2005, Keysers et al. 2004), reward (Mobbs et al. 2009), and social exclusion (Masten, Morelli, & Eisenberger 2011). See Boris Bernhardt and Tania Singer (2012) for an authoritative review.

Further readings

Coplan, A. 2011. Understanding empathy: Its features and effects. In: A. Coplan & P. Goldie (Eds.) *Empathy: Philosophical and Psychological Perspectives*. New York: Oxford University Press, 3–18. An interesting and philosophically demanding account of empathy, which draws a hard line between the different aspects of empathic affect.

Davis, M. 1994. *Empathy: A Social Psychological Approach*. Boulder, CO: Westview Press. The best overview of the psychological research on empathy up until the early 1990s.

Eisenberg, N. 2005. The development of empathy-related responding. In: G. Carlo & C.P. Edwards (Eds.) *Nebraska Symposium on Motivation. Volume 51. Moral Motivation Through the Life Span*. Lincoln, NE: University of Nebraska Press, 73–117. An authoritative account of empathy development in children by one of the foremost empathy researchers in psychology.

Heal, J. 1986. Replication and functionalism. In: J. Butterfield (Ed.) *Language, Mind and Logic*. Cambridge: Cambridge University Press, 135–150. This was one of the first papers on simulation theory. It explains what simulation is, what problems it solves, and how it is a superior alternative to theory theory.

Maibom, H.L. 2007. The presence of others. *Philosophical Studies*, 132, 161–190. It suggests that the distinctive contribution of simulation might not be as a wholesale alternative to theory theory. *Instead*, it is an approach that is more likely to induce empathic affect than other ways of thinking about others.

Preston, S & de Waal, F. 2002. Empathy: Its ultimate and proximal bases. *Behavioral and Brain Sciences*, 25, 1–72. This is an account of empathy which emphasizes the emotional contagion aspect. It is encompassing enough to account for empathic phenomena in nonhuman animals as well.

References

Anieskiewicz, A.S. 1979. Autonomic components of vicarious conditioning and psychopathy. *Journal of Clinical Psychology*, 35, 60–67.

Baron-Cohen, S. & Wheelwright, S. 2004. The empathy quotient: An investigation of adults with Asperger Syndrome or High Functioning Autism, and normal sex differences. *Journal of Autism and Developmental Disorders*, 34, 163–175.

Batson, C.D. 2011. *Altruism in Humans*. New York: Oxford University Press.

Batson, C.D. 2014. Empathy-induced altruism and morality: No necessary connection. In: H.L. Maibom (Ed.) *Empathy and Morality*. New York: Oxford University Press, 41–58.

Batson, C.D., Duncan, B., Ackerman, P., Buckley, T., & Birch, K. 1981. Is empathic emotion a source of altruistic motivation? *Journal of Personality and Social Psychology*, 40, 290–302.

Batson, C.D., Early, S., & Salvarini, G. 1997. Perspective taking: Imagining how another feels versus imagining how you would feel. *Personality and Social Psychology Bulletin*, 23, 751–758.

Batson, C.D., Eklund, J.H., Chermok, V.L., Hoyt, J.L., & Ortiz, B.G. 2007. An additional antecedent of empathic concern: Valuing the welfare of the person in need. *Journal of Personality and Social Psychology*, 93, 65–74.

Bernhardt, B. & Singer, T. 2012. The neural bases of empathy. *Annual Review of Neuroscience*, 35, 1–23.

Blair, R.J.R., Jones, L., Clark, F., & Smith, M. 1997. The psychopathic individual: A lack of responsiveness to distress cues? *Psychophysiology*, 34, 192–198.

Blakemore, S.J., Bristow, D., Bird, G., Frith, C., & Ward, J. 2005. Somatosensory activation during the observation of touch and a case of vision-touch synaesthesia. *Brain*, 128, 1571–1583.

Bryant, B. 1982. An index of empathy for children and adolescents. *Child Development*, 53, 413–425.

Cacioppo, J. & Sandman, C. 1978. Psychological differentiation of sensory and cognitive tasks as a function of warning, processing demands, and reported unpleasantness. *Biological Psychology*, 6, 181–192.

Carrera, P., Oceja, L., Caballero, A., Muñoz, D., Lópes-Pérez, B., & Ambrona, T. 2013. I feel so sorry! Tapping the joint influences of empathy and personal distress on helping behavior. *Motivation and Emotion*, 37, 335–345.

Chemero, A. 2016. Sensorimotor empathy. *Journal of Consciousness Studies*, 23, 138–152.

Cheng, Y., Lin, C., Liu, H.L., Hsu, Y., Lim, K., Hung, D., Decety, J. 2007. Expertise modulates the perception of pain in others. *Current Biology*, 17, 1708–1713.

Cialdini, R.B., Schaller, M., Houlihan, D., Arps, K., Fultz, J., & Beaman, A.L. 1987. Empathy-based helping: Is it selflessly or egoistically motivated? *Journal of Personality and Social Psychology*, 52, 749–758.

Coke, J.S., Batson, C.D., & McDavis, K. 1978. Empathic mediation of helping: A two-stage model. *Journal of Personality and Social Psychology*, 36, 752–766.

Coplan, A. 2011. Understanding empathy: Its features and effects. In: A. Coplan & P. Goldie (Eds.) *Empathy: Philosophical and Psychological Perspectives.* New York: Oxford University Press, 3–18.

Curwen, T. 2003. The importance of offense characteristics, victimization history, hostility, and social desirability in assessing empathy of male adolescent sex offenders. *Sexual Abuse: A Journal of Research and Treatment*, 15, 347–364.

Darwall, S. 1998. Empathy, sympathy, care. *Philosophical Studies*, 89, 261–282.

Davis, M. 1983. Measuring individual differences in empathy: Evidence for a multidimensional approach. *Journal of Personality and Social Psychology*, 44, 113–126.

de Greck, M., Wang, G., Yang, X., Wang, X., Northoff, G., & Han, S. 2012. Neural substrates underlying intentional empathy. *Social Cognitive and Affective Neuroscience*, 7, 135–144.

Eisenberg, N. 2005. The development of empathy-related responding. In: G. Carlo & C.P. Edwards (Eds.) *Nebraska Symposium on Motivation. Volume 51. Moral Motivation Through the Life Span.* Lincoln, NE: University of Nebraska Press, 73–117.

Eisenberg, N. & Lennon, R. 1983 Sex differences in empathy and related capacities. *Psychological Bulletin*, 94, 100–131.

Eisenberg, N., Schaller, M., Fabes, R., Bustamante, D., Mathy, R., Shell, R., & Rhodes, K. 1988. Differentiation of personal distress and sympathy in children and adults. *Developmental Psychology*, 24, 766–775.

Eisenberg, N., Spinrad, T.L., & Sadovsky, A. 2006. Empathy-related responding in children. In: M. Killen & Smetana, J. (Eds.) *Handbook of Moral Development.* Mahwah, NJ: Lawrence Erlbaum Associates, 517–549.

Gelder, B., Snyder, J., Greve, D., Gerard, G., & Hadjikhani, N. 2004. Fear fosters flight: A mechanism for fear contagion when perceiving emotion expressed by a whole body. *Proceedings of the National Academy of Science of the USA*, 101, 16701–16706.

Gordon, R. 1986. Folk psychology as simulation. *Mind and Language*, 1, 158–171.

Grossi, G. & Fine, C. 2012. The role of fetal testosterone in the development of the "Essential Difference" between the sexes: Some essential issues.

In: R. Bluhm, A.J. Jacobsen, and H.L. Maibom (Eds.) *Neurofeminism*. New York: Palgrave Macmillan, 73–104.

Harrison, N.A., Singer, T., Rotshtein, P., Dolan, R.J., & Critchley, H.D. 2006. Pupillary contagion: Central mechanisms engaged in sadness processing. *Social Cognitive and Affective Neuroscience*, 1, 5–17.

Hastings, P.D., Zahn-Waxler, C., Usher, B., Robinson, J., & Bridges, D. 2000. The development of concern for others in children with behavior problems. *Developmental Psychology*, 36, 531–546.

Hatfield, E., Cacioppo, J.T., and Rapson, R.L. 1994. *Emotional Contagion*. Cambridge: Cambridge University Press.

Heal, J. 1986. Replication and functionalism. In: J. Butterfield (Ed.) *Language, Mind and Logic*. Cambridge: Cambridge University Press, 135–150.

Heal, J. 1998. Understanding other minds from the inside. In: A. O'Hear (Ed.) *Current Issues in Philosophy of Mind*. Cambridge: Cambridge University Press, 83–99.

Hoffman, M. 2000. *Empathy and Moral Development*. New York: Cambridge University Press.

Hogan, R. 1969. Development of an empathy scale. *Journal of Consulting and Clinical Psychology*, 33, 307–316.

Jabbi, M., Bastiaansen, J., & Keysers, C. 2008. A common anterior insula representation of disgust observation, experience, and imagination shows divergent functional connectivity pathways. *PLoS One*, 3, e2939.

Jabbi, M., Swart, M., & Keysers, C. 2007. Empathy for positive and negative emotions in the gustatory cortex. *NeuroImage*, 34, 1744–1753.

Jolliffe, D. & Farrington, D. 2006. Development and validation of the basic empathy scale. *Journal of Adolescence*, 29, 589–611.

Keysers, C., Wicker, B., Gazzola, V., Anton, J.L., Fogassi, L., & Gallese, V. 2004. A touching sight: SII/PV activation during the observation and experience of touch. *Neuron*, 42, 335–346.

Krach, S., Cohrs, J.C., de Echeverria Loebell, N.C., Kircher, T., Sommer, J., Jansen, A. & Paulus, F.M. 2011. Your flaws are my pain: Linking empathy to vicarious embarrassment. *PLoS One*, 6, e18675.

Liew, J., Eisenberg, N., Losoya, S., Fabes, R., Gurthrie, I., & Murphy, B. 2003. Children's physiological indices of empathy and their socioemotional adjustment: Does caregivers' expressivity matter? *Journal of Family Psychology*, 17, 584–597.

Lipps, T. 1903. 'Empathy', inward imitation, and sense feelings. In: E.F. Carritt (Ed.) *Philosophies of Beauty: From Socrates to Robert Bridges, Being the Sources of Aesthetic Theory.* Oxford: Clarendon Press, 252–256.

Maibom, H.L. 2007. The presence of others. *Philosophical Studies*, 132, 161–190.

Maibom, H.L. 2014. (Almost) everything you ever wanted to know about empathy. In: H.L. Maibom (Ed.) *Empathy and Morality.* New York: Oxford University Press, 1–40.

Maibom, H.L. 2017. Affective empathy. In: H.L. Maibom (Ed.) *Routledge Handbook of Philosophy of Empathy.* New York: Routledge, 22–32.

Maibom, H.L. Manuscript. *Knowing Me, Knowing You: Adventures in Perspective Taking.*

Masten, C.L., Morelli, S.A., & Eisenberger, N.I. 2011. An fMRI investigation for empathy for 'social pain' and subsequent social behavior. *NeuroImage*, 55, 381–388.

Mehrabian, A. & Epstein, N. 1972. A measure of emotional empathy. *Journal of Personality*, 40, 525–543.

Mobbs, D., Yu, R., Meyer, M., Passamonti, L., Seymour, B., Calder, A.J., Schweizer, S., Frith, C.D., & Dalgleish, T. 2009. A key role for similarity in vicarious reward. *Science*, 324, 900.

Patrick, C., Cuthbert, B., & Lang, P. 1994. Emotion in the criminal psychopath: Fear image processing. *Journal of Abnormal Psychology*, 103, 523–534.

Prehn-Kristensen, A., Wiesner, C., Bergman, T.O., Wolf, S., Jansen, O., Mehdorn, H.M., Ferstl, R., & Pause, B.M. 2009. Induction of empathy by the smell of anxiety. *PLoS*, 4, e5987.

Preston, S. & de Waal, F. 2002. Empathy: Its ultimate and proximal bases. *Behavioral and Brain Sciences*, 25, 1–72.

Schramme, T. 2017. Empathy and altruism. In: H.L. Maibom (Ed.) *Routledge Handbook of Philosophy of Empathy.* New York: Routledge, 201–214.

Shamay-Tsoory, S., Harari, H., Aharon-Perez, J., & Levkovich, Y. 2010. The role of orbitofrontal cortex in affective theory of mind deficits in criminal offenders with psychopathic tendencies. *Cortex*, 46, 668–677.

Singer, T., Seymour, B., O'Doherty, J., Kaube, H., Dolan, R.J., Frith, C.D. 2004. Empathy for pain involves the affective but not sensory components of pain. *Science*, 303, 1157–1162.

Sober, E. & Wilson, D.S. 1998. *Unto Others.* Cambridge, MA: Harvard University Press.

Spinrad, T. & Eisenberg, N. 2014. Empathy and morality: A developmental psychology perspective. In: H.L. Maibom (Ed.) *Empathy and Morality.* New York: Oxford University Press, 59–70.

Vischer, R. 1873. On the optical sense of form. In: H.F. Mallgrave & E. Ikonomou (Eds.) *Empathy, Form, and Space: Problems in German Aesthetics, 1873–1893.*

Wicker, B., Keysers, C., Plailly, J., Royet, J-P., Gallese, V., & Rizzolatti, G. 2003. Both of us disgusted in my insula: The common neural basis of seeing and feeling disgust. *Neuron,* 40, 655–664.

Zahavi, D. 2017. Phenomenology, empathy, and mindreading. In: H.L. Maibom (Ed.) *The Routledge Handbook of Philosophy of Empathy.* New York: Routledge, 33–42.

2

EMPATHY AND
UNDERSTANDING OTHERS

'Cognitive empathy' refers to empathy that is directed towards understanding others. It is thought to involve mainly, or exclusively, cognitive mental structures. Affective empathy, by contrast, necessarily involves emotions. In some cases, cognitive empathy is taken to cover what is also known as 'theory of mind,' namely our practice of ascribing mental states and properties more broadly. Understood in its more narrow sense, it describes only one form of this practice, which philosophers call 'simulation.' It is a way of understanding others through the means of transposing oneself imaginatively into their situation. Psychologists tend to call this 'perspective taking.' There is a somewhat vigorous debate about how we do this, whether it is really possible, and if so, what the use is.

In this chapter, we discuss the theory theory versus simulation theory debate, mirror neurons, perspective taking, and self-knowledge. We also consider some of the most common objections to the use of perspective taking, such as the objection from impossibility and from transformative experience, and get an idea of how to meet those challenges.

§2.1 Knowing other minds

In psychology, cognitive empathy is typically called 'perspective taking.' In philosophy, we talk more frequently of 'simulation.' It is important that we do not confuse perspective taking, as I shall call it henceforth, with theory of mind. 'Theory of mind' describes the ability to understand others in terms of mental phenomena. Doing so does not require one to shift one's perspective. Moreover, simulation is but *one* method of divining what another person thinks or feels. Theory of mind, then, is the superordinate category under which falls perspective taking and simulation.

Philosophers often call 'theory of mind' 'folk psychology' or 'common sense psychology.' In the last century, there was a period where analytic philosophers seemed to agree that the way we understand others is by use of something like a folk *theory* of mind. Paul Churchland (1970), Jerry Fodor (1987), and Daniel Dennett (1987) all supported this idea in their own ways.

To understand how this idea was so appealing, think of the task of understanding others this way. Whereas we seem to be aware of our own thoughts, wants, and feelings more or less directly, we only have access to those of other people *indirectly*. We see the way that they move, the expressions they make, and we hear what they say. But we are never aware of their thoughts, feelings, or intentions in the direct way we are of our own. Yet, we are not consciously aware of first *seeing* a piece of behavior and then figuring out what the person is doing. How is that? Well, the argument from analogy was once thought to be what did the job. We have direct awareness of our own inner mental goings on, and we are aware of the way such psychological states correlate with what we do and certain bodily expressions. We are also aware that we respond to what happens in our environment with certain thoughts, feelings, and so on. When, then, we observe these same behavioral manifestations in others, we assume that they are caused by the same things that cause them *in us*. In other words, we assume that others have 'inner' reactions to what happens in the environment that are largely commensurate to our own.

There are two levels to this analogy. At the first and most general one, we simply infer that *others have minds*. By comparison, we don't suppose that stones or trees do. At the second level, the analogy gets more specific. We infer that similar types of mental states cause similar types of behaviors, and similar states of the environment cause similar mental states. The argument from analogy rests on what is often thought to be a Cartesian idea that we have direct and privileged access to the contents of our own minds but not to the minds of others. That idea came under pressure during the middle and last part of the last century, particularly with the work of Wilfrid Sellars (1963) and Gilbert Ryle (1949). Sellars doubted that we had anything like the *direct* access to our own mental states that the Cartesian picture supposes. This formed part of a larger doubt concerning what is 'given' in experience. According to Sellars, most of what seems to be deliverances of perception are the results of intense mental processing. Something similar might be said about the idea of mental states. Instead of their being given to us directly in introspection, mental states are our own reconstructions of what gives rise to behavior. These are ideas we have formed because doing so turns out to be useful in interacting with others. We have become so familiar with this way of thinking of ourselves—in terms of beliefs, desires, emotions, and intentions—that we are no longer aware that it is based on an inference. But in actual fact, *all* our psychological ascriptions, whether to others or to ourselves, are based on inferences.

From here it is a short step to supposing that we have a *theory* of mind, later known as 'theory theory.' Churchland (1970) was instrumental in trying to flesh out what such a theory would look like. He suggested that it is like a scientific theory, consisting of a list of counterfactual supporting generalizations or law-like statements. In such statements, 'belief,' 'desire,' and 'intention' feature as theoretical terms. These are terms introduced by the theory and are often used to refer to so-called 'unobservables'—i.e. objects or properties that we cannot perceive. This seems to fit nicely with this new way of conceiving of the mind. However, it is doubtful that someone like Sellars, let alone Ryle, believed that there actually are inner mental episodes or dispositions that correspond to what we call beliefs and desires. In this case, our folk psychological theory is a *bad* theory of human psychology. Sellars and Ryle formed part of an older generation much influenced by behaviorism. After it became respectable to posit inner mental processes again, someone like Fodor proudly announced that the idea that there *are* real inner episodes that correspond largely to our folk psychological theory was "the only game in town" (Fodor 1975). A student of Ryle's, Dennett would continue to insist that mental states are real only to the extent that something like 'the equator' is real. They are calculation-bound entities, which is to say that they are interpretations of patterns that are useful for the purposes of explaining and predicting behavior but that do not exist as such (Dennett 1987, 53).

From then on, the debate started revolving around whether we knew such a theory tacitly or whether it was really like a scientific theory at all (Gopnik & Wellman 1992, Maibom 2001, Stich & Nichols 1992). There were also suggestions that we should not understand the theoriticity of folk psychology as involving a body of counterfactual supporting generalizations but instead embrace the idea that we have knowledge of folk psychological *models* (Godfrey-Smith 2005, Maibom 2003). At this point, a new theory of folk psychology had been introduced. Jane Heal (1986) in England and Robert Gordon (1986) in the United States arrived at the idea of simulation more or less simultaneously. The idea is closely related to the argument from analogy but with important modifications inspired by modern technology. The idea was that we use ourselves to understand others by a process of mental simulation. There ensued about a decade of intense debating (Davies & Stone 1995a, 1995b), after which most parties settled on agreeing that when we ascribe mental states to others we do a bit of both. What remained unresolved was whether theory or simulation was the most fundamental capacity.

How does this theory of mind debate relate to cognitive empathy? Simulation describes the same ability that psychologists often call 'perspective taking.' Theory theory could, technically speaking, count as cognitive empathy, but, as I said, the more common assumption is that cognitive *empathy* refers to perspective taking, not simply psychological attribution. Simulation, therefore, is the method of greatest interest to us and is the topic of the rest of the chapter.

Although these are the two main competitors in the theory of mind domain, there are alternatives. One is Dan Hutto's idea that folk psychological practices are essentially narrative practices. Narratives engage with individuals in particular situations, whereas theories engage with classes of things and their generalized behavior (Hutto 2008, Hutto & Jurgens 2019).

Another position, and one that is gaining increasing traction, comes from phenomenology and researchers excited about enactive, embodied, extended, and embedded cognition. The idea is that empathy constitutes a form of *direct* perception of other minds. In other words, the assumption is exactly the opposite of Sellars'. According to Dan Zahavi, who builds on Husserl, knowledge of other minds is a special kind of *knowledge by acquaintance*.

> We can see the other's elation or doubt, surprise or attentiveness in his or her face, we can hear the other's trepidation, impatience, or bewilderment in her voice, feel the other's enthusiasm in his handshake, grasp his mood in his posture, and see her determination and persistence in her actions.
>
> (Zahavi 2017, 40)

It is important to note, however, that this is an account of folk psychology that is restricted to the personal encounter with the other person.

It is not always easy to tell how much of the disagreement with the other views of theory of mind relies on an over-reading of what an inferential process is or does, or of the idea that if we theorize about another, we have made her merely one object among others. And it is not always easy to know what purchase 'direct' as in 'direct perception' has. In what follows, I put these alternative views aside and focus on the idea of perspective taking or simulation, as this is less of a controversial notion.

§2.2 Simulation and pretending to be someone else

As mentioned, Gordon (1986) and Heal (1986) suggest that instead of our relying on a *theory* of mind to predict and explain the behavior of others, we actually use our own ability to make decisions, or to reason counterfactually, to understand others. How do we do it? Here the two accounts differ somewhat. In the most straightforward case, suppose that you are faced with an individual whose actions you would like to predict. According to Heal, you start with an initial move of full projection. That is, you project yourself fully into his or her situation, complete with all your desires, emotions, thoughts, and so on. Then you make adjustments. Suppose you know that the other person differs from you in ways that seem relevant to understanding her here and now. Let's say she is an inveterate smoker. What you do is 'quarantine' your dislike of smoking and instead adopt a positive attitude such as you imagine a smoker would have. Only then do you imagine that you are in the situation that the other person is in and see what happens. If things go right, you should end up thinking, wanting, or intending to act as she does. The last step is to ascribe your own thoughts, wants, or intentions, arrived at in the context of the simulation, to the other person, on the assumption that you and she are sufficiently alike to justify this move.

As the debate advanced, Heal retreated to a position where she argued that belief simulation was the most useful, perhaps even the primary, approach to simulation (Heal 1998). This is understandable. Two people are more likely to differ in their desires than in their beliefs, and so a simulation that only involves the latter is more likely to be right. Moreover, it may make an important difference to one's imagination whether one *actually* desires something or merely *supposes* one does. It seems to make no difference to the kinds of inferences one is likely to perform whether one *actually* believes something or whether one merely supposes that it is true.

Gordon is famous for claiming that it is no good simply projecting *ourselves* into the other person's situation. We have to actually pretend *to be* the other person (Gordon 1992). I have never quite understood what Gordon means, but here are two plausible interpretations. First, we might suppose that we try really hard to become the other person, much as a method actor lives the character of the person he plays. Perhaps we go to all the places and engage with all the people he did, like the detective in the movie *The Element of Crime*. This, of course, is impractical, if not impossible. It may not do much for the understanding either, since understanding does not typically involve self-transformation (Maibom 2019). The second interpretation is more modest: when we imagine being someone else, we move our center of agency into the other person. Gordon sometimes says we reset our 'egocentric map.' We each have an egocentric map, the idea goes, which relates stuff out there in the world to us. We see things as close or far. These are clearly not intrinsic features of objects or the environment. They are ways of representing the world *relative to* us. When we reset our egocentric map, we move it to the person we are trying to understand. We imagine what happens to him, happens *to us*, that his 'I' refers to us, and so on. Because I am already imagining *being* the other person in my simulation, I don't subsequently need to base my ascription to the other on a sort of analogy. This interpretation does not require self-transformation of the sort just discussed. But just like Heal's suggestion, it would involve our imagining being at least somewhat different from how we are.

Gordon maintained that simulation is special because it allows us to understand people's reactions in a way that would not be possible were we merely using a psychological theory. He gives the following example. Mr. Crane and Mr. Tees are both late to the airport. Mr. Crane misses his flight by half an hour. Mr. Tees, however, misses his by 5 minutes. Who is going to be more upset? Most people find this question easy to answer: Mr. Tees, of course. But it does not seem to make a lot of sense to suppose that we consulted a theory to figure this out. Rather, we rely on our own experience of missing planes, trains, or busses and come up with the right answer.

This brings out one of the central features of simulation. It is simpler. Whereas theory theory seems to require us to know a large number of counterfactual supporting generalizations, such as 'if A wants to p, and A believes that to p, she must q, then A will q (ceteris paribus),' simulation requires no special knowledge. All that is required is the ability to use our imagination to figure out what we would or might do, think, or want. We already know that we have a capacity to make decisions, namely to reflect on counterfactual scenarios and come up with good solutions, since this is required to plan ahead. Simulation is just a special use of this pre-existing capacity. Simulation theory, then, is a more parsimonious theory of our competence than is theory theory.

One can imagine a host of other reasons to suppose simulation is a method we use for understanding others. One might appeal to introspection. Do you not sometimes try to understand what someone will do by thinking about what you would do if you were that person? If you answer yes, it seems to provide us with strong reasons to suppose that you actually do use simulation. Another line of thinking appeals to how we explicitly relate to one another. People do sometimes ask that others put themselves in their shoes. This does not show that simulation is the most fundamental way of relating to others as psychological beings, but it does provide strong evidence that it is a method people like to use.

Simulationists differ in their opinions about what capacity, exactly, simulation relies on. Heal insists that it is our ability to reason counter-factually. Martin Davies (1994) focuses on what he calls our ability for practical deliberation. These are both relatively reasoned and orderly approaches to thinking about what our capacity for simulating others con-sist in, much as one would expect from philosophers working in England. Across the pond, however, more industrial-type thinking is the order of the day. We have a decision-making system that can operate either online or offline, says Alvin Goldman (1989). Online use is the normal use. We reflect on our preferences, our beliefs, and so on, and come up with a plan of action. Offline use of our decision-making system, however, is what simulation is made of. We merely pretend to have certain beliefs and desires or, as Stephen Stich and Shaun Nichols put it, we "feed" pretend beliefs and pretend desires to our decision-making system and wait for it to churn out a pretend decision (Stich & Nichols 1992). This is a decidedly more automatic operation than what Heal or Davies appears to have in mind. The idea comes from online and offline uses of programs in computers. An offline use of a program is one in which the program does not interface with the other programs of the computer on which it runs. One runs a program offline to test its performance before it is introduced into the larger system. This means that in its offline use, the program does not have the same input and output as it usually has. The same thing is true of an offline use of our decision-making system. Instead of ending up *deciding* to do something, we merely end up with a *pretend* decision or intention.

There is, of course, a question as to whether Stich and Nichols use the term 'decision-making system' somewhat metaphorically, without committing themselves to the existence of anything like a unified *system* in the mind. The problem is that even if the term is shorthand for whatever it is that enables us to make decisions, using it certainly gives the impression that there is a unified set of capacities that allow us to reflect rationally on our decisions. To my knowledge, we have little reason to think that anything equivalent exists. In fact, I have argued elsewhere that there are at least two different ways of making decisions (Maibom 2016). One of these we might call short-term or immediate decision-making. Here we have access to a rich array of perceptual information that gives us much to work with in choosing what to do. When, however, we make decisions further in advance, what I call 'longer-term decision-making,' we *imagine* being in situations unlike the one we are currently in and therefore no longer have access to perceptual information. Instead, we use our imagination to re-create the relevant scenario. But here we rely on a different kind of information; one that is mostly abstract, general, and de-contextualized. This makes a significant difference to our choosing.

Karsten Stueber (2006) has a different way of making simulation central. His idea is that we can only understand what constitutes a reason for action from the inside. This means that unless we simulate others, we cannot truly appreciate their beliefs and desires as reasons for them to act the way they do. The thing is that thoughts can only be ascribed against a background of other thoughts. Suppose that you ascribe to your ailing aunt the belief that 'President Kennedy was assassinated,' in part because she sometimes utters these words. But, due to progressing dementia, she has little or no grasp of the idea of what a president is and what it is for someone to be assassinated. Does it not now seem that you are wrong to ascribe to her the belief that President Kennedy was assassinated? In Stueber's words, "Individual thoughts function as reasons for rational agency only relative to a specific framework of an agent's thoughts that are relevant for consideration in a specific situation" (2006, 156). It seems fairly obvious that were we to ascribe to others *whole networks* of beliefs in order to think of them as acting for certain reasons, we would not get very far. It is simply too labor intensive. How to get around this? We import the thoughts and desires we believe the other person to have into our own psychological economy, which is already heavily populated by other beliefs and desires that can double as the relevant framework. This is why we *have to* simulate others in order to think of them as acting for reasons.

If Stueber is right, simulation does not simply rely on *pretend* beliefs and desires. At the very least, it *also* relies on *our* background beliefs and desires. Moreover, when we simulate, not only must we to pretend to have beliefs and desires that we do not actually have; we must also pretend *not* to have beliefs and desires that we have. In other words, we need to quarantine them. How we accomplish this feat is under-discussed in the literature. And there are some reasons to think that this might be the hardest aspect of getting a simulation right.

It is important to notice that although simulation was first suggested as an alternative to theory theory and is therefore typically thought of as *cognitive* empathy, it really does not exclude *affective* empathy. For, as someone like Goldman pointed out, when we simulate someone experiencing affect, we thereby come to experience affect ourselves (Goldman 1992). Affect within the context of a simulation is affect nonetheless. And so simulation really straddles the cognitive versus affective empathy divide.

Another issue that has been raised in the context of the simulation theory is whether simulation is exclusively a conscious activity. Might we not sometimes run 'covert' or 'tacit' simulations? Someone like Goldman (2006) has argued that we do. According to him, we should distinguish between what he calls 'low-level' and 'high-level' simulation. 'High-level' simulation is pretty much how I have described simulation above, namely as a conscious activity where we attempt to change our perspective. 'Low-level' simulation, however, may involve a variety of different things, such as imitation, motor mimicry, or mirror neuron activity. This adds a whole new dimension to thinking about simulation.

To sum up, philosophers think of simulation as a process whereby we imagine being in someone else's situation, which leads to our figuring out what we would do, think, feel, etc. in that situation. This may involve, at a minimum, a transformation of our egocentric map, or it may require some more thoroughgoing imaginative change into the other. The latter might be done purely in terms of imagining having beliefs and desires one does not currently have. Simulation is often thought of either as a straightforward, and cognitively cheaper, alternative to theory theory or as an essential aspect of understanding other people as acting for reasons. Some have argued that simulation is perfectly poised for producing empathic feelings for others, by contrast to theory theory, which may be more exclusively concerned with producing understanding (e.g. Maibom 2007).

§2.3 Mirror neurons and low-level simulation

In the late 1980s, Giacomo Rizzolatti and his team in Parma discovered that the same neuron fired in a monkey's exposed and wired-up brain when it reached for an object and when it observed an experimenter do so (Rizzolatti et al. 1988). They called these neurons 'mirror neurons.' Neuroscientist Vittorio Gallese and philosopher Alvin Goldman (1998) were quick to connect the activity of such neurons with the simulation theory. Because simulation really is a matter of using our own capacities to understand the thoughts and actions of others, mirror neurons seem to be simulation devices par excellence. It is certainly hard to deny that mirror neurons show there is a basic mapping system in the brain that codes both self-generated and other-generated actions as belonging to the same type, hence the name 'common coding.' We do not simply see movements and then have to process them post facto. We already see such movements as movements of a certain type: reaching for a banana or closing a door. Gallese and Goldman went a step further and argued that mirror neurons allow us to see the intention with which an action is performed. For instance, I don't see you simply reaching for a glass, but see you as intending to drink what is in the glass. Since the very same capacity is used to parse our own actions and those of others, mirror neuron activity seems to provide evidence in favor of our simulating others to understand what they do. This activity is not, however, taking place at the conscious level. And so Goldman ends up calling it 'low-level simulation' to be contrasted with the more conscious form we have discussed so far, which he calls 'high-level simulation.'

It is important to note that very few studies have found definitive evidence of mirror neurons in humans. Why? Because to find them, you need to saw off parts of the person's skull and insert electrodes directly into the brain. While this is too invasive and dangerous to be thought fit to do to humans, it's apparently just fine to do to monkeys. I know of only one study that has found mirror neurons in a human, and they were found in different areas (medial frontal cortex and temporal lobe, Mukamel et al. 2010) than the ones so heavily studied in monkeys (premotor and parietal posterior areas). Nonetheless, it is generally thought that fMRI studies that demonstrate activation in overlapping areas in the person who is doing or feeling something and the person who is simply observing him show that these areas contain mirror neurons. It is a fact, though, that we know relatively little about the location of human mirror neurons. In particular, it is unclear whether they are present in some of the areas most associated with empathy (see Ugazio, Majdandžić, & Lamm 2014). Anthony Jack, for instance, argues that perspective taking engages the default mode network and inhibits the functioning of the task positive network, where mirror neurons are the most active. In other words, taking another's perspective depresses mirror neuron activity (Friedman & Jack 2018).

Various people have been highly critical of the idea that mirror neurons give us information about the intention with which an action is performed (Csibra 2007, Hickock 2014). Moreover, whereas it is fairly well established that mirror neurons code for certain gross motor actions, such as grasping, holding, tearing, and placing (Jeannerod et al. 1994), it is less clear that they code for more precise actions, such as the reason why one is holding or tearing an object. After all, I might reach for a cup to throw it on the floor, or to use it as an ashtray. This does not seem to be the sort of thing that mirror neurons code for. We should note, however, that mirror neurons' firing pattern shows that they are sensitive to points of view and the value of the action, which shows that they are not simply bottom-up structures but can be modulated top-down (Kilner & Lemon 2013). What does this mean? It means that mirror neuron functioning is not purely perceptual. It is likely to be more centrally engaged with meaning making, even if of a kind that does not quite amount to ascription of intentions.

Another concern one might have is how to interpret 'common coding.' Simulationists have been quick to claim that it supports their theory. In actual fact, it is not clear that it does. For recall that mirror neurons code equally for your actions and for mine but with no obvious priority between the two. Simulation requires priority of coding for our own action compared to the coding of other people's actions. And it might initially seem that mirror neurons do just that because of their connection to motor responses. But it is important to remember that what reaching looks like from a first-person perspective and a third-person one is really quite different. And when it comes to things like expression of emotions, things get even worse because whereas we have a partial view of our hands and arms, we have almost no immediate visual access to our own faces. But understanding what *we* do is heavily influenced by our perceptual representations of what *others* do (what smiling looks like, say). It is therefore not obvious that the connection with motor responses shows any clear prioritizing of one's own self-understanding compared to the understanding of others. If so, is it right to call mirror neuron activity simulation even if it is just low-level simulation?

However skeptical you might be about what mirror neurons actually *do*, there is little doubt that their existence shows that it is problematic to suppose that we *see* others' actions as actions and not behaviors only because we *interpret* them. Action may, indeed, be 'given' in experience in a way not foreseen by Sellars or his followers.

One last question one might have concerns the connection between high-level and low-level simulation. They may seem like very different processes. And, indeed, they are. However, they are supposed to have one thing in common; they are both *mirroring processes*. In both types of simulation, the thought goes, do we have processes that are *re-using* or *(re)enacting* another, more original version of that process. The two differ, though, in the degree to which they are conscious, automatic, and driven by stimulus (Barlassina & Gordon 2017).

§2.4 Putting the 'perspective' back into perspective taking

Psychologists talk less of simulation and more of *perspective taking*. As we saw in the previous chapter, 'perspective taking' appears alongside 'empathic concern,' 'fantasy,' and 'personal distress' in *The Interpersonal Reactivity Index*. People who express a high degree of agreement with statements such as: "Before criticizing somebody, I try to imagine how I would feel if I were in their place" and "I believe that there are two sides to every question and try to look at them both" (Davis 1980) score high on perspective taking. As such, perspective taking seems to be just a different term for the phenomenon that philosophers call 'simulation' (high-level simulation). There are two important differences, however. First, psychologists' perspective taking seems to be just *one* of several approaches to understanding others. At least originally, simulation was not. Second, psychologists tend to make a distinction between imagine-self and imagine-other perspective taking.

Imagine-self perspective taking encourages people to imagine that they are in the other person's situation and what that would mean to them. This personal element tends to be strongly emphasized in the instructions. Here is the version Batson typically uses:

> try to *imagine how you yourself would feel about what has happened to the person* [...] *and how this experience would affect your life.*
>
> (Batson, Early, & Salvarini 1997, 753)

It turns out that this kind of instruction leads to greater focus on the self (Davis et al. 2004), more personally felt distress when exposed to someone in need, and a greater tendency to escape a situation where another is in need, if it is easy to do so, without helping them (Batson 1991).

Imagine-other perspective taking simply describes a process where a person uses his or her imagination to think about the other person's feeling and her situation. This does not require perspective taking in the sense of taking up a first-person perspective on the other person's situation. Consider these instructions, also taken from Batson:

> imagine how the person [...] feels about what has happened and how it has affected his or her life.
>
> (Batson, Early, & Salvarini 1997, 753)

Notice that this feat can be accomplished by imagining the other person's feelings and the consequences of those feelings without having to transpose oneself into their situation. That is not to say that doing so would not be a great way of following the instructions, only that it is not necessary. Imagine-other perspective taking leads to greater focus on the other person (Davis et al. 2004), less personal distress compared to empathic concern (sympathy) when exposed to a person in need, and more helping of the person in need, even when escape from the upsetting situation is easy (Batson 1991).

How should we think of this distinction as philosophers? I think that neither imagine-self nor imagine-other perspective taking are particularly realistic portrayals of perspective taking in the wild. They certainly describe activities that we can engage in, and obviously doing one as opposed to the other has interestingly different consequences. But that does not show that when we take another person's perspective we usually do one or the other. Consider the imagine-self instructions. They encourage an almost exclusive focus on the self. But, when we take the trouble to put ourselves in other people's shoes, we do so to understand *the other person*, not simply to see what *we* would feel or think. Imagine-other perspective taking, on the other hand, does not help us distinguish between simulating the other and other 'close readings' of another person (using theory theory, for instance). Ordinary perspective taking is most likely somewhere between imagine-self and imagine-other perspective taking (Maibom 2019).

To get a little closer to what is really going on in perspective taking, we might start reflecting on why we call it 'perspective taking' in the first place. Taking a perspective is originally a *visual* activity. When we take other people's *visual* perspectives, it helps us understand not only *what* people see but also *how* they see it. Psychologists sometimes call this level 1 and level 2 perspective taking, respectively (e.g. Michelon & Zacks 2006). When we take other people's visual perspectives, we perform transformations on the visual scene by means of our own visual system and thereby come to 'see' what the visual scene looks like to the other person. There are two central elements to visual perspective taking: 1) a *shift* in perspective, whereby one *moves* one's own perspective to that of the other person, and 2) an imaginative engagement of one's visual system. This has the result of 3) providing information about what something *looks like*. It seems quite plausible that when we take another person's perspective more generally (and not simply visually) we: 1) move our first-person perspective to the other person, 2) we *imagine* the other person's situation, the result of which is that we 3) acquire information about what *it is like* to be in that situation. We might call this 'agent perspective taking' to distinguish it from 'visual perspective taking,' although I shall continue to use 'perspective taking' as a short-hand for the former (Maibom manuscript).

It is worth dwelling briefly on the idea of change of perspective. In the visual case, the difference may easily be demonstrated by considering videogames. Back in the day, one's avatar in a game was merely one object among others. The main difference was that you had some control over its movements (vertical and horizontal). In first-person shooter games, on the other hand, the game world is seen from the perspective of one's avatar; you can only see what is in front of you, more or less—i.e. your arms and the gun. The first-person visual perspective is, then, quite specific and involves a radically different experience than a third-person one. From your own perspective, you are mostly *implicitly* represented. You are the unrepresented focal point of what you see. The visual world seems to radiate out from your person, and all objects are seen in relation to your body. Space itself is represented on an egocentric frame of reference (Campbell 1994, Eilan 1995). Moreover, you see *less* from this perspective than you do from what we might call an observer, or third-person, perspective.

The first-person *agent* perspective is similarly unique. According to research carried about by Bertram Malle and colleagues (e.g. Malle, Knobe, & Nelson 2007), when someone thinks about herself normally, and therefore from a first-person perspective, she tends to: 1) focus more on her experiences and feelings than on her actions; 2) think her actions are reasoned and relatively uninfluenced by outside factors, such as her environment and her past; and 3) think that her beliefs directly reflect the nature of the world. By contrast, when a person thinks about other people—i.e. takes a third-person perspective—she usually: 4) focuses more on their reasons for action than on their experiences and feelings; 5) thinks their environment and past experiences have a greater role to play in their actions than her own do in hers; 6) considers them to be driven by desire as much as by reason; and 7) she thinks of others' beliefs about the world *as beliefs*, i.e. as potentially false.[1]

It can be a bit hard, on the basis of a list of these features alone, to figure out what impact perspective taking has. Turning to the victim versus perpetrator literature helps. Victims maximize the seriousness of the wrongdoing, moralize it, and see it as essentially incomprehensible. The event continues to produce anger, which is conceived of as righteous anger by the victim. Perpetrators, on the other hand, minimize the wrongness of the act and/or justify it, see it as unavoidable, and focus on extenuating circumstances. The victim is often thought to have provoked the action and/or is seen to be overreacting, despite the fact the perpetrator regrets the action. One can easily effect a switch of perspectives by giving people a story of a wrongdoing and asking them to identify with either the victim or the perpetrator (Baumeister, Stillwell, & Wotman 1990, Stillwell & Baumeister 1997).

Keeping these differences in mind, it is easy to see that if we actually manage to take up someone else's perspective, as in taking up her first-person perspective, it would make a significant difference to how we think about things. It should be noted that Malle and colleagues did not find support for the fact that people experienced these benefits when asked to change their perspective (Malle & Pearce 2001). However, the study was not well designed. In it, they asked people to switch their perspective while interacting with the target. Most subjects reported finding this difficult to do. Either they were thinking about the other person's point of view, or they were interacting with him or her. This suggests that other tests, where the person does not have his or her attention divided, may be needed to discover whether we are actually able to switch our perspectives. Common experience suggests that we are, however, so I don't think we ought to be too disconcerted about the lack of evidence provided by one study.

It is important to note that the third-person perspective is sometimes used to describe a disengaged and scientific point of view. The first-person point of view is the subjective one, and the third-person one, the objective. The way I have used the terms here does not imply that the third-person point of view is particularly objective or disengaged. It is simply how one person regards another from *her own* point of view. It is the viewpoint of an observer of another person, to be distinguished from an engaged agent point of view.

§2.5 Introspection, perspective, and self-understanding

As we saw, many early forms of simulation theory assumed that we could rely on knowledge of our own mental states to ascribe mental states to others based on a simulation of them. This assumes that simulation is for simulating *others* exclusively. But can we simply help ourselves to our own mental states, as it were? Are we *directly* aware of our mental states? Goldman has argued so, with some justification (Goldman 1989). Recall, for instance, Descartes' *cogito* argument. I think, therefore I am. This argument works because thoughts are self-verifying in the following sense. To doubt that I am thinking, I must be doubting. But doubting is a form of thinking. And so, by necessity, I think when I doubt. Might I not be hallucinating that I'm doubting, and therefore thinking? Perhaps, but hallucinating doubting would still be a way of thinking. It is impossible, it seems, that there should be doubting when there is no thinking at all going on. This suggests that there is something special about first-person access to mental states. It is direct in a way that is fairly undeniable.

This does not mean, of course, that we have access to all let alone most of our mental states or processes. It also does not imply that when we ask ourselves: "why did I say that?" the answer that we provide is the correct one. Knowing *why* we thought or did something is very different from knowing *that* we think or do something. Psychological research suggests that we often confabulate when giving our reasons for acting (Ross & Nisbett 1991, Wilson 2002). A reason, such as "I said what I said because I was trying to ameliorate a bad situation," may be *directly* accessible, but this thought need not be causally connected to the *actual* reason for saying what you said. This suggests that we are often in need of interpreting ourselves in addition to others. And here perspective taking can do some work.

Just as we saw taking another person's perspective ought to reverse the asymmetry between a first-person and a third-person perspective, so should taking a third-person perspective on oneself. If successful, it corrects the self-interested and often self-flattering interpretations we often give of our own actions, motives, and accomplishments. It might turn out to be particularly important when it comes to intentional action. It is here that we tend to be overly focused on our own interpretations of what we do. This easily creates problems because responsible agency requires us to consider not only how what we do impacts those around us but also how others would see what we do. We don't always see eye to eye with those others, however. This is one important reason to think that the ability to take an outside perspective on one's own action is required for responsible agency (Maibom 2014). After all, as Socrates once pointed out, no one does wrong knowingly (Plato 380BCE). If that is right, it means that actions that we see as obviously wrong or problematic are conceived differently by the actors performing them. What is needed is for these actors to take an alternative perspective on what they do. Clearly, if they had taken ours, they would have viewed things differently. Conversely, we might sometimes find that what we thought was wrong is not so bad after all, once considered from the perspective of the actor.

When it comes to who we are, knowing how we appear to others is also central, Western individualism notwithstanding. There is a beautiful passage in Sartre's *Being and Nothingness* where he asks us to imagine that we are peeking through a keyhole to see what is going on behind the locked door (Sartre 1943/1956, Part III, Chap. 1). As we peek, we don't think of this act of peeking much, or if we do, we do so in a fairly innocent way. We are, after all, merely trying to inform ourselves about something important. Suddenly, we hear footsteps in the hall. This immediate threat of another intruding into the scene reverses our perspective so that we come to see ourselves as we imagine the other person would: as a *peeping Tom*. This is a rather powerful demonstration of the difference taking another perspective on ourselves can have.

§2.6 Can we ever really understand others from the inside?

The most popular objection to simulation and perspective taking is that it is impossible for us to imaginatively transform ourselves enough to capture

what something is like for another person. This type of objection takes
many forms. During the height of the simulation theory versus theory
theory debate in the nineties, the worry was that people differ quite widely
from one another, and to know *what* beliefs and desires someone else has
so that we can incorporate their imaginative counterparts into our simulation is impossible without already having some access to such states inde-
pendent of simulation.

A more recent objection is from Peter Goldie (2014), who maintains
that we can never fully succeed in taking another person's perspective
because to do so we would have to represent her *background* beliefs, moods,
attitudes, and other features of her personality. This is impossible, both in
theory and in practice. It would be so cognitively onerous as to be impossible for any normal person to carry out, quite apart from it being
impractical in everyday life. More seriously, it is also impossible in principle, Goldie insists. Why? Because the functional roles of explicitly represented beliefs, desires, etc. are different from the functional roles of
implicitly represented beliefs, desires, etc. For instance, a simulator who
pretends to be a male chauvinist is going to get different results from a
simulation than he would were he, himself, a male chauvinist. In the latter
case, he could simply rely on the relevant background assumptions about
women in his simulation and get results similar to the target. In the former
case, these assumptions are going to be widely available to cognitive, in
addition to motivational, systems. Imagine, for instance, that you are
simulating someone whom you know acts imperiously and dismissively
towards women when it comes to institutional decision-making. You are
trying to figure out what that person might say or do in a certain woman-
involving situation, and to do so you imagine being a male chauvinist. You
find yourself having all sorts of derogatory thoughts about the particular
woman, and women in general. It turns out, however, that the person you
are simulating does not. Why? Because he does not *think* of himself as a
male chauvinist.

Goldie thinks that these reflections raise concerns about the entire
enterprise of imagining being in someone else's position, unless we simply
assume that what we imagine is what *we* would think or feel in her situation (full projection). I think that concern is overblown. There are at least
two problems with Goldie's approach. First of all, Goldie thinks of perspective taking as *either* imagining *ourselves* in someone else's situation or
imagining *being the other person* in her situation. But it is unclear that perspective taking falls under either one of these descriptions or, indeed, that

it ought to. It is fairly easy to see how wholesale projection goes astray. Even people who are very similar to us have different tastes, sensibilities, and predilections, all of which will be lost in egocentric simulation. It may get us accurate results some of the time for some people, but it would be hard to know when. Moreover, projecting ourselves into other people's situations often defeats its own purpose. After all, the situations where projection would be helpful are typically situations where we would not find what others do puzzling at all (because they are already so similar to us). The situations where we do find what others do puzzling, however, are exactly the types of situations where we differ and so we cannot rely on our own psychological make-up to simulate them (Maibom 2019).

It is harder to see why imagining being the other person, which Goldie calls 'empathic imagining,' is problematic. Goldie seems to think that in the absence of full identification with the subject, we cannot hope to get good results from a simulation. The problem is that full identification is both counterproductive and beside the point. Take Lars von Trier's movie *The Element of Crime*, for example. In it, the detective uses a method of identification to find a serial killer. He reconstructs the killer's earlier travels and encounters. He takes the same drugs. He sleeps with the same woman. In the end he succeeds. But what does he do? He kills the next victim. Moreover, the more he identifies with the killer, the less he understands him. He does, however, embody his actions and quirks. How is this? Perhaps because the traits, beliefs, etc. that would have helped such an understanding are no longer explicitly represented but have become part of the detective's own psychology (i.e. are now implicit). This captures the problem beautifully. The point of taking another person's perspective is not to transform me into you. It is to *understand* you. Once I have become you, I no longer understand you because there's nothing left of *me* to do so.

I have suggested elsewhere that the aim of perspective taking it neither self-transformation nor projection (Maibom 2019). Rather, we try to make sense of the other person on the basis of our own current capacities and understanding. We meet somewhere in the middle, where I can still make sense of you from my own standpoint but where I will also find patterns of reactivity that are different from my own. I am neither projecting myself wholesale into your situation nor attempting to transform myself into you (even if for just a moment). This process involves a complex mix of projections, substitute beliefs, desires, etc. *explicitly represented*, as well as a decided *shift* in perspective, which changes the relevance of things so that they gravitate towards *the other person*. There is no reason to think that this shift needs explicit representing.

Another thing to note is that Goldie uses the very thing that some simulationists think is the virtue of simulation theory against it: its reliance on background beliefs. Recall that for Stueber, it is the very fact that the simulator imports his or her own background beliefs into her simulation that makes simulation useful in the first place. Among other things, the reliance on these background assumptions solves what is sometimes called the epistemological *frame problem*. The problem is this. When you decide what to do or think, there are almost infinitely many things that might turn out to be relevant. Unless you have some sense of what to consider in making your decision about what to do or think, you will be stuck needlessly considering *everything*. To avoid this predicament, you must have some sense of *relevance*. It would be absurd to suppose that we *explicitly* represent such relevance. Moreover, it appears to lead to an infinite regress. Instead, our grasp of relevance is widely supposed to be the result of lived experience. This is why simulation is superior to theorizing according to some philosophers, such as Stueber. We can simply rely on information we already have, implicit or explicit. On Goldie's account, empathic perspective shifting would defeat the very purpose of simulation in the first place.

§2.7 What about transformative experience?

A concern not unlike the one we have just looked at may arise from the work of Laurie Paul (2014) on transformative experience. Experiences that are rather major, such as having a child or moving to another country, change your preference structure. That is, as a parent you are likely to relinquish old standing preferences and to acquire desires that you did not previously have, *as a result* of having the child. Moreover, you won't know beforehand just how your preferences will change. So you cannot factor these preferences into your decision-making. This means that when you make choices that involve personal transformation, it is impossible for you to do so rationally. Why? To make rational choices, you need to consider your so-called priors—namely, your desires, beliefs, and standing preferences—to see whether engaging in the relevant action will satisfy enough of them to be worth it. This presupposes that your desires and preferences do not undergo radical change over time. But, as a matter of fact, they do. There is, therefore, no way of making a rational decision about whether or not to have a child. You have to throw yourself into it, as it were. Put simply, standard accounts of rational decision-making are flawed because they do not take into account such personal change.

Why is this relevant to our discussion, you might ask? If *we* cannot cal-culate rationally what we ought to do in cases of transformative experiences because there is no way to know what they are like and how they will change you before having them, we cannot use our ability to make such decisions to understand those of others either. And supposing we did manage to imagine being in a very similar situation to the other agent—including having similar beliefs and desires—we could still not count on understanding him. We cannot *know what it is like* until we have tried it ourselves. What something is like for someone else is at least sometimes something of a mystery.

There is little doubt that life changes us and, at times, in surprising ways. As Kierkegaard said, life is understood backwards, but must be lived forwards.[2] I no longer desire the sorts of things I desired when I was younger, and I am much more concerned about things that I thought little about then, such as the welfare of nonhuman animals or environmental degradation. In fact, it seems like we change a little all the time with aging, experience, and our changing environment. If that is true, is it not also true that pretty much any choice can change us just enough to make it the case that we can *never* rationally choose anything at all? Since it seems that we *do* make rational choices at least some of the time, the model of decision-making Paul criticizes must be wrong. If so, we can be hopeful that a new account will tell a decent story about choice, including the one to have transformative experiences.

Personally, I think that any criticism of the possibility of perspective taking or simulation based on the transformative experience argument misses the point of perspective taking in much the same way Goldie does. Whoever thought that we can know *exactly* what it is like for others to have the experiences they do, or *exactly* what difference having them makes to their lives? I certainly do not, enthusiastic though I may be about the epistemic potential of perspective taking. The idea is to engender an imaginative counterpart of the other person's experience that *approximates* it. The same presumably applies when we, personally, face a transformative choice. We approximate and probably end up making our decision in a space between who we are now and who we will become. Vague though it may be, this suggestion points to a larger question. Can we get information that is *good enough* to decide whether or not to choose to have a transformative experience? My suspicion is that many of us think that we can. Long ago, I decided not to have children myself. I was never particularly into children, and when I learnt that women bear the brunt of child rearing on top of already doing more housework than their male partners, I knew it was not for me. Does that mean that I claim to *know* what the experience would be like on this basis? Not really. But I think I knew enough to understand that this experience was not one I wanted to have.

But won't I now be in a situation where I cannot possibly understand what a parent might do, feel, or want? Not necessarily. It strikes me as quite plausible that I can concoct an imaginative scenario out of my love for other people, for pets, and so on. If my aim is *for me* to understand a parent better, this may be very effective indeed. I am not saying that I can imagine *exactly* what it is like for a parent to have parent-related experiences. The point is rather to argue that it can be helpful from the point of view of *understanding* to imagine that I am a parent, *even* if I have never had children myself. It is quite plausible that I must be capable of certain feelings and that I must have had certain experiences in order to be able to simulate such a scenario. If I cannot love another being so much that its death will seem like an unmitigated disaster to me, or if I have never experienced the sense that I would die for the one I love, I may not be able to get very close to what most parents feel. But it is unclear to me why we should suppose that we must have had *the very same experiences* as someone else to be able to understand, in some reasonable sense of 'understand,' what it is like for her.

§2.8 Take-home message

Cognitive empathy is a broad term for what is usually known as 'simulation' in philosophy of mind or 'perspective taking' in social psychology, although it also sometimes describes any form of theory of mind activity. Perspective taking or (high-level) simulation is a process wherein we imagine that we are in someone else's situation and thereby generate imaginative responses to it. Those responses are then assumed to be like those of the other person: what they think or will do, for instance. Some simulation theorists talk as if one simply needs to imagine having different beliefs, desires, and so on, whereas others insist that simulation involves an egocentric shift or a perspective change. For something to be perspective *taking*, however, it must involve such a shift or change in one's perspective.

There are broad concerns about the possibility of success of such an imaginative enterprise. The difference between people, there being transformative experiences, and the difficulties imagining correctly even in our own case have been thought to present serious difficulties for the success of simulation or perspective taking. I have presented some reasons not to be overly impressed with such arguments.

To sum up, in this chapter, we have discussed:

- The difference between theory theory and simulation theory
- What it is to simulate another person
- What it is to take another's *perspective*
- The difference between high-level and low-level simulation
- How perspective taking can help you understand yourself as well as other people
- Some of the difficulties simulating others, such as transformative experiences
- How to overcome challenges to the usefulness of perspective taking/ simulation

Notes

1 The authors talk of the actor versus observer perspective, which, as far as I can see, comes to the same thing as a first-person and third-person perspective, respectively.

2 This is a common condensation of the following passage from his journal: "Det er ganske sandt hvad Philosophien siger, at Livet forstås baglænds. Men derover glemmer man den anden sætning, at det må leves forlænds" (Kierkegaard: Journalen JJ: 167, *Søren Kierkegaard's Skrifter*, http://www.sks. dk/forside/indhold.asp). In other words, "it is true what philosophy says that life must be understood backwards. But people forget the other sentence, namely that it must be lived forwards" (my translation).

Further readings

Gallese, V. & Goldman, A. 1998. Mirror-neurons and the simulation theory of mind-reading. *Trends in Cognitive Science*, 2, 493–501. *The classical paper that links the existence of mirror neurons with the simulation theory.*

Goldie, P. 2014. Anti-empathy. In: A. Coplan & P. Goldie (Eds.) *Empathy: Philosophical and Psychological Perspectives*. New York: Oxford University Press, 218–230. *A paper highly skeptical of the possibility of imagining 'from the inside' what it is like to have another person's experiences.*

Gordon, R.M. 1986. Folk psychology as simulation. *Mind and Language*, 1, 158–171. *One of the two first defenses of the simulation theory.*

Heal, J. 1998. Understanding other minds from the inside. In: A. O'Hear (Ed.) *Current Issues in Philosophy of Mind*. Cambridge: Cambridge University Press, 83–99. *A later development of Heal's distinctive form of simulation, this time focusing on simulating beliefs.*

Maibom, H.L. 2019. What can we learn from taking another's perspective? In: D. Matravers & A. Waldow (Eds.) *Philosophical Perspectives on Empathy*. New York: Routledge, 74–90. *A paper that explains what might be special about taking another person's perspective as opposed to thinking about their psychological states using some other method.*

Paul, L. 2014. *Transformative Experience*. New York: Oxford University Press, Chaps. 2–3. *This book presents a serious challenge to the prevalent way of thinking about rational decision-making. It shows that there is a shift in desires as a result of choices that we make, which makes it difficult to base our decisions to have transformative experiences on rational deliberation.*

References

Barlassina, L. & Gordon, R.M. 2017. Folk psychology as mental simulation. In: E.N. Zalta (Ed.) *The Stanford Encyclopedia of Philosophy*. https://plato.sta nford.edu/entries/folkpsych-simulation/#ex-proc.

Baumeister, R.F., Stillwell, A., & Wotman, S.R. 1990. Victim and perpetrator accounts of interpersonal conflict: Autobiographical narratives of anger. *Journal of Personality and Social Psychology*, 59, 994–1005.

Batson, C.D. 1991. *The Altruism Question: Toward a Social-Psychological Answer*. Hillsdale, NJ: Lawrence Erlbaum Associates.

Batson, C.D., Early, S., & Salvarini, G. 1997. Perspective taking: Imagining how another feels versus imagining how you would feel. *Personality and Social Psychology Bulletin*, 23, 751–758.

Campbell, J. 1994. *Past, Space, and Self*. Cambridge, MA: MIT Press.

Churchland, P. 1970. The logical character of action-explanations. *The Philosophical Review*, 79, 214–236.

Csibra, F. 2007. Action mirroring and action interpretation: An alternative account. In: P. Haggard, Y. Rosetti, & M. Kawato (Eds.) *Sensorimotor Foundations of Higher Cognition (Attention and Performance XII)*. Oxford: Oxford University Press.

Davies, M. 1994. The mental simulation debate. In: *Proceedings of the British Academy, 83*. Oxford: Oxford University Press, 99–127.

Davies, M. & Stone, T. (Eds.) 1995a. *Folk Psychology*. Oxford: Blackwell.

Davies, M. & Stone, T. (Eds.) 1995b. *Mental Simulation*. Oxford: Blackwell.

Davis, M.H. 1980. A multidimensional approach to individual differences in empathy. *JSAS Catalog of Selected Documents in Psychology*, 10, 85.

Davis, M.H., Soderlund, T., Cole, J., Gadol, E., Kute, M., Myers, M., & Weihing, J. 2004. Cognitions associated with attempts to empathize: How do we imagine the perspective of another? *Personality and Social Psychology Bulletin*, 30, 1625–1635.

Dennett, D.C. 1987. *The Intentional Stance*. Cambridge, MA: MIT Press.

Eilan, N. 1995. The first person perspective. *Proceedings of the Aristotelian Society*, 95, 51–66.

Fodor, J. 1975. *The Language of Thought*. Cambridge, MA: MIT Press.

Fodor, J. 1987. *Psychosemantics*. Cambridge, MA: MIT Press.

Friedman, J.P. & Jack, A. 2018. Mapping cognitive structure onto the landscape of philosophical debate: An empirical framework with relevance to problems of consciousness, free will and ethics. *Review of Philosophy and Psychology*, 9, 73–113.

Gallese, V. & Goldman, A. 1998. Mirror-neurons and the simulation theory of mind-reading. *Trends in Cognitive Science*, 2, 493–501.

Godfrey-Smith, P. 2005. Folk psychology as model. *Philosophers' Imprint*, 5, 1–16.

Goldie, P. 2014. Anti-empathy. In: A. Coplan & P. Goldie (Eds.) *Empathy: Philosophical and Psychological Perspectives*. New York: Oxford University Press, 218–230.

Goldman, A.I. 1989. Interpretation psychologized. *Mind and Language*, 4, 161–185.

Goldman, A.I. 1992. Empathy, mind, and morals. *Proceedings and Addresses of the American Philosophical Association*, 66, 17–41.

Goldman, A.I. 2006. *Simulating Minds*. New York: Oxford University Press.

Gopnik, A. & Wellman, H.M. 1992. Why the child's theory of mind really is a theory. *Mind and Language*, 7, 145–171.

Gordon, R.M. 1986. Folk psychology as simulation. *Mind and Language*, 1, 158–171.

Gordon, R.M. 1992. The simulation theory: Objections and misconceptions. *Mind and Language*, 7, 11–34.

Heal, J. 1986. Replication and functionalism. In: J. Butterfield (Ed.) *Language, Mind and Logic*. Cambridge: Cambridge University Press, 135–150.

Heal, J. 1998. Understanding other minds from the inside. In: A. O'Hear (Ed.) *Current Issues in Philosophy of Mind*. Cambridge: Cambridge University Press, 83–99.

Hickock, G. 2014. *The Myth of Mirror Neurons: The Real Science of Cognition and Communication*. New York: W.W. Norton and Company.

Hutto, D. 2008. *Folk Psychological Narratives: The Sociocultural Basis of Understanding Reasons*. Cambridge, MA: MIT Press.

Hutto, D. & Jurgens, A. 2019. Exploring enactive empathy. In: D. Matravers & A. Waldow (Eds.) *Philosophical Perspectives on Empathy*. New York: Routledge, 111–128.

Jeannerod, M., Arbib, M.A., Rizzolatti, G., & Sakata, H. 1994. Grasping objects: The cortical mechanisms of visuomotor transformation. *Trends in Neuroscience*, 18, 314–320.

Kilner, J.M. & Lemon, R.N. 2013. What we know currently about mirror neurons. *Current Biology*, 23, PR1057–R1062.

Maibom, H.L. 2001. Tacit knowledge & folk psychology. *Danish Yearbook of Philosophy*, 35, 95–114.

Maibom, H.L. 2003. The mindreader and the scientist. *Mind & Language*, 18, 296–315.

Maibom, H.L. 2007. The presence of others. *Philosophical Studies*, 132, 161–190.

Maibom, H.L. 2014. Knowing what we are doing. In: D. Jacobson & J. D'Arms (Eds.) *The Science of Ethics: Moral Psychology and Human Agency*. New York: Oxford University Press, 108–122.

Maibom, H.L. 2016. Knowing me, knowing you: Failure to forecast and the empathic imagination. In: A. Kind & P. Kung (Eds.) *Knowledge Through Imagination*. New York: Oxford University Press, 185–206.

Maibom, H.L. 2019. What can we learn from taking another's perspective? In: D. Matravers & A. Waldow (Eds.) *Philosophical Perspectives on Empathy*. New York: Routledge, 74–90.

Maibom, H.L. Manuscript. *Knowing Me, Knowing You: Adventures in Perspective Taking*.

Malle, B.F., Knobe, J.M., Nelson, S.E. 2007. Actor-observer asymmetries in explanations of behavior: New answers to an old question. *Journal of Personality and Social Psychology*, 93, 491–514.

Malle, B.F. & Pearce, G.E. 2001. Attention to behavioral events during interaction: Two actor-observer gaps and three attempts to close them. *Journal of Personality and Social Psychology*, 81, 278–294.

Michelon, P. & Zacks, J.M. 2006. Two kinds of visual perspective taking. *Perception and Psychophysics*, 68, 327–337.

Mukamel, R., Ekstrom, A.D., Kaplan, J., Iacoboni, M., & Fried, I. 2010. Single-neuron responses in humans during execution and observation of actions. *Current Biology*, 20, 750–756.

Paul, L. 2014. *Transformative Experience*. New York: Oxford University Press.

Plato. 380BCE. *Gorgias*. Trans. B. Jowett. http://classics.mit.edu/Plato/gorgias.html.

Rizzollati, G., Camarda, R., Fogassi, L., Gentilucci, M., Luppino, G., & Matelli, M. 1988. Functional organization of inferior area 6 in the macaque monkey. II. Area F5 and the control of distal movements. *Experimental Brain Research*, 71, 491–507.

Ross, L. & Nisbett, R.E. 1991. *The Person and the Situation: Perspectives of Social Psychology*. New York: McGraw-Hill Inc.

Ryle, G. 1949. *The Concept of Mind*. London: Hutchinson.

Sartre, J-P. 1943/1956. *Being and Nothingness*. Trans. H.E. Barnes. New York: Washington Square Press.

Sellars, W. 1963. Empiricism and the philosophy of mind. In: *Science, Perception and Reality*. London: Routledge & Kegan Paul, 127–196.

Stich, S. & Nichols, S. 1992. Folk psychology: Simulation or tacit theory? *Mind and Language*, 7, 35–71.

Stillwell, A. & Baumeister, R. 1997. The construction of victim and perpetrator memories: Accuracy and distortion in role-based accounts. *Personality and Social Psychology Bulletin*, 23, 1157–1172.

Stueber, K. 2006. *Rediscovering Empathy: Agency, Folk Psychology, and the Human Sciences*. Cambridge, MA: MIT Press.

Ugazio, G., Majdandžić, J., & Lamm, C. 2014. Are empathy and morality linked? Insights from moral psychology, social and decision neuroscience, and philosophy. In: H.L. Maibom (Ed.) *Empathy and Morality*. New York: Oxford University Press, 155–171.

Von Trier, L. 1984. *The Element of Crime (Forbrydelsens Element)*.

Wilson, T.D. 2002. *Strangers to Ourselves: Discovering the Adaptive Unconscious*. Cambridge, MA: Harvard University Press.

Zahavi, D. 2017. Phenomenology, empathy, and mindreading. In: H.L. Maibom (Ed.) *The Routledge Handbook of Philosophy of Empathy*. New York: Routledge, 33–43.

3

EMPATHY AND FEELING FOR AND WITH OTHERS

Being able to share the affect of our fellow creatures is arguably one of our more remarkable capacities. We may be infused with a mood as we enter into a room; we sometimes seem to feel the pangs of anguish of our friends; and we sympathize with victims of war. These are all ways in which we are affected by others' feelings or their situations. We called these affective responses to empathy emotional contagion, empathy 'proper,' and sympathy in Chapter 1. Are they fully distinct, or are some, or all, modifications of the same basic sensibility? Is empathy, for instance, a later stage of emotional contagion, or sympathy a development of empathy?

In this chapter, I discuss mimicry and contagion, the differences and similarities between emotional contagion, empathy proper, and sympathy, the likely evolutionary origin of these responses, the importance of altruistic and egoistic motivation to the empathy debate, and what sharing might amount to in empathy.

§3.1 Vicarious affect

As we saw in Chapter 1, vicarious affect or emotional contagion is so central to empathy that some people have defined empathy in such a permissive way as to include it in its scope. That was (D3) we looked at, suggested by primatologists Preston and de Waal. Since most definitions of empathy proper include a condition that the empathizer understands that what she feels is either the result of what another feels, or has as its object what that person feels, it is natural that primatologists would not lean towards such a definition. After all, we cannot *ask* an animal whether it feels distress for the other animal whose suffering it witnesses or whether it merely feels it personally. To be fair, though, when you ask some people the same question, they have no idea what you're talking about either. But I digress.

The first thing to note about vicarious affect is that it is an affective reaction that is largely *consonant* with that of the other person. Ideally, it involves the same type of emotion; for instance, sadness, happiness, or disgust. If the emotions between two people differ greatly, we can safely assume that neither one of these emotions is vicarious. There is currently no agreement on what counts as similar enough, although all agree that if someone's sadness makes you happy, you're not empathizing.

Second, vicarious affect is an emotional *reaction* to the emotions of another. It is because I am aware, in some sense, of your experiencing the emotion that you are that I experience the (largely consonant) emotion I am. This is a special instance of experiencing emotions with other people. We can do so without experiencing emotions *vicariously*. For instance, if you and I are both in a scary situation and we are afraid as a result of that, but not because we observe that we are each afraid, our fear is not vicarious but what psychologists call 'direct.' It is likely that direct and vicarious affect operate jointly in many situations. Catching your fear, I may become fearful myself, and knowing that you are afraid can enhance the fear I already feel. My resultant state is, then, best conceived of as a mix of direct and vicarious affect. Nonetheless, it is reasonable to distinguish between the two types of reactions, since in many cases they do not co-occur.

Third, vicarious affect is not meant to apply to all types of reactions to other people's emotions. For instance, when you are angry with me and I become angry as a result, I am reacting to your emotion. It is the same emotion; it is a reaction to your emotion; but it has the wrong object. You are angry with me and I am angry with you. If my anger were vicarious, truly speaking, should it not be anger with myself? It is hard to say, since vicarious affect may only transmit the affective *quality* but not the object of the originator emotion. It is therefore *possible* that many instances of people getting angry with angry people are actually the result of anger contagion. Having said that, the current consensus is that if your anger makes me angry *with you* it is not vicarious anger. It is *reactive* anger.

To these three features, one might add a fourth: that vicarious affect is *affiliative*. Ursula Hess and Agneta Fischer (2014) propose this addition. Why? Because when we are with people we do not like, we do not automatically respond to their emotions with vicarious affect. In fact, we often feel the opposite; if they are suffering, we are happy, and so on. And so sometimes our sensitivity to what others feel causes us to feel emotions that are contrary to what they are feeling. At other times, though, we are moved by the plight of our enemy, and this causes us to see him as a fellow human. Whether or not affiliation comes before or after vicarious affect, it is clearly closely associated with it. The tendency to experience vicarious affect and having a positive, or perhaps a neutral, attitude toward the other go hand in hand.

Some people talk of affective *mimicry* and distinguish this from emotional contagion. It is well known that people mimic others' emotional expressions (Dimberg 1990; Dimberg, Thunberg, & Elmehed 2000). Mimicking does not necessarily involve an affective response, however, but only the behavioral expressions associated with the emotion that is mimicked. For instance, you smile and I either smile back or engage the same muscles that I would use for smiling. Moreover, much mimicry is below the threshold of awareness and is not always visible. We cannot therefore conclude that I *feel* happy or pleased because I engage the relevant muscles. Some theories hold that emotional mimicry is the first step towards emotional contagion. The idea is that by mimicking the facial expressions associated with an emotion, you induce that very emotion in yourself (e.g. Hatfield, Cacioppo, & Rapson 1994). This is known as the matched motor hypothesis or the facial feedback hypothesis (Laird & Bressler 1992; Tomkins 1962). We will talk more about mimicry when we move to empathy with art in Chapter 5.

Contagious affect does not appear to be a dumb automatic process. It is sensitive to the context of expression, the communicative intent of the expression, the nature of the relationship with the other person, and may only work for *some* emotions, such as happiness, anger, and sadness (see Hess & Fischer 2014).

Emotional contagion may be traced back to early infancy. Reactive crying is the phenomenon of children crying as a result of hearing other children cry (Sagi & Hoffman 1976, Simner 1971). Like emotional mimicry, reactive crying is also discriminate and is age and species specific (Martin & Clark 1982). It is hard not to see reactive crying as a developmental precursor to empathic distress or empathic sadness. But, as we have seen, reactive emotionality is not simply an early step in a person's normal empathic development. It seems to constitute a basic affective sensitivity to what other people feel that remains active throughout life, at least in people without developmental or psychiatric disorders. It is a part of ordinary human life that is often overlooked.

Some people have used the phenomena of emotional mimicry and contagion to argue for the simulation theory. Alvin Goldman, for instance, maintains that we learn to *recognize* that others experience the emotions they do on this basis (Goldman & Sripada 2005). It is easy to see why such a view would be appealing. If we have evidence that people mimic each other's facial expressions, and if such mimicking facilitates emotion recognition, then we have good grounds for expecting Goldman to be right. However, as we have seen, Hess and Fischer (2014) have shown that not all emotions are mimicked and that people don't mimic the facial expressions of those they dislike. Moreover, facial mimicry does not necessarily improve emotion recognition. This suggests that facial mimicry may not, in the end, play a large role in emotion *recognition*. Perhaps its role in social interaction is different.

Although emotional contagion is often talked about in the literature on intersubjectivity, it does not appear as its own category in major tests of empathy, such as the IRI. Out of the IRI's four facets of empathy, 'personal distress' is the one most likely to be, or be the result of, emotional contagion. Why? Because a person who experiences it does so as a result of another person's distress or distressing situation and yet experiences it as self-directed and is more likely to act selfishly than were she feeling sympathy for the other person. One can imagine spending an hour with a really depressed person and walking away wondering why one is feeling so downcast. And one can equally imagine hitting on a scheme to cheer oneself up, such as stopping by the pub for a pint, or going for a brisk walk. These reactions indicate that one 'owns' the depressed feeling, which is therefore 'personal.' According to this logic, personal distress is clearly just one form of emotional contagion.

Emotional contagion can easily turn into affective empathy. It is a simple step accomplished by the empathizer becoming aware that the emotion she experiences really is about the other person, in a sense soon to be explicated. So perhaps personal distress is neither self- nor other-directed. If so, it is a highly unusual state. Indeed, it is so unusual that it is hard to comprehend what it would be like. As soon as we reflect on our emotions, it seems that we must either own them, and so they are 'personal,' or we must think of them as being about the other, in which case they are empathic. If that is right, then emotional contagion may be a brief transitory state on the way to our either owning the emotion or not. An alternative interpretation is simply to say that emotional contagion is *always* a self-directed emotion even if it is *caused* by another person's affect or their situation.

§3.2 Empathic affect

As we saw in Chapter 1, empathic affect is different from emotional contagion because it involves a recognition that the affect felt is for another. What, exactly, that means has been the subject of some dispute. Some insist that in empathy you do not feel *for* anybody but only *with* that person. The idea is, I think, that 'feeling *for*' better characterizes sympathy than empathy. I'm not so sure that is true. Here is why. It is regularly assumed that torturers and other nasty folk are good at feeling empathy because that helps them hurt others better (e.g. Bubandt & Willerslev 2015). This is taken to be a conceptual truth of sorts. And yet psychopaths, who do have deficient empathy, still manage to be quite nasty to other people. Moreover, I don't know of any evidence that shows that torturers *feel* empathy for their victims and that this allows them to torture them better. All they need to know is that what they do *hurts*. This does require some theory of mind ability, but it does not necessitate either perspective taking or affective empathy. Pushing this point further, we can note that when people feel antipathy towards others, they tend not to empathize with them. Tania Singer found that when players in economic games watched people who had cheated them receive electric shocks, their reward centers, not their empathy centers, lit up (Singer et al. 2006). This dovetails nicely with Hess and Fischer's observation, mentioned above, that emotional mimicry is *affiliative*. And if we suppose that one type of empathy is a development of a contagious affective response, presumably it would be affiliative also. This does not exclude, of course, that empathy caused by *knowing* or *imagining* what someone feels is not affiliative also. It might be a relatively brute fact that we only empathize with someone in a caring way, or as someone we care about. In response to people we dislike, we have *reactive* emotions, such as indifference to, or joy at, their suffering. Empathy may always be a feeling *for* in addition to being a feeling *with*.

Empathy, then, requires not only an emotional response that is consonant with that of the other person but one that must also be experienced as being *for* her in some sense. If we want to avoid partisan interpretations of the 'for' or 'with,' we can instead talk of the *object* of the empathic emotion. The object should not be me or my situation narrowly defined. Rather, it should at a minimum *include* the target, his affect, or his situation more narrowly construed. Specifying that the construal is 'narrow' is necessary because a narcissist may be affectively aroused by what happens to his friend or partner, not for their sake but purely for his own. The object of his affect is himself primarily. This does not seem to be what we think of as empathy. Instead, when I empathize with your sadness, I am sad *because* either you are sad or whatever makes you sad happened *to you*, or both. Probably it is usually both. There are, of course, cases where something bad happens to you and you are not sad, or where you are sad when nothing bad has happened to you, and I can feel empathically sad in both these cases. But in the first case, I must focus on your situation, and in the latter I focus on your feeling.

Someone might object that unless my sadness is caused by your sadness then my sadness is not empathic sadness. Most people, however, accept a broader definition of empathy whereby I can empathize with you because I have an emotional response that is more appropriate to your situation than to my own. This is Martin Hoffman's pithy definition of empathy (Hoffman 2000). The idea is that your situation is as good an indicator of what you feel, as is your emotional expression. Although not invariably true, it is true enough. The idea should be familiar from Adam Smith's (1759/1976) suggestion that we imagine the entire situation someone is in when we empathize with him. This contrasts with Hume, who focused on the apparent emotion as it is expressed (see Hume 1739/1978, Ilyes 2017). There might, of course, be interesting borderline cases where I feel sad because something bad has happened to you and you are happy. What we should say in such cases is not easy to determine, but it does not strike me that we need to solve such problems in order to have a reasonable grasp on empathy as a psychological phenomenon.

There are many ways to induce empathy, but the three big ones are: (a) by *witnessing* another experience an emotion or being in an emotion-inducing situation (getting kicked in the nuts, say), (b) by *imagining* being in that person's situation, or (c) by *knowing* about the other person's feelings or emotion-inducing situation (Maibom 2007). Because we started with emotional contagion, we have already mostly discussed (a). What is needed in addition to emotional contagion is awareness of the provenance and object, or target, of the experienced emotion.

Adam Smith thought that imaginative projection of some sort formed an essential part of empathy. In his *The Theory of Moral Sentiments*, he argues that:

> As we have no immediate experience of what other men feel, we can form no idea of the manner in which they are affected, but by conceiving what we ourselves should feel in the like situation. Though our brother is upon the rack, as long as we ourselves are at our ease, our senses will never inform us of what he suffers. They never did, and never can, carry us beyond our own person, and it is by the imagination only that we can form any conception of what are his sensations. [...] By the imagination we place ourselves in his situation, we conceive ourselves enduring all the same torments, we enter as it were into his body, and become in some measure the same person with him, and thence form some idea of his sensations, and ever feel something which, though weaker in degree, is not altogether unlike them. [...] For as to be in pain or distress of any kind excites the most excessive sorrow, so to conceive or to imagine that we are in it, excites some degree of the same emotion, in proportion to the vivacity or dullness of the conception.
>
> (Smith 1759/1976, Part I, Sect. I, Chap. I, par. 2)

This is quite a strong position. And it is similar to one of the definitions we started with (D2). It seems to rule out that empathy can be produced (more or less) *directly* by means of what we have called emotional contagion. In actual fact, Smith acknowledges that it might take place sometimes but views it as the exception rather than the rule. Why one would want to favor such a restricted view of empathy is not entirely clear. But it is interesting to observe that Smith seems to assume that to understand that others experience what we do we have to first *personally* experience an emotion that is consonant with theirs. We then suppose that what we experience is what the other person experiences. This is a straightforward example of perspective taking or simulation. The passage quoted suggests that this type of simulation is a precursor to affective empathy, even if it *seems* that we experience it directly upon seeing, say, our brother on the rack. Theodore Lipps' (1907) original formulation of Einfühlung also involved at least something like projection, much like Smith's account.

The phenomenological tradition, however, favors the idea that we are directly acquainted with other people's emotions when we are with them. We saw a version of this in my discussion of emotional contagion, imitation, and mimicry. But phenomenologists go a more Wittgensteinian route than do psychologists, who typically assume that the expressions are signs of the underlying emotion. Phenomenologists are more likely to insist that it is a mistake to think that there is some mental reality *behind* what we find expressed in the body. Others' psychological states are directly visible to us because they are not hidden in the mind, which is itself hidden in the body. Instead, we should recognize the body itself as being expressive and emotional (for more on this tradition, see Jardine & Szanto 2017 and Zahavi 2017).

This leaves us with the route to empathy *via* knowledge (c). Quite simply, when I know that you are in pain, I can sometimes come to experience the unpleasant emotional counterpart to that pain. Alternatively, I can learn that you are in a situation where people typically feel a certain emotion, say pain, and experience that affect as a result (but with you as the object of that emotion). Many experiments in the laboratory use a design where the subject is simply informed about what another person feels, or her situation (many of Batson's studies, for example). An early experiment in neuroscience meant to establish the neural reality of empathy also used such a design. Tania Singer and colleagues (2004) brought a romantically involved couple to the laboratory. One person was exposed to a painful shock while the other was alerted to this fact by a blinking light, which they were told indicated each shock. To the extent that you find the neuroscience convincing, you should also be persuaded that merely knowing that someone experiences a certain emotion/is exposed to a strong emotion-inducing situation is sufficient for you to empathize with her. It is therefore quite reasonable to be ecumenical about how empathy comes about; all of the three routes suggested above (a–c) are firmly established.

One thing that is under-discussed is empathy as a process. Most people deal with empathy as if it were a momentary and discrete occurrence. It is quite unlikely that this is the case (Schulz 2017). In fact, I have suggested that empathy often arises from emotional contagion or even emotional mimicry. In some cases, we might be able to describe the process as involving, first, emotional mimicry, then emotional contagion, and then empathy. What drives this process is of great interest to empathy researchers. It is likely to be quite a complex matter and one that can differ substantially from person to person. Tracy Spinrad and Nancy Eisenberg (2014) have begun exploring the idea that one's ability to regulate emotions generally plays a rather important role in how an empathic process unfolds. Emotion regulation is, as we saw above, the ability to regulate one's emotional response to a situation. Typically, it is thought of as regulating the *strength* of the response. Eisenberg and Hoffman both believe that when empathic arousal is too strong, as it might be in response to a person undergoing a horrific experience, it turns into personal distress. The idea therefore seems to be that being able to experience *less* distress allows a sympathetic response to develop.

The idea might also be applicable to other forms of empathic affect, such as empathic anger, empathic joy, or empathic disgust. Perhaps feeling *any* of these emotions strongly makes one focus more on the self-directed aspects of the emotion—that I am disgusted, angry, and so on—than the other-directed ones—that *the other person* is disgusted, angry, and so on.

Common ways to emotionally regulate include averting one's gaze from the suffering and adopting a conscious strategy of reminding oneself that this is happening to another person, not to oneself. Regulating one's emotions by the distancing that is involved in locating the relevance of the event to the other person can have a downside, of course. Psychopaths are good at regulating their distress reactions to other people in distress. So much so that they quickly lose interest in what the other person is going through (Decety, Lewis, & Cowell 2015).

We should also keep in mind the paramount importance of how a person *thinks about* what she feels when it comes to empathy. If I think of the affect as my own, then it cannot develop into true empathy. My other attitudes are also important in the unfolding of empathy-like responses. I might welcome the thought that I am sad because you are sad with anger and irritation because I care only about how I feel. This attitude channels the response in a different direction compared to a typical empathic response. In my view, the exploration of empathy as it unfolds over time is the most important aspect of affective empathy yet to be understood.

§3.3 Empathy and personal distress in psychology

Armed with these distinctions, you might go to the psychology literature and see what the experimental data say about what empathy does, for instance. And the transition seems straightforward, as you will find liberal use of the terms 'empathy' and 'empathic concern.' Empathic concern is an item in the IRI, we saw, and is widely researched by someone like Batson when it comes to its altruistic effects. But most philosophers would call 'empathic concern' sympathy. Why? 'Empathic concern' refers to a range of emotions that are of the same affective polarity but that do not usually match the actual or expected affect of the target person. Moreover, these emotions constitute a more objective assessment of the situation the person is in. 'Personal distress', by contrast, has all the features of affective empathy *except* that it is thought to be self-directed. This is *despite* the fact that it is caused by the other person's affect and has it as its object. What makes it personal rather than empathic, then?

According to Batson, personal distress differs from empathic distress in two ways. It is felt for the self, insofar as people *report* that they feel it for themselves, *and* it motivates action to reduce that distress even if the target has not been helped in any way. In other words, personal distress provokes a desire to get rid of *one's own* distress more than that of the other. It leads to egoistic motivation, Batson would say.

Although the psychological literature talks about personal distress a fair amount, particularly as a foil against which the positive features of empathic concern are highlighted, it tends to ignore its role in more complex emotional episodes. When Batson measured the degree to which being exposed to another person in need caused distress, people would invariably report feeling distress *both* for themselves and for the other person (Batson, Early, & Salvarini 1997). And yet Batson goes on to ignore this other-directed aspect of distress in his future studies and classifies *all* distress reactions as 'personal' (Batson 2011). A person who scores high on feeling alarmed, grieved, upset, worried, disturbed, and perturbed compared to feeling sympathetic, moved, or compassionate is said to feel personal distress. As far as I can tell, the justification is that when people feel more distress than empathic concern for someone, the degree to which they feel distress for themselves or the other does not make a difference to the resultant motivation. They are still more likely to try to escape the upsetting situation—even if doing so leaves the target in the lurch—than someone who feels as much, or more, empathic concern compared to distress. Note, however, that we don't know what a *particular* person who experiences more distress for the target than for herself ends up doing. We just know averages.

It would seem, then, that quite a number of psychologists think of empathic distress as *personal* distress (Batson et al. 1981). And so if we look to psychology to tell us what the effects of empathic distress are, we are better off looking for the effects of personal distress than those of empathic concern. Distress for self and distress for other are most likely two sides of the same coin (Maibom 2014). When one's distress is caused by another person's affect or situation, one never just feels personal or empathic distress; one always feels *both*. Why?

The explanation is simple. You are feeling an emotion even if the other person is *also* feeling an emotion very much like it. An empathic emotion is a personally felt emotion, even if that emotion is more appropriate to the other person or her situation. If we are ever capable of experiencing empathic distress, therefore, it *must* be felt *both* for the self and for the other in the sense that when you are distressed for the other, you are thereby also distressed yourself. Personal distress, as measured on many tests, is therefore likely to be empathic distress.

§3.4 Sympathy

By contrast to two-faced empathy, finely balanced as it is between feeling for oneself and feeling for another, sympathy is robustly other-oriented. This is why sympathy, more than empathy, is favored as a uniquely *moral* emotion. Stephen Darwall (1994) thinks of sympathy as being foundational to our notion of a person's good or wellbeing, including our own. Neither reason nor self-interest, he says, require us to be concerned for our own good or wellbeing, let alone for that of others. However, in the act of sympathizing with someone, we are concerned with that person for her own sake. More precisely, if bad things happen to her, we are negatively affected by it, and when good things happen to her, we are positively affected. Moreover, these negative and positive sympathetic sentiments *motivate* us. This capacity to be concerned for someone *for her sake* is special to our forming, or even grasping, the concept of the good of a person. Compared to other other-directed or other-caused emotions, sympathy is the only one through which the wellbeing of others is represented as mattering categorically. If we follow Darwall, therefore, we could say the following. Empathy represents the other person as mattering because by feeling affect consonant with hers, her wellbeing matters to us *through* those feelings. Sympathy is different. In sympathy, the target matters to us *not* by evoking strong affect in us through which we can feel some of what she feels but by making her matter *for her own sake*. Sympathy is an emotion of caring *par excellence*.

The psychology literature, as we have seen, talks of empathic concern. For Batson, it is not so much an emotion in its own right as a family of feelings of concern for another in need; the person feels "sympathetic, kind, compassionate, warm, softhearted, tender, empathetic, concerned, moved, and touched" (Batson 2011, 103). It is common to think that sympathy develops out of emotional contagion or empathy (Eisenberg 2005, Hoffman 2000, Scheler 1973/2009). But some insist that all three concepts are more strictly distinct (Batson 2011, Coplan 2011).

One reason to think that sympathy is *not* a development of empathy is the fact that people typically report feeling *both*. People do not report one type of affect *replacing* the other kind altogether. In his studies, Batson finds that personal distress and sympathy co-occur. Another reason is that studies that measure the degree to which people feel distress and sympathy across an extended emotional episode indicate that there is no general resolution after which only one emotion is experienced. Rather, people report feeling *more* of the one emotion compared to the other. Pilar Carrera and colleagues (2013) found that, on average, people report sympathy throughout the emotion process. They also found that what mattered to helping was not whether the person felt more sympathy *throughout* the episode but whether the person felt a preponderance of sympathy *at the end* of it, or at least an equal amount of sympathy and personal distress. By contrast, people who experienced a preponderance of distress at the end of the episode were significantly less likely to help the target than were people who experienced a preponderance of distress during the beginning or middle of it.

Batson links sympathy—which he calls empathic concern, or empathy for short—with altruistic motivation. This is a psychological cousin of Darwall's view. He shows that people exposed to a person in need are quite likely to offer to help that person, particularly if they have been induced to feel sympathy (empathic concern) for him. Of course, Batson needs to rule out that people are helping for ultimately egoistic reasons. The most important alternative hypothesis he is concerned to rule out is that people are helping so as to reduce their own empathic distress. Should this be the case, people ought to prefer to help only when it is difficult to escape the situation where they are exposed to the other person's distress (and where their own empathic distress is constantly evoked). When it is easy for them to leave the upsetting situation, they ought to do that. Batson finds that people who experience more personal distress than sympathy are more likely to escape the situation where they are exposed to the other's distress if it is easy to do so. By contrast, people who experience a preponderance of sympathy are as likely to help whether escape is easy or hard. Batson has made a career out of showing that the main egoistic interpretations of helping behaviors are not supported. This includes the ideas that people help to reduce personal aversive arousal, to look good socially, to make themselves feel morally better, or because of the *rewards* of helping (for this and more, see Batson 2011).

Although Batson has provided a good *prima facie* case in favor of sympathy leading to altruistic motivation, he has not definitively established the so-called empathy-altruism hypothesis (see Schramme 2017 for an overview). The problem is that there are potentially endless egoistic motivation alternatives to each act that appear to be altruistically motivated. Some people think that so-called psychological egoism is more plausible than psychological pluralism because it only posits one basic kind of desire. People who believe in altruistic motivation are pluralists and believe that there are at least two basic kinds of motivations: one that is self-directed and another that is other-directed. They therefore have to posit two types of basic motivational states—not simply one type. However, as Elliott Sober and David Sloan Wilson (1998) point out, if you hold an egoistic view of motivation, you must posit a preponderance of *beliefs* concerning why helping others ultimately serves your own interests. It is unclear, therefore, who has the simplest explanation.

§3.5 Acting together: the origin of vicarious affect

There can be a tendency to construe emotions along ideological lines, particularly if those emotions are moral. Thus, an author will characterize a particular emotion—say, shame—in ways that fit his or her favored moral theory. To avoid such undue influences on our accounts of morally relevant emotions, it can be helpful to look at them from outside such moral frameworks as much as possible. How might we do that? One option is to look at similar emotions in nonhuman animals, since there is little temptation to moralize affect in nonhuman animals. This can be helpful because animal and human emotions might have the same descent or have evolved independently to serve similar functions. And so looking at the latter can help us understand the former better. Some philosophers detest evolutionary explanations. If you are one of those, you might want to skip the next two sections.

Flock animals often act together in such a concerted way that it can hardly be an accident. One interpretation, particularly of flight behavior, is that perceiving fear in a member of one's group causes one to feel fear and mimic the other's fleeing, freezing, or fighting. This looks a lot like what we call emotional mimicry, if not emotional contagion, in humans. What other evidence do we have? Not much, unfortunately. Up until recently, it was not even thought that animals could experience emotions at all, let alone empathy-like emotions. While working on my PhD in London two decades ago, I watched a BBC program that raised the 'radical' question: do animals experience emotions? Because crude behaviorism has taken longer to disappear from the study of animal behavior and psychology than from human psychology, there is precious little work conducted on empathy-like emotions in nonhuman animals. However, here is what we have.

According to Frans de Waal, contagious laughing and yawning is found in other species; for instance, the chimpanzee (Campbell & de Waal 2011, de Waal 2009). Reactions to pain in conspecifics have been found in rats and mice too. Russell Church (1959) found that a rat will starve itself if to obtain food it has to push a lever that delivers it but also shocks another rat it is acquainted with. The same has been found in rhesus macaque monkeys (Masserman Wechkin, & Terris 1964). Dale Langford and colleagues (2006) report that mice evince pain responses when they see a cage mate exhibit those very same responses. In other words, mice show pain contagion (notice that they show the same discrimination Hess and Fischer argue is true of emotion mimicry in humans). It is possible that in many nonhuman animals emotional responsiveness of this kind only applies to fear, pain, anger, and a couple of other emotions. But then again, no systematic review of human empathy or emotional contagion has established that we can 'catch' or empathize with any emotion whatsoever.

The fact that many different animals experience something like mimicry and contagion is decent evidence that they are adaptations. We cannot rule out that they are side effects of other traits that were selected for, but it seems unlikely. It's just hard to see what they could be. If this is right, what is emotional mimicry or contagion an adaptation for? For a while, it was popular to think that empathy and mindreading gave organisms a leg up on conspecifics and were therefore competitive mechanisms. According to the Machiavellian Intelligence hypothesis, being able to understand other minds allows an organism to deceive and cheat them and generally get ahead at their expense (Byrne & Whiten 1988). There are less nasty accounts of the evolution of empathy. But many of these also regard empathy as providing the organism with a competitive advantage. Armin Schulz (2017), for instance, argues that "if it is adaptive for A to feel X, then it is often also adaptive for B to feel X, simply because A and B are subject to the same sort of environmental contingencies" (2017, 68). An example of this type of non-cooperative account includes the one suggested above: fleeing when other members of one's group flee or acting excitedly when others are (mobbing in birds). There is strength in numbers, as they say.

There is plenty of evidence that humans interact much better with one another when their behavioral expressions, linguistic utterances, and emotional reactions align with one another (for an overview, see Hatfield, Cacioppo, & Rapson 1994 and Anderson, Keltner, & John 2003). De Waal, who has long been concerned to move beyond behaviorism when it comes to explaining animal behavior, also argues that staying 'in tune' with other group members is essential for survival and swift responses to environmental dangers (de Waal 2009). Although this capacity can still be understood to be selfish and self-advantageous, it is nonetheless interweaved with an account of the adaptiveness of group living and interaction. It is, if you like, a nicer explanation of contagion.

Genuinely cooperative accounts of the evolution of empathy suppose that emotional contagion enables cooperation, which will be for the benefit of each individual. Cooperation can be adaptive for parents and their children, for kin, and for close-knit groups. It is important to note, however, that according to Schulz, the two types of environment that exert adaptive pressures on organisms to evolve "the ability to mirror an emotional state upon detecting evidence of that emotional state in others" (2017, 71) are significantly different. One involves group living as a strength in numbers situation. The other involves genuinely cooperative groups. And not all contagious affect is as easily explained on each account. In competitive environments, being able to 'catch' fear and aggression would be the most important. By contrast, in cooperative environments, contagious joy could be a real advantage. One might, of course, maintain that contagion, once unleashed, can transmit any emotion. Currently, we don't have the answer.

Above, I suggested that mimicry enables or increases good interactions in humans, and so one might think that a non-cooperative story might be able to account for contagious joy. After all, getting on well with the people one interacts with is an important element in surviving and thriving. It is quite possible that emotional mimicry, contagion, and empathy are all part of the same evolved response to non-cooperative adaptive pressures. Sympathy, however, seems to be different. As we shall see, it might have evolved as a more cooperative response, perhaps mainly in the context of rearing offspring. The easiest way to respond to the potential conflict of differing adaptive pressures is to accept that empathy (including contagion and mimicry) and sympathy evolved separately, each one to different pressures. Empathy evolved along the competitive lines described above, whereas sympathy is the result of much more cooperative pressures. Alternatively, sympathy could have evolved first for parental care (see below), after which it was pressed into use for more cooperative purposes. Any story along these lines would also account for why we mostly observe both empathy and sympathy in response to people in need.

§3.6 Cooperation and the evolution of sympathy

One of the most prominent proposals regarding the evolutionary origin of sympathy is that sympathy has descended from an emotional mechanism of care for offspring. Sober and Wilson (1998) have argued as much, and something like it has been championed by Batson (2011). The idea is quite simple. In animals that have offspring with extended infancy, substantial parental care is needed in order for the offspring to survive and thrive (Hrdy 2011). It behooves the animal, therefore, to have certain psychological solutions at hand for ensuring proper infant care.

If an animal only cares for its own survival, then many kinds of offspring would not make it. Take mammals, for instance, where nursing drains the mother of valuable resources. It is evidently not in the mother's interests to nurse, unless she believes that her ultimate interests include not only her own survival but also the survival of her offspring, its offspring, and so on. As far as we know, humans are the only animals who could understand such a thing. Nonetheless, fitness considerations do not typically play much of a role in child rearing. The solution to the problem of infant survival seems to have taken the form of parental feelings of care for their children. It is from this type of care that sympathy has descended. Or so the story goes.

Batson frequently observes that empathic concern/sympathy is greatest for close others, such as family, friends, or other people one affiliates with. This is why he chooses the stories he does in his laboratory studies. Most typically, his stories explicitly state that the person in need is another student at the university. This, he says, enhances the sympathetic response. If sympathy evolved from parental care as a process of extending that care outwards to others, then it should reach close others before it reaches those less familiar to us. This is, in fact, what we observe.

If parental care is the origin of sympathy, is parental care altruistic? And why should we not suppose that empathy has its origins in parental care? Here are some reasons. Empathy has an unfortunate tendency to become personal. Many have suggested that the stronger the empathy, at least when it comes to aversive affect, the more likely it is to turn personal. And personal distress, we have seen, is more associated with escaping the unpleasant situation than with staying and helping if escape is easy. Why would an animal not abandon its young, which at any rate slows it down and depletes its resources? Suppose its plight also leads to terrible empathic distress. Why wouldn't this distress lead to more frequent abandonment? These are all reasons to think that sympathy may be better suited for the all-important task of providing infant care.

Sober and Wilson argue that sympathy, understood as an altruistic emotion, may have evolved from parental care, but not because they think it is a better candidate than empathy. They do not consider empathy as we have discussed it here. Rather, the idea is that the task of raising offspring is so important that having more than one mechanism in play is adaptive. Sober and Wilson ask us to consider the following two options for care of offspring. One might be motivated to care for one's offspring out of purely egoistic concerns, or one might be so motivated out of altruistic concerns: concerns for the offspring's welfare. We have plenty of reasons for thinking egoistic motivation exists. Egoistic motivation can be coupled with beliefs regarding the importance of the offspring's welfare to parental interests (much as we saw above). So why posit altruistic motivation?

There are a couple of reasons. First, two mechanisms are better than one when it comes to taking care of a basic survival or reproduction need. For instance, having several ways of detecting oxygen content helps an organism survive better than having just one. Being able to detect when care is needed is another instance where more ways are better than one. Second, more direct pathways are better than less direct ones. For example, having an oxygen detection mechanism is better than having a mechanism that detects the effects of oxygen levels on something else. This is because each link introduces a possible confound and the possibility of malfunction. In a similar fashion, ensuring offspring welfare is better accomplished by an organism if it is directly motivated by *its offspring's* welfare than it is by its being indirectly motivated to do so because of how it affects *its own* welfare. If this is right, then as long as the right kinds of conditions were in place and the right kinds of mechanisms were available for selection to work with (*availability*), we should expect altruistic motivation to evolve.

We should also consider how reliable (*reliability*) and how resource-demanding (*efficiency*) these mechanisms are for producing offspring care. Sober and Wilson argue that if egoistic motivation was available in the ancestral environment, so was altruistic motivation, since both exploit the same basic desire structure. Desire is the same in both cases; the only thing that changes is its *object* (you or me). And there is no reason to think that having two basic types of motivational states is substantially less efficient than having just one state. After all, for egoism to be true, parental care must be the result of egoistic motivation *plus* a bunch of different beliefs about the adaptive relevance of the other organism's wellbeing.

Sober and Wilson also make the reasonable observation that in animals that have offspring that require care, particularly longer care, it would be very strange for evolution to select egoistic motivation exclusively. Recall that from the point of view of evolution and life on earth, an organism's success is not a matter of it being happy and not feeling bad; it is a matter of its *survival* and *reproductive success*. If these were your goals, what would you choose? Egoistic motivation only? I think not. A judicial mix of the two allows the organism to seek what is beneficial to it, avoid that which causes suffering, and provide good care for its offspring (for a fuller version of the argument, see Sober & Wilson 1994). Sober and Wilson call this idea 'motivational pluralism.'

Why do we need sympathy if we already have empathy? Can't the two types of affect serve the same purpose? They can. But they won't always. For, as we have seen, empathic distress goes hand in hand with personal distress, and once the latter takes over, the focus may well turn to escaping the upsetting situation. This is not necessarily good for the offspring in question. The parent would now have to hang on to the belief that its fitness, or *raison d'être*, is intimately tied to the wellbeing of its offspring. This seems to be a much thinner thread than the one provided by sympathy. In other words, even if we already have empathy, it might still be useful to evolve sympathy for the reasons outlined above.

I don't think anything I've said so far should make us think that empathy involves purely *egoistic* motivation. Instead, it seems to be a state that has *both* an egoistic component and an altruistic one. Recall that people report feeling distress *both for themselves and for the other person*. The object that is assigned the emotion has an enormous influence on the resultant, or constituent, motivation. If I'm afraid of the bear, I will try to escape the bear. If I'm empathically afraid that the bear will eat you, I will try to *help you* escape the bear. If we think of empathy this way, it makes this type of affective responding to others less schizophrenic. It is an experience of your distress *as if it were mine*. This is what makes it such a fascinating emotion. But it is also what makes it so liable to turn egoistic, as in its transition into wholesale personal distress.

In conclusion, empathy and sympathy are two fairly distinct emotional reactions to others, which have likely evolved due to different evolutionary pressures. As Schulz stresses, one type of adaptive pressure comes from the competitive advantage of being *a member of a group*, and some pressures are purely cooperation oriented. Perhaps empathy fits the former, having ultimately descended from emotion contagion and mimicry. Parental care is another matter altogether. This line of thinking dovetails with many of the other reasons for thinking that sympathy and empathy are much more distinct than are emotional contagion and empathy. The latter are distinguished mainly in terms of their object, whereas the former differ partly in terms of object (self + other *versus* other) but also in emotional tone and intensity.

§3.7 Against sharing

Some people insist that when we empathize with someone we always only feel what we feel, and it therefore makes no sense to say that *we feel what the other person feels*. Max Scheler, for instance, spends some time bewailing this terrible error, which he ascribes to Lipps (Scheler 1973/2009). More recently, Dan Zahavi and Philippe Rochat (2015) have insisted that empathy ≠ sharing, as they put it. What is it that they are so intent on denying? Quite simply that since sharing necessarily involves reciprocation, and empathy does not, empathy does not necessarily involve sharing. Of course, it does not follow that *no* form of empathy involves sharing, but I suppose the idea is that sharing is not an intrinsic feature of empathizing.

I am less impressed with this line of reasoning. I doubt that all forms of sharing require reciprocity. And clearly many empathic episodes involve reciprocity. Suppose your friend is having a hard time. She is sad and you are sad for her too. As she describes her woes, she watches your facial expressions and listens to you expressing how sad it all is. In other words, she is aware that you are empathizing with her, and that makes a difference. This is an instance of sharing sadness about a situation according to Zahavi and Rochat's definition, surely, but it is also clearly a case of empathy. Are all instances of empathizing with someone like this? Clearly not. We often empathize with someone *in absentia*. But even in these cases, it strikes me that there is a looser sense in which we share some of the travails or joys of the person we empathize with. We do so by experiencing affect that is appropriate to that situation and by focusing on her situation. In fact, the whole experience is a way of *our* living through what we believe *she* is or has been experiencing. It is not reciprocal, but is reciprocity really essential to sharing?

Zahavi and Rochat's suggestion hints at another fundamental disagreement in the empathy literature. I have suggested that empathy is, or can be, an emotional reaction that can, at times, be almost undifferentiated between the target and the experiencer. Some people disagree quite strongly with such a construal. Rochat, for instance, insists that the sort of coordination we observe in infant-caretaker interactions, such as early forms of reciprocal exchange of gestures or two-way mutual gaze (2 months of age), are prototypical cases of sharing but already show differentiation. To share is to reciprocate, but one can only reciprocate with a genuine *other* (as it were). In other words, there is no undifferentiated *we* even in young infants but always an I and a *you*. It is when these two separate individuals come together in a co-created experience that we find a new type of experience arising—one of sharing—which is irreducible to the experiences of the 'I' and the 'you' added up.

There is a big and interesting debate hiding here that I can only touch on. The fact is that our sense of self is quite malleable. We are quite easily duped into incorporating physical objects into our bodily sense of self, for instance. Take the rubber hand illusion. It is created by placing a person so that she cannot see her left hand but only a left rubber hand placed where the left hand would plausibly be (and next to where it actually is). The real left hand and the rubber hand are then simultaneously stroked, and within a minute or so, the person begins to feel the strokes *in the rubber hand*. Thomas Metzinger (2009) reports a number of other fascinating experiments where a subject's sense of bodily self 'jumps' into another object or, if you like, incorporates that other object. This shows that our bodily sense of self is by no means fixed but is in fact quite flexible. Why should we suppose that our sense of self is any different? It may be that, as Tony Chemero (2016) suggests, we sometimes form temporary systems together with other people, and in the moment of doing so, our sense of individuality dissipates. This does not mean that we do not have a more robust sense of separateness at other times. Whether anything actually corresponds to this sense, namely a real self, is yet another fascinating question, worth exploring further in the context of a full exploration of empathy. In that context, the phenomenon of mirror touch synesthesia would be quite relevant. This is a condition that as many as 2 in 100 people have (see Medina & DePasquale 2017), in which the person feels in her own body where another person is being touched.

One final point. Suppose you agree with me that empathy involves sharing in the sense of my feeling what you are feeling *as if* it were myself feeling what you are feeling. If so, where is the sharp self-other differentiation that we saw is central to most accounts of empathy? And so, even if one disagrees with Zahavi and Rochat's particular construal of empathy, they have certainly unveiled a basic tension in many accounts of this ability. I agree that there is a tension, but it may be a virtuous one. We need to be able to think that we feel what we feel because the other feels what he feels, but this may not change *the experience in the situation*, which is not as clear-cut as the corresponding thought. Perhaps there is a point in the empathic episode where there is no sharp self-other differentiation, but for the full experience to count as empathy it must finish with a relatively clear understanding of *who* the original target is and what one's own emotion is about (the other). This is another under-explored topic in the study of empathy.

§3.8 Take-home message

In Chapter 1, we saw that 'affective empathy' covers a number of *prima facie* different emotional states, including emotional contagion, empathy, and sympathy. In this chapter, we looked at each of these emotional reactions in more detail. I suggested that empathy is sometimes a natural development of emotional contagion. There are other ways to empathize with someone than first catching her emotion, of course. These involve either knowing what the other person is experiencing, or imagining being (her) in her situation. We saw that in the psychological literature, personal distress is the emotion closest to what philosophers call empathic distress.

Sympathy appears to be different from both emotional contagion and empathy. It is robustly other-directed and does not require, and usually does not involve, emotion matching. In addition to these differences, we also have reason to think that empathy and sympathy have evolved in response to different evolutionary pressures, one to do with group living and the other concerned with caring for offspring. Interestingly, people report experiencing *both* sympathy and distress for those in need. This suggests that one does not simply develop into the other, contrary to what is sometimes thought to be the case. Lastly, we considered some objections to the idea that empathizing with someone is a way of *sharing* what that person feels. This last discussion unveiled a fundamental tension in what people commonly believe about empathy: that it is *both* a way of sharing what another feels *and* that it involves a strict distinction between the affect of the target and the affect of the empathizer.

In this chapter, we have explored:

- What emotional mimicry and contagion is
- What empathy is and how it differs from contagion and sympathy
- Where to find philosophers' empathy in psychological research (personal distress)
- What's special about sympathy
- How altruistic and egoistic motivations figure in the empathy debate
- The evolutionary origins of vicarious affect and sympathy
- What sharing amounts to in empathy

Further readings

Darwall, S. 1994. Sympathy, empathy, care. *Philosophical Studies*, 89, 261–282. *Darwall argues that our concept of the good of a person derives from our ability to sympathize with her.*

Hatfield, E., Cacioppo, J.T., & Rapson, R.L. 1994. *Emotional Contagion*. Cambridge: Cambridge University Press. *The classic book on all things contagion, including behavioural mimicry and vicarious affect.*

Hess, U. & Fischer, A. 2014. Emotional mimicry: Why and when we mimic emotions. *Social and Personality Psychology Compass*, 8, 45–57. *A paper that shows that a person's tendency to mimic emotions is influenced by a range of factors, including affiliation.*

Jardine, J. & Szanto, T. 2017. Empathy in the phenomenological tradition. In: H.L. Maibom (Ed.) *Routledge Handbook of Philosophy of Empathy*. New York: Routledge, 86–97. *A comprehensive and clear overlook of empathy in the phenomenological tradition.*

Schulz, A. 2017. The evolution of empathy. In: H.L. Maibom (Ed.) *Routledge Handbook of Philosophy of Empathy*. New York: Routledge, 64–73. *A fascinating account of the various adaptive pressures that might have given rise to empathy.*

Sober, E. & Wilson, D.S. 2000. Summary of Unto Others: The Evolution and Psychology of Unselfish Behavior. *Journal of Consciousness Studies*, 7, 185–206. *It's hard to find a better account of the altruism versus egoism debate in evolution and psychology, and this summary shows why.*

References

Anderson, C., Keltner, D. & John, O.P. 2003. Emotional convergence of people over time. *Journal of Personality and Social Psychology*, 84, 1054–1068.

Batson, C.D. 2011. *Altruism in Humans*. New York: Oxford University Press.

Batson, C.D., Duncan, B., Ackerman, P., Buckley, T., & Birch, K. 1981. Is empathic emotion a source of altruistic motivation? *Journal of Personality and Social Psychology*, 40, 290–302.

Batson, C.D., Early, S., & Salvarini, G. 1997. Perspective taking: Imagining how another feels versus imagining how you would feel. *Personality and Social Psychology Bulletin*, 23, 751–758.

Bubandt, N. & Willerslev, R. 2015. The dark side of empathy: Mimesis, deception, and the magic of alterity. *Comparative Studies in Society and History*, 57, 5–34.

Byrne, R.W. & Whiten, A. 1988. (Eds.) *Machiavellian Intelligence*. Oxford: Oxford University Press.

Campbell, M. & de Waal, F. 2011. Ingroup-outgroup bias in contagious yawning by chimpanzees supports link to empathy. *PLoS One*, 6, e18283.

Carrera, P., Oceja, L., Caballero, A., Muñoz, D., López-Pérez, B., & Ambrona, T. 2013. I feel so sorry! Tapping the joint influence of empathy and personal distress on helping behavior. *Motivation and Emotion*, 37, 335–345.

Chemero, A. 2016. Sensorimotor empathy. *Journal of Consciousness Studies*, 23, 138–152.

Church, R.M. 1959. Emotional reactions of rats to the pain of others. *Journal of Comparative Physiological Psychology*, 76, 893–910.

Coplan, A. 2011. Understanding empathy: Its features and effects. In: A. Coplan & P. Goldie (Eds.) *Empathy: Philosophical and Psychological Perspectives*. New York: Oxford University Press, 3–18.

Darwall, S. 1994. Sympathy, empathy, care. *Philosophical Studies*, 89, 261–282.

de Waal, F. 2009. *The Age of Empathy*. Toronto: McClelland & Stewart Ltd.

Decety, J., Lewis, K.L., & Cowell, J.M. 2015. Specific electrophysiological components disentangle affective sharing and empathic concern in psychopathy. *Journal of Neurophysiology*, 114, 493–504.

Dimberg, U. 1990. Facial electromyography and emotional reactions. *Psychophysiology*, 27, 481–494.

Dimberg, U., Thunberg, M., & Elmehed, K. 2000. Unconscious facial reactions to emotional facial expressions. *Psychological Science*, 11, 86–89.

Eisenberg, N. 2005. The development of empathy-related responding. In: G. Carlo & C.P. Edwards (Eds.) *Moral Development Through the Lifespan: Theory, Research, and Application. The 51st Nebraska Symposium on Motivation*. Lincoln, NE: University of Nebraska Press, 73–117.

Goldman, A. & Sripada, C. 2005. Simulationist models of face-based emotion recognition. *Cognition*, 94, 193–213.

Hatfield, E., Cacioppo, J.T., & Rapson, R.L. 1994. *Emotional Contagion*. Cambridge: Cambridge University Press.

Hess, U. & Fischer, A. 2014. Emotional mimicry: Why and when we mimic emotions. *Social and Personality Psychology Compass*, 8, 45–57.

Hoffman, M. 2000. *Empathy and Moral Development: Implications for Caring and Justice*. New York: Cambridge University Press.

Hrdy, S.B. 2011. *Mothers and Others: The Evolutionary Origins of Mutual Understanding*. Cambridge, MA: Harvard University Press.

Hume, D. 1739/1978 *A Treatise of Human Nature*. L.A. Selby-Bigge (Ed.) & P.H. Nidditch (2nd Ed.). Oxford: Clarendon Press.

Ilyes, I. 2017. Empathy in Hume and Smith. In: H.L. Maibom (Ed.) *Routledge Handbook of Philosophy of Empathy*. New York: Routledge, 98–109.

Jardine, J. & Szanto, T. 2017. Empathy in the phenomenological tradition. In: H.L. Maibom (Ed.) *Routledge Handbook of Philosophy of Empathy*. New York: Routledge, 86–97.

Laird, J.D. & Bressler, C. 1992. The process of emotion experience: A self-perception theory. In: M. Clark (Ed.) *Review of Personality and Social Psychology*, 13. New York: Sage, 213–234.

Langford, D.J., Crager, S.E., Shehzad, Z., Smith, S.B., Sotocinal, S.G., Levenstadt, J.S., Chanda, M.L., Levitin, D.J., Mogil, J.S. 2006. Social modulation of pain as evidence of empathy in mice. *Science*, 312, 1967–1970.

Lipps, T. 1907. Das Wissen from fremden Ich. In: *Psychologische Untersuchungen*. Leipzig: Engelmann, 694–722.

Maibom, H.L. 2007. The presence of others. *Philosophical Studies*, 132, 161–190.

Maibom, H.L. 2014. (Almost) Everything you ever wanted to know about empathy. In: H.L. Maibom (Ed.) *Empathy and Morality*. New York: Oxford University Press, 1–40.

Martin, G.B. & Clark, R.D. 1982. Distress crying in neonates: Species and peer specificity. *Developmental Psychology*, 18, 3–9.

Masserman, J., Wechkin, M.S., & Terris, W. 1964. Altruistic behavior in rhesus monkeys. *American Journal of Psychiatry*, 121, 584–585.

Medina, J. & DePasquale, C. 2017. Influence of the body-schema on mirror-touch synesthesia. *Cortex*, 88, 53–65.

Metzinger, T. 2009. *The Ego Tunnel: The Science of the Mind and the Myth of the Self*. New York: Basic Books.

Sagi, A. & Hoffman, M.L. 1976. Empathic distress in the newborn. *Developmental Psychology*, 12, 175–176.

Scheler, M. 1973/2009. *The Nature of Sympathy*. New Brunswick, NJ: Transaction Publishers.

Schulz, A. 2017. The evolution of empathy. In: H.L. Maibom (Ed.) *Routledge Handbook of Philosophy of Empathy*. New York: Routledge, 64–73.

Schramme, T. 2017. Empathy and altruism. In: H.L. Maibom (Ed.) *Routledge Handbook of Philosophy of Empathy*. New York: Routledge, 203–214.

Simner, M.L. 1971. Newborn's response to the cry of another infant. *Developmental Psychology*, 5, 136–150.

Singer, T., Seymour, B., O'Doherty, J.P., Kaube, H., Dolan, R.J., & Frith, C.D. 2004. Empathy for pain involves the affective but not the sensory components of pain. *Science*, 303, 1157–1162.

Singer, T., Seymour, B., O'Doherty, J.P., Stephan, K.E., Dolan, R.J., & Frith, C.D. 2006. Empathic neural responses are modulated by the perceived fairness of others. *Nature*, 439, 466–469.

Smith, A. 1759/1976. *The Theory of Moral Sentiments*. D.D. Raphael & A.L. Mackie (Eds.). Indianapolis, IN: Liberty Fund.

Sober, E. & Wilson, D.S. 1998. *Unto Others: The Evolution and Psychology of Unselfish Behavior*. Cambridge, MA: Harvard University Press.

Sober, E. & Wilson, D.S. 2000. Summary of Unto Others: The Evolution and Psychology of Unselfish Behavior. *Journal of Consciousness Studies*, 7, 185–206.

Spinrad, T. & Eisenberg, N. 2014. Empathy and morality: A developmental psychology perspective. In: H.L. Maibom (Ed.) *Empathy and Morality*. New York: Oxford University Press, 59–70.

Tomkins, S. 1962. *Affect, Imagery, Consciousness: The Positive Affects, Vol. 1.* New York: Springer.

Zahavi, D. 2017. Phenomenology, empathy, and mindreading. In: H.L. Maibom (Ed.) *Routledge Handbook of Philosophy of Empathy.* New York: Routledge, 33–43.

Zahavi, D. & Rochat, P. 2015. Empathy ≠ sharing: Perspectives from phenomenology and developmental psychology. *Consciousness and Cognition*, 36, 543–553.

4

EMPATHY AND MORALITY

One of the most important roles empathy is thought to play is enabling, or affecting, moral judgment and action. The Scottish sentimentalists, such as David Hume and Adam Smith, were the most famous proponents, arguing that empathy (what they called 'sympathy') was foundational to our caring about the weal and woe of others. In the last couple of decades, the idea has been revived in various forms. But it has also been exposed to more or less vehement criticisms (Bloom 2016, Prinz 2011). That being said, there is a fair amount of empirical evidence that supports the claim that empathy plays an important role in interpersonal relations and in moral considerations and motivations. And so it would be extremely surprising to find that empathy played *no* role in morality.

In this chapter, I discuss Hume and Smith's ideas about the foundational role of empathy in morality and some modern views according empathy an important role in moral judgment, moral motivation, or moral perception. I then move on to criticisms of the idea that empathy is central to morality, after which I present some evidence for sentimentalism. I conclude by suggesting how one might defend the role of affective empathy, perspective taking, or sympathy in moral responding.

§4.1 Fellow feeling, or sympathy, in Hume and Smith

Although the term 'empathy' really derives from the German *Einfühlung*, the modern preoccupation with empathy as a morally relevant category owes most to the works of David Hume (1739/1978) and Adam Smith (1759/1976). Both of these authors talked about 'fellow feeling' as lying at the root of our ability to be moved by each other's plight. They also called this fellow feeling 'sympathy.' This term, however, was understood much as we have defined 'affective empathy,' wherefore I shall simply use that term unless I'm quoting. Although they are largely in agreement about the role of empathy, Hume and Smith differ when it comes to the degree to which the imagination is involved.

Hume thought that we pick up on other people's emotions not quite directly but via a process of association. First we observe people expressing an emotion or we observe them in a situation typically associated with a passion. For instance, I see someone crying or I see a strike aimed at someone's face. This causes the idea of that emotion to arise in me. Because of the vivacity connected with that idea, it turns into an impression—i.e. it becomes itself a passion of the sort I discern in you. Why? The only difference between ideas and impressions (i.e. feelings and perceptions) is their degree of vivacity. Vivacity is influenced by contiguity and resemblance, both of which are often operative in empathic situations. Not only am I often face to face with the people I empathize with, but they are people just like me and subject to the same range of emotions as am I. I am therefore immediately brought to reflect on my own prior experience of that emotion, the vivacity of which is sufficient to transform the idea of the other person's emotion into a personally felt emotion of the same type. In a way, then, the other person becomes included in my self-concern through this process. This is not meant to exclude the possibility that we can empathize with others more immediately when we are face to face with their strong emotion. The more usual process, however, is the one just described.

So where does morality enter? Well, our tendency to empathize with others is what makes us care about what they do, who they are (their character), and what happens to them. Without it, we could not explain why we would care about what happens to others that are not directly connected to us. But empathy, on its own, is not sufficient to explain our sentiments of approbation and disapprobation. These sentiments are our judgments of right and wrong, according to Hume. They are pleasurable, in the case of approbation, or painful or unpleasant, as in the case of disapprobation. What we approve or disapprove of are someone's character traits or actions. Depending on how beneficial or agreeable, or harmful or disagreeable, they are to the person who has them and to others, we approve or disapprove of them (Treatise 3.3.1.2–3). For instance, when considering the effects of someone's generosity, we see the good effects it has on others and that person, and we come to approve of it.

For Hume, empathy is a relatively weak force by comparison to our self-love. We don't like to empathize with those who suffer because it makes us feel bad. So we do so only when the idea of others' experiences is powerful enough to displace our immediate concern with ourselves and what is going on with us. This may occur because the person is an intimate, or because the emotion is expressed very powerfully. But since our empathy is limited by contiguity, similarity, etc., we cannot simply rely on our own present and momentary experience of the other to form the basis of our moral judgment of them. People have to adopt "some common point of view, from which they might survey their object, and which might cause it to appear the same to all of them" (Treatise 3.3.1.30). This is why our moral judgments typically align. What Hume is working up to is the idea that it is disinterested consideration of someone's character, or their actions, which is morally relevant.

Interestingly, Hume thought that empathy's effect on moral judgment is different from its effect on moral motivation. When it comes to moral judgment, we overlook the limitedness of empathy by taking the general point of view. But when it comes to moral motivation, our natural limitation seriously comes into play, and we can only be motivated by the welfare of those close to us. Indeed, we need other passions to keep us motivated by benevolence, such as the desire for societal approval.

Smith has his eye on the other person's situation much more so than does Hume. We project ourselves into the other person's situation and imagine what we would feel in it. In other words, we typically use something like imagine-self perspective taking to empathize with other people. In certain situations, we can rely on that person's expression, but this is relatively rare. So where Hume posits a process of association, Smith posits imaginative projection. There is an additional difference. Smith claims that as we imagine ourselves in another's situation, we also either agree with, or dissent from, the other person's actual emotion. This affects whether or not we empathize with that person in that situation. If, for instance, I imagine having been denied the opportunity to have a nose job, I might not feel particularly distressed. If so, I do not empathize with my friend, and, moreover, I dissent from her distress. I think it is inappropriate. So where Hume's empathic process is largely one of descriptive psychology, Smith's is already evaluative.

Another important difference is that whereas Hume thought suffering with others is simply unpleasant, Smith thought that although empathic suffering is unpleasant, experiencing emotional harmony with others is itself pleasing. The pleasure of achieving this harmony is sufficient to counterbalance the unpleasantness of the suffering. In fact, the harmony is so valued that we do not shy away from empathizing with others that suffer. Hume famously thought this was absurd, since it seems to imply that we would be as happy to spend an evening in the hospital as at a party (see Raynor 1984).

For Smith, the moral import of empathy is in the extra evaluative element, which is strictly speaking an emotion that accompanies the empathic affect. When we enter into someone's situation and find that we share the emotion that motivated a certain action of his, we approve of that action. We can also view the situation from the point of view of those affected by it. In that case, we may come to empathize with someone's gratitude, grief, or resentment as a result of imaginatively entering into her situation.

When it comes to our own desire to be or to do good, the approbation of others matters. However, what is most important is not that they approve of us and what we do but that they do so *rightly*. This requires more than what a relatively uninformed person can do simply by putting himself in our situation. What is needed is *an impartial spectator*—i.e. someone who is unbiased and fully informed about a person's motivation, their character, and the consequences of their action for others. This person does not actually exist, but we can imagine being such a person, and when we do, we can overcome our own and others' limitations. The point of view of this impartial spectator is, ultimately speaking, all we need for moral judgment *and* moral motivation.

Despite their differences, Hume and Smith agreed that our ability to feel what others feel lies at the foundation of our moral sentiments. Our sentiments of approbation and disapprobation arise from basic concerns regarding the welfare of others, which is itself the result of empathy. Put in contemporary ethical terms, the ability to empathize with others is a pre-condition for moral judgment. Moreover, for Smith the imagined approbation or disapprobation of the impartial spectator is sufficient to motivate someone to act. In other words, empathy-enabled approbation or disapprobation, but from a general point of view, is necessary and sufficient for moral judgment and, for Smith, moral motivation. For Hume, empathy's motivational pull is quite weak and so often needs buffering from other sources.

§4.2 Modern views

If we skip ahead to the last couple of decades, empathy in its various forms has seen a revival, particularly in more empirically oriented moral psychology. The idea is to show that empathy plays a central role in morality, broadly conceived, although the ways in which it is thought to do so vary quite significantly from proposal to proposal.

Michael Slote (2009, 2017) has long defended a sentimentalist view of ethics based in (affective) empathy. He agrees with Hume that the prototypical form of empathy is when we are with others who express emotions. However, he takes a more phenomenological approach and maintains that we can be *directly* aware of what the other person feels. This stands in contrast to Hume, who posited a process of association. But like Hume, and contra the typical phenomenologist line, he thinks we get to *experience* the emotion of the other through this process. Moral judgment comes in this way. How precisely?

When we consider the nature of an action, Slote says, we focus on the person who performed it. We catch his or her emotion. The way he puts it is that we empathize with their empathy. If their feelings are warm, we feel warm, and if they are cold, we are chilled. As he says: "my suggestion is that we empathetically warm to empathic agential warmth toward others and that approval consists in our having such a reaction" (Slote 2009, 35). This account, he says, is inspired by Hume describing our being moved to tears by tender sentiments and those who have them. Moral approval, then, is a certain liking of, or affection for, "certain agential affections" (ibid.)

If, on the other hand, the agent expresses cold indifference (or worse) towards the person affected by his actions, Slote says we are chilled. And we therefore disapprove of it. The focus on the agent should be familiar from Hume and Smith, but there are a number of notable differences. Slote's focus seems to be *entirely* on the actor to the exclusion of those affected by the action. And that is not only surprising but also quite different from someone like Hume, who thought moral judgments involved a consideration of the *usefulness to others* of the character trait possessed, or the action performed.

It is also difficult to evaluate the hot/cold claim. People might say of an action "that was cold," meaning that the action was inconsiderate or even cruel, but this seems to rely on a metaphorical notion of cold. Presumably an action can be neither hot nor cold. But if hot and cold describe the affective quality of the intention with which the action was performed, we have another issue. Most violence is committed in anger. Anger is hardly a cold emotion. Nor is it indifferent to the target. It is *very* interested in causing harm to the person. So, if anything, anger is hot. But if we feel a hot emotion, we ought to *approve* of the other person's actions. This is not what we observe. And so there is often a mismatch between what a perpetrator feels while, or immediately prior to, acting and how we feel as a result of observing that action (Furlane & Maibom 2017).

Another strand of research originates with the early work of James Blair on psychopathy. Blair argued for the existence of a Violence Inhibition Mechanism, which takes distress in others as input and produces inhibition of aggression as output (Blair 1995). If a person attacks another, who expresses distress as a result, the aversiveness of that distress to the attacker is often sufficient for him or her to stop the attack. The Violence Inhibition Mechanism probably works by means of causing vicarious distress, which, combined with the relevant cognitive abilities, becomes empathic distress. Empathic distress together with more reflection gives us moral emotions, such as guilt and remorse, and moral judgments. We should probably not understand the suggestion as a description of how moral judgment comes about in adults but as a characterization of the moral development of the child. Blair argued that the absence of a Violence Inhibition Mechanism is what is at the roots of the amorality of psychopaths (see Chapter 6). These days, Blair believes that more cognitive systems are also affected in psychopathy, although it is unclear how he thinks they affect morality other than in a relatively superficial manner (such as impulse control) (Blair, Mitchell, & Blair 2005).

Although Shaun Nichols (2004) is sympathetic to Blair's idea, he thinks it has some shortcomings. Most importantly, it is simply not true that all forms of distress give rise to judgments of moral wrong. The distress of victims of natural disasters does not provoke judgments of moral wrong, for instance. To be fair, this is a bit of an uncharitable interpretation of the operation of the Violence Inhibition Mechanism, as pointed out by Blair (2008). However, Nichols proposes that we remedy the short-comings of what he thinks Blair's view is by making the mechanism a bit more flexible and adding knowledge of harm-prohibiting norms. Nichols calls his mechanism the Concern Mechanism. It is much like a Violence Inhibition Mechanism in being responsive to distress in others and, when combined with a normative theory, in providing motivation to refrain from harming them.

One thing that is noteworthy about Nichols's approach in particular is that he is concerned that moral judgment not be isolated from moral motivation. If moral judgments are beliefs or, when expressed verbally, statements expressing beliefs, it does seem that they cannot motivate on their own. This is a fundamental assumption of modern belief-desire psy-chology to which Nichols subscribes. He is far from being alone in this; indeed one will be hard-pressed to find an empirically oriented philoso-pher who thinks beliefs can motivate on their own. Desires are motivating, as are emotions. Although these states are typically thought to be content-ful, or have intentional objects, they are not thought to be sufficient for action on their own. Usually, they must be combined with beliefs, which specify how to satisfy them. What is tricky about moral judgments is that they seem a) to constitute beliefs about what is right or wrong, and b) to motivate to action. But according to belief-desire psychology, mental states are either motivating—which means that they are desires, sentiments, or passions—or cognitive, and therefore beliefs or thoughts. This forms part of what Michael Smith calls 'the moral problem' (Smith 1994).

Hume, himself, was adamant that moral judgment consists in approba-tion or disapprobation, both of which are passions. He famously claimed, "reason is and ought to be the slave of the passions" (*Treatise*, II.3.3 415). This is one way to solve the problem. Sentimentalism in ethics has its own problems, of course. For instance, we are not always aware that we experience affect when we make moral judgments; moral judgments are the kinds of things we use for inferences, but it is unclear that emotions can play this role, and there is a normativity to moral judgment (we say things like "he ought to feel bad about that") that is harder to place in affectivity. For many, such issues are enough for them to look for a different solution to how moral judgments motivate. This is why Nichols introduces the idea that for us to make moral judgments our Concern Mechanism must combine with our *knowledge of norms or rules*. In other words, on this picture you have *both* reason and emotion operating in the formation of a moral judgment.

Although Nichols' account seems to overcome problems associated with sentimentalist thinking while still holding on to the connection to motivation through concern, other aspects of his proposal are potentially problematic. Most importantly, Nichols relies on Batson's (1991) work for much of his experimental evidence. Batson, however, focuses on sympathy, as we have seen. Empathic distress is almost exclusively conceptualized as *personal*, and therefore egoistically motivated. This is presumably not the best ground upon which to base morality. We should therefore expect Nichols to have sympathy in mind. But sympathy, according to Batson, is welfare oriented and produces altruistic motivation to help those in need. Being motivated to *help* others in need seems quite different from being motivated *not* to harm them. And so we need more of an explanation of how this Concern Mechanism is supposed to work before it makes sense to accept this account.

David Shoemaker (2015, 2017) has recently proposed that affective empathy is required for moral *responsibility*. Now, to be morally responsible, a person must be able to understand the difference between right and wrong, and his actions must conform to that knowledge. What is required to do both, Shoemaker argues, is empathy. Why? Well, an essential ingredient in a moral orientation towards others is *regard*. To show someone regard is to be willing to take up her perspective on things (cognitive empathy). This involves treating what we find are her interests as reasons for us to act in certain ways, *and* being sensitive to her *affect*. The latter amounts to affective empathy, according to Shoemaker. As he puts it "[e]motional regard is typically enabled by *emotional empathy*, wherein we take up others' normative perspectives in opening ourselves up to *feeling* what they do or would feel in various circumstances" (2015, 101). To put things more simply, if we cannot see things from another person's point of view, and if we are not able or willing to affectively empathize with them, we lack the central ingredients in showing regard for that person (Shoemaker 2017). Psychopaths, he claims, show this lack of regard very clearly, and so although we can *attribute* wrongful actions to them, we cannot blame them because they are neither answerable nor accountable for their actions (see Chapter 6 for more on psychopaths).

There are some problems with Shoemaker's approach. One of the reasons he can maintain that empathy is required for regard is because he demands a lot from understanding right and wrong. According to him:

> [t]o have a good sense of humor requires both that one fully appreciate the reasons why things are funny and also that one be disposed to respond to such things with amusement (and for those reasons). To have a good moral sense, by analogy, one must both fully appreciate the reasons why things are right and wrong and also be disposed to respond to those things with the right attitudes and motivations (and for those reasons).
>
> (2017, 243)

First of all, even philosophers cannot agree *why* things are right or wrong. Suppose a Kantian believes something is wrong because she could not consistently will it. Suppose she does it anyway. If she is taken to court, she should be able to maintain that she does not understand right and wrong, since her right and wrong does not involve empathizing with others. Consequently, we cannot hold her responsible for her action. But this just seems plain wrong. Second, even supposing that we have one account of right and wrong, who fully appreciates those reasons? Certainly not most of the people we hold morally responsible in everyday life. And so one might want to demand less from knowing the difference between right and wrong (Maibom forthcoming).

A very different approach to empathy and morality is found in the work of Peggy Des Autels. She argues that empathy plays a role in what she calls *moral perception*. Des Autels (2012) points out that moral philosophers tend to ignore not only *how* people determine what situations are morally relevant but also *what* it is about such situations that is relevant. Morally relevant actions do not come with a label such that anyone can recognize them. Instead, actions have to be *perceived* to be so. Why perceived, you might ask. Can't we just *conceptualize* them as moral or not? Well, sometimes we can, when given sufficient time. But in real life, we rarely have such time. We have to be able to pick up on the relevant cues right away. Have we not often passed someone on the street and only later recognized that we should have helped them?

One way we can learn to train our moral perception is by practicing taking other people's perspectives. Sometimes, we can do so by taking *one* person's perspective. At other times, I might have to take several people's perspectives to see what is morally relevant. Perspective taking brings out what is relevant and important to people. That is at the heart of its moral importance. Des Autels is only too aware that taking other people's perspectives is time consuming and won't get the job done on its own. I need to double check that my perspective taking gets things right, and I need to find a way of responding immediately in the situation to the needs of others. This may require my engaging in a practice of noticing the types of situations that are less obvious but nonetheless morally relevant. Now, Des Autels is not explicit about whether or not she thinks perspective taking is necessary or sufficient for good moral perception. But she certainly thinks it plays an important role in it.

Modern ideas about the role of empathy in morality tend to focus on: moral judgment, moral motivation, moral development, or moral perception and less on the sort of foundational role Hume and Smith seem to have accorded affective empathy. And although most are concerned with affective empathy, perspective taking does seem to play a prominent role in some of these ideas whether with or without affective empathy.

§4.3 Criticisms of the moral import of empathy

Not everybody is enthusiastic about the moral potential of empathy. Some argue that empathy is not required for a range of moral judgments (Maibom 2009, Prinz 2011), that empathy better accounts for super-erogatory acts than morally required ones (Maibom 2010), or that empathy is actually bad morally speaking (Bloom 2016, Prinz 2011). This is a backlash against the recent prominence of emotions and empathy in moral psychology. What kind of empathy do these people usually have in mind? Affective empathy.

A commonality of these views is that they tend to focus on moral judgments or moral motivation. They also appear to assume that the idea that empathy is required for either of these two is simply an updated version of Hume and/or Smith. But, as we saw, it may be more correct to say that for Hume and Smith empathy is the reason we care about what happens to others in the first place. It is, if you like, a pre-condition for morality. It is therefore not clear how serious these criticisms are for the theories of these historical figures.

Keeping this in mind, let's move on to the criticisms. The first, and most modest, objection to dispense with is the idea that empathy is not sufficient for moral judgment or moral motivation. I'm not sure anybody actually holds this view. Smith and Hume did not; nor is it clear that any of the views we have just considered would either. Almost everyone would agree that empathizing, or sympathizing, with someone is different from judging that what happened to them is *wrong*. Seeing somebody's action from her point of view is hardly sufficient to make it right. Nor is moral motivation simply a matter of being motivated to act out of empathic affect, such as helping someone in need. For instance, you might be motivated to hide a criminal from the police because you feel sorry for her. You might be motivated to take away valuable resources from others because you feel sympathy for a certain person (see Batson 2014). In short, maintaining that perspective taking, affective empathy, or sympathy is sufficient for moral judgment or motivation appears to be a non-starter.

It is therefore usually the idea that (affective) empathy is *necessary* for moral judgment or motivation that is the target of the above criticisms. Should we really think that empathy is *necessary* to make any kind of moral judgment, though? Here are some reasons to think that this is not the case. First, there are different views of morality, such as Kantian ones, that explicitly rely on *reasoning* in accordance with certain principles, such as the Categorical Imperative. It seems unlikely that such a popular ethical tradition could have been so wrong that reason cannot provide the basis for *any* moral judgments. Furthermore, one would have thought that at the very least *some* people—a Kantian, for instance—could make moral judgments based on categorical reasoning, and not on empathy. Second, moral judgments are not all made the same way. It is harder to see how empathy forms the basis of a judgment that some distribution of resources is wrong because it is unequal than it is to see how it could be at the foundation of judging that *harming* someone is wrong. Alternatively, one might think of Jonathan Haidt's moral foundations, which include purity norms. How can moral judgments concerning the permissibility of eating certain things because they are unclean spring from empathy (Haidt 2001)? Third, not even judgments that it is wrong to harm must always rely on empathy. Luke Skywalker, for instance, in *The Return of the Jedi* is moved by fear of moving to the dark side were he to kill the Emperor. This is what motivates his judgment that it is wrong, for he clearly feels no empathy for the Emperor (Maibom 2009). Fourth, some people who have deficient empathy still seem to be able to make moral judgments, such as people with autism.

It is not clear that empathy is required for us to be morally motivated by moral judgments or norms either. First, all emotions motivate, so if what we are interested in is primarily motivation, why should we privilege *empathically* felt emotion? Second, a range of emotions may be even *more motivating* than empathy; namely, anger, indignation, or happiness (Prinz 2011). Of course, the emotions have to provide the *right kind* of motivation. But philosophers have long preached the virtues of the so-called reactive attitudes, such as resentment, indignation, hurt, anger, gratitude, and forgiveness. And so, there is no obstacle in principle to emotions other than empathetic ones being of the right kind to motivate moral action.

However, one could argue that empathy is necessary for *moral development*. Perhaps without the ability to experience empathy one cannot have the right kind of attitudes towards others. The work of both Nancy Eisenberg and Martin Hoffman show that children tend to engage in empathic reasoning when they make moral judgments and that empathy and prosocial behavior correlate (e.g. Eisenberg 2005, Hoffman 2000). Nonetheless, both Jesse Prinz and Paul Bloom insist that there is no evidence that empathy is *essential* to moral judgment. Prinz points out that children draw the moral-conventional distinction before they associate empathy with morality (Prinz 2011). Bloom (2016) argues that children don't need to empathize to help, so there is no reason to think they need empathy to engage in that kind of moral behavior.

Pathological populations, such as psychopaths, have been thought to provide additional evidence that without empathy a person won't develop a moral sense (e.g. Nichols 2002). Blair's evidence that psychopaths do not draw the moral-conventional distinction combined with his account of the VIM provides reason to believe in the developmental necessity claim. However, Prinz points out that the existence of a VIM in humans is controversial to say the least, and there are other possible explanations for psychopaths' moral deficits, such as deficient fear and sadness. Lastly, since many moral norms are not concerned with proscribing violence, a malfunctioning VIM cannot explain the general disregard for morality exhibited by psychopaths.

In the works of Prinz (2011) and Bloom (2016), these criticisms that empathy is not sufficient for moral judgment, motivation, or development spill into a more thoroughgoing critique of its relevance to morality. Whereas others, such as myself, have been content to point out that empathy alone cannot account for the *full range* of our moral judgments or motivations, Prinz and Bloom take it to the next level. Empathy is actually *morally bad!*

What is the problem? Well, first of all, empathy is just not that motivating. Hume, himself, was clear on this point. Other emotions that one might feel in response to morally relevant scenarios or actions are *more* motivating, such as anger, indignation, gratitude, and so on. So if you want motivation, shouldn't you go for the stronger stuff? (Prinz 2011). Second, as Batson has pointed out, empathy or sympathy often motivates someone to help *one* person over others. This can lead to serious injustice, in skewing distribution towards the few and away from the many. To make things worse, empathy is *typically* directed towards just *one* other person, not towards many (Bloom 2016). Third, we empathize more with those we agree with, feel similar to, or who belong to our own group. And so empathy tends to perpetuate biases, partiality, partisanship, and so on. This is hardly a glowing recommendation (Bloom 2016, Prinz 2011). Fourth, collectivism, liberalism, and feminism all stress empathy towards others. But they have dark sides, Prinz says. Collectivism often involves little respect for the individual (bullying, suicide-bombing, communist ideology), liberalism clings to social programs like welfare programs that might actually be counterproductive in the long run (people get 'stuck' in them), and feminist ethics focuses on emotions that perpetuate female subjugation and ultimately prevents radical change (Prinz 2011).

To sum up, affective empathy, far from being essential to morality, is actually *bad* as a guide to moral judgment or motivation, according to Prinz and Bloom.

§4.4 The empirical evidence

You would have thought that with this barrage of objections to empathy having anything to do with morality, the case would be closed. It is not. There is plenty of evidence that Empathy has positive interpersonal effects, particularly perspective taking and sympathy. Before moving on to a defense of the importance of affective empathy to morality, it is worth looking at that.

Let us start with perspective taking. Perspective taking increases interpersonal liking (Dovidio, Allen, & Schroeder 1990 and Goldstein, Vezich, & Shapiro 2014), helping (Carlo, Allen, & Buhman 1999, Dovidio, Allen, & Schroeder 1990, Fennis 2011, Goldstein, Vezich, & Shapiro 2014, Myers, Laurent, & Hodges 2014, and Pahl & Bauer 2013), desire for justice (Berndsen & McGarty 2012 and Decety & Yoder 2016), tendency to make prosocial moral judgments (Eisenberg, Zhou, & Koller 2001 and Hoffman 2000), moral reasoning (Eisenberg, Zhou, & Koller 2001 and Walker 1980), and forgiveness (Konstam, Chernoff, & Deveney 2001, Takaku, Weiner, & Ohbuchi 2001, and Zechmeister & Romero 2002). Moreover, perspective taking reduces stereotyping (Galinsky & Moskowitz 2000 and Todd, Galinsky, & Bodenhausen 2012), bias and prejudice (Moore 2005, Shih, Stotzer, & Gutiérrez 2013, Shih, Wang, Bucher, & Stotzer 2009, Todd et al. 2011, and Vescio, Sechrist, & Paolucci 2003), and anger and interpersonal aggression (Mohr et al. 2007, Nemerovski 2010, and Richardson, Green, & Lago 1998).

Batson has provided quite an impressive body of research that shows that sympathy increases helping, more so than what he calls personal distress but what we have conceptualized as empathic distress (summarized in Batson 2014). He interprets the motivation to help as altruistic because he has ruled out a long list of alternative egoistic explanations (reward, social regard, etc.). Eisenberg and Davis have both found that sympathy correlates with prosocial behavior, by which is typically meant helping (Davis 1994, Eisenberg & Miller 1987). Of course, helping is not always good, but the fact that sympathy tends to motivate us to come to the aid of others is surely an indication of its positive effects. There is some evidence that it also reduces aggression, but that evidence is quite mixed (for an overview, see Maibom 2014).

Affective empathy is harder to get information about because it is typically only measured as 'personal distress.' Personal distress is typically found to have a smaller effect than sympathy when it comes to prosocial behavior (e.g. Eisenberg et al. 1989). Nonetheless, it is a significant predictor of helping when it is difficult to escape the situation in which one is exposed to the other person in need (for a summary see, Batson 2014). This does depend somewhat on whether it is dispositional or situational personal distress that is measured. Relatively little research has been done on other types of affective empathy. It seems that empathic sadness is an important predictor of helping those in need (Eisenberg et al. 1989); it makes it less likely that a person will bully others (Barlińska, Szuster, & Winiewski 2018, Kokkinos & Kipritsi 2017, Stavrinides, Gergiou, & Theofanous 2010).[1] Empathic anger makes one desire to help the victim and punish the perpetrator (Vitaglione & Barnett 2003) and is connected strongly with personal values and ethical competence (Pohling et al. 2016).

To sum up, much as empathy detractors argue that empathy is not necessary or sufficient for moral judgment, plays no central role in moral development, and might actually sometimes conflict with the morally right thing to think or do, empathy in its various forms is associated with an impressive range of behaviors and attitudes that are typically regarded as being *good*. And not just any kind of good; they are *morally good*.

§4.5 Defending empathy

Let's bring together what we have discussed so far. We have a range of different proposals as to how empathy is necessary for, central to, or important in moral judgment, motivation, or perception. But enthusiasm about these claims is tempered by the many objections that empathy is not *necessary* for moral judgment, motivation, or development. More seriously, we have seen that some people even argue that empathy ought not to play *any role whatsoever* in morality. That idea, however, seems somewhat strained in the light of the extensive empirical research that shows that perspective taking, affective empathy, and sympathy all contribute positively to a range of moral concerns. What should we conclude?

Let us begin with the most severe criticism—i.e. that empathy is morally bad, since if that is true, there is little use considering the other criticisms. The big issue Prinz and Bloom have with empathy is that it is partial and biased; we empathize more with those that are close to us physically, that we identify with, or who are a member of our group or family. Morality, however, is supposed to be *impartial*. The first thing to note is that even if empathy is sometimes biased, it is not always biased. Nor is it the case that reason is never biased. And so the fact that empathy is biased may not be a decisive strike against it. Another thing to consider is that morality is itself biased insofar as you have a greater duty to provide for, and aid, your spouse, your child, or your relatives than you have towards a stranger in a foreign land. The same thing is true of friends. This does not, of course, mean that we do not have *any* duties towards people far away from, or unrelated to, us. However, to the extent that varying degrees of empathy track these relations that *are* morally relevant, we should not be concerned about bias.

More important, perhaps, is the fact that there is quite a bit of evidence that empathy makes you *less* biased. In addition to the studies mentioned in the previous section, Jellie Sierksma, Jochem Thijs, and Maykel Verkuyten (2015) found that encouraging children to imagine how a recipient of help would feel had the effect of reducing or preventing in-group favoritism. Moreover, taking the perspective of an out-group member makes a person feel more positive towards them. Interestingly, this attitude *transfers to the group at large* (Shih et al. 2009). If bias is bad, the fact that empathy makes you less biased is surely a good thing. Indeed, it is a point in favor of it, morally speaking. And so contrary to the claims of Bloom and Prinz, bias does not sound the death knell for the role of empathy in morality. The concern is overblown.

Hume and Smith were both aware of the fact that empathy is felt more strongly towards people close to us. And they did suggest means for overcoming lagging empathy towards those we may not be naturally disposed to feel much for. Hume suggested we take the common view, and Smith that we adopt the point of view of an impartial spectator, as we have seen. Is there any reason to think this won't work? I don't think so, and I'm not the only one. Antti Kauppinen (2014) has developed what he calls 'Neo-Classical Explanatory Sentimentalism.' *Explanatory* sentimentalism refers to the foundational role both Hume and Smith accord (affective) empathy, although Kauppinen sides with Smith on the necessary involvement of the imagination (he calls it *combined* empathy, which he takes to include both imagine-self and imagine-other perspective taking). He thinks neither Hume nor Smith thought empathy directly gives rise to moral judgments, wherefore arguments assuming that this is the case miss the point. Kauppinen goes on to argue that although empathy sometimes gives rise to moral judgments, this is not the typical role it plays in morality. Rather, the fact that we make moral judgments *at all* about certain types of actions is the result of what Kauppinen calls "more or less successful ideal-regulated empathy" (2014, 111), usually with the recipient of some action. 'Ideal-regulation' is a different way of saying that when we empathize, we do so from the perspective of an ideal observer, at least when it comes to evaluating the normative dimension of the action performed. This is very much in line with classical sentimentalism.

The fact that empathy is *regulated* is exactly what allows Kauppinen to avoid many of Prinz's and Bloom's objections. Ideal-regulation moves us beyond biases and other provincialisms. But Kauppinen envisages further restricting the type of empathy he talks about, making it truth- and aim-adjusted also. The emotion we experience as a result of putting ourselves in the situation of the other has to be correct, *to our knowledge*. Moreover, the kinds of emotion that are relevant to moral judgment are the *reactive attitudes*. Kauppinen focuses on just two such emotions: resentment and gratitude (2014, 109). When I imagine myself in the other person's situation, I set aside other types of concerns, interests, feelings, and so on (this is *aim-adjusted* empathy). From the point of view of the criticisms leveled against the empathy-as-central-to-morality project, this is very interesting. Prinz promotes 'righteous' anger as being better than empathy when it comes to moral motivation. But if we can empathize with someone's resentment, which is surely a form of righteous anger, is there any difference worth having?

It does rather seem that the main target for both Prinz and Bloom is *certain types* of empathy, such as empathic distress, empathic pain, empathic sadness, or empathic fear. If anger is what they want, Kauppinen can provide it, as can, in principle, *any* sentimentalist theory that is based in empathy. For recall, we can empathize with many emotions, at least in principle. Moreover, if we can allow for the types of adjustments that Kauppinen has in mind (and adjustments were considered necessary even by Hume and Smith), most of Prinz's and Bloom's concerns are dispelled. Adding support to this is that Batson conducted several studies trying to find evidence of righteous anger. He did not succeed. Instead, what he found was that people are made *empathically angry* by unjust and harmful treatment of others (Batson, Chao, & Givens 2009, Batson et al. 2007). Just how did he do that, you might wonder. Well, he looked at the *appraisal conditions* of the anger that he measured.

In emotion research, it is widely accepted that emotions contain, or are preceded by, appraisals. An appraisal is a type of judgment typically about how the environment impacts your wellbeing. Empathic emotions, however, concern how something in the environment impacts a cared-for person, such as a friend or family member. Consequently, the appraisal in personal anger is that my interests have been thwarted, and in empathic anger it is that the interests of someone I care about have been thwarted. If there is such a thing as moral outrage, Batson reasons, it must be due to, or contain, an appraisal that a moral standard or principle has been violated. But it turns out that people make just the same fairness judgments no matter how angry they feel. Moreover, they are more angry when they or a cared-for other are treated unfairly. This suggests, Batson says, that the anger experienced is not *moral outrage* but instead empathic anger (Batson et al. 2007). The effect extends in ways that track the empathy biases criticized above: American university students are angrier about a US marine being tortured than they are about a Sri Lankan soldier undergoing the same (Batson, Chao, & Givens 2009).

In a recent paper, however, Helen Landmann and Ursula Hess (2017) claim to have found evidence for moral outrage. They, too, used appraisal patterns and degree of affect to try to disentangle empathic anger and moral outrage. What they found was people's anger was affected purely by the fact that there was a moral violation and not by the outcome for the victims. Since empathic anger should be provoked by a person's thwarted goals, which in the study would be evidenced by the victim outcome, we should conclude that the anger experienced by third-party observers is *not* empathic anger but, instead, moral outrage.

The one limitation that I see in the study is that empathic anger is measured purely in terms of *outcome*. The example that Landmann and Hess use is of an old couple who are heavily pressured by their banker to invest in an equity fund. In some conditions, the banker knows that doing so is a high-risk investment, but he hides this fact from the couple. In one condition, the couple end up losing a lot of money; in the other they lose, but the fund eventually recovers. Because, Landmann and Hess say, third-person observers are still angered even in the condition where there is no ultimate loss, this provides evidence that the appraisal condition concerns a moral violation. But it is not obvious to me that the reaction cannot be explained as empathic anger after all. For imagine how you would feel about the situation even if you made it out okay. Would you not feel angry? And if so, empathizing with the old couple, would you not feel empathic anger? If your answer is yes—and I know that mine is—then it is too simple to say that the appraisal condition of empathic anger is only actually thwarted goals. It may well concern the *threat* of thwarted goals too for instance.

However you interpret the evidence—as supporting the idea that there is such a thing as moral outrage or not—there are some problems with this lionization of anger in its various forms. Since when was anger regarded a good thing and sadness ignored as being morally relevant? Almost all religions agree that anger is a bad emotion: wrath is one of the seven deadly sins in Christianity; a direct outcome of one of the three poisons in Buddhism; was advised against by Muhammad; and the Stoic Seneca wrote a treatise on how to get rid of it. The lynchings in the American South were frequently fueled by 'righteous anger,' as was the Holocaust and the Rwandan genocide. Riots of all kinds are fueled by the sense of righteous indignation. You might argue that such anger really isn't 'righteous.' Even so, it felt righteous to the ones experiencing it. There is unlikely to be any phenomenological difference between anger that is justified and anger that is not justified. It is in the nature of anger, someone like Seneca would say, that it makes it appear to you that you have been wronged, even if you have not. Anger has terrible consequences. It leads to aggression, violence, and death. If you think empathy has potentially bad effects, anger is infinitely worse. Presumably anger can be useful at times, but most of the time it probably is not. Were we to compare the bad consequences of empathy to the bad consequences of anger, anger would win hands down. This goes for *empathic anger* or *empathic resentment* also. Bloom would presumably agree because he points out that a lot of aggression against people who are Jewish or African-American has been fueled by empathic anger with supposed victims of their depraved behavior (2014, 191–195). Incidentally, this is another reason Bloom thinks empathy is problematic and why he thinks we should hitch our moral wagon to compassion instead. The problem, though, is that there is now evidence that compassion *also* increases third-party punishment (Pfattheicher, Sassenrath, & Keller 2019).

Pointing out that affective empathy is not a perfect emotion, that it does not apply equally to everybody, that it is partial, and so on is fair as far as it goes. We find it easier to imagine being in someone else's situation when we see them as similar to us (Williams, Parker, & Turner 2007), when it is easy to do so (Chambers & Davis 2012), or when we have a particular interest in understanding them (Ickes et al. 1990, Klein & Hodges 2001). But, as we saw, perspective taking, affective empathy, and sympathy have a host of positive effects also. So far, it looks like they outweigh the negative ones. We can now turn to how what we have just discussed is relevant to morality.

§4.6 Cautious conclusions about empathy and morality

It seems fair to conclude that neither perspective taking nor affective empathy nor sympathy is individually necessary for us to be able to make moral judgments or be morally motivated. Not only is morality notably diverse across times and cultures but even within our own culture there is a range of moral norms and ideas that are not easily assimilated to empathic responding to others. Take, for instance, prohibitions related to certain sexual practices that do not appear to harm anyone, such as sex with (some) nonhuman animals or with dead bodies, or the strong desire many feel to act in accordance with natural, cosmic, or divine principles (respect for nature, respect for religious practices) (Maibom 2009). This suggests that Empathy is not necessary to make *any* kind of moral judgment or to be motivated to act in accordance with any kind of moral norm. This is why many modern proponents such as Nichols limits their accounts to the class of actions and prohibitions that concern welfare, or non-religiously motivated moral judgments, as in the case of Kauppinen.

As we have seen, it is less clear that Hume and Smith are subject to these concerns because of the rather foundational role they accorded empathy when it comes to moral considerations. One way to look at this is to ask: why should we care about what happens to people not immediately associated with us? If someone's suffering does not hurt me or mine personally, either directly or by means of affecting my livelihood, etc., why should it make any difference to me? Perhaps the two questions have two different answers. Sympathy makes us care about others for their sake, as Stephen Darwall has suggested (1998). It involves an experience, or appearance, of the welfare of another mattering *categorically*. Affective empathy, on the other hand, allows us to understand what it is like to experience the relevant emotions and what they say about our situation. Both are needed for morality. Alternatively, perhaps sympathy could answer the first question but not the second one, whereas affective empathy might be able to answer both.

But is morality purely about caring about the wellbeing of others? Many moral systems, including our own, contain something like purity norms, for instance. These norms seem primarily self-protective. It is noticeable, however, that we do not only judge what we do as disgusting but also what others do *even when what they do cannot possibly harm or contaminate us*. So our question arises again. Why should we care that others do things that we find impure or disgusting? Sympathy or empathy can explain it; pure disgust cannot. Suppose we care about doing or not doing certain things because we believe it is dharma or because God said so. Why should we care about whether others engage in those behaviors if they do not directly impact us? If they go off to their certain doom, what is that to us? Again, we need a reason to care, over and above our own selfish reasons to care.

But what about fairness and justice, you ask. Is not the concern about others built into the very core of these structures? And yet, they do not appear to be empathy driven. In my mind, this comes closest to an objection to this idea that empathy explains the moral. And it is easy to see that we should care about reciprocity for purely self-interested reasons. We do not need empathy for this. But now think of how you feel about lack of reciprocity among others not related to you? Is this a matter of indifference to you, or do you not judge such actions as wrong, and would you not be at least somewhat motivated to do something about it if you could? My hope is that the answer is 'yes.' I know mine is. And so now we must ask why. Again, empathy or sympathy can provide the answer.

Someone might object that I have silently replaced 'empathy' with 'caring' and that it is not legitimate, since caring involves something over and above simply feeling with someone else. If we are to push a classical sentimentalist idea about the foundation of morality, we cannot help ourselves to care. There are a couple of responses one might make. First, one might be ecumenical about what form of empathy is required for morality and insists that all of perspective taking, affective empathy, and sympathy are in the mix. After all, someone like Adam Smith's notion involves both perspective taking and affective empathy, since he requires that we imagine being in the other person's stead. Second, one can simply deny that anything nefarious has taken place. 'Caring' is not used in its philosophically loaded sense here and could be replaced with 'being moved by' or whatever notion is thought appropriate to express empathic affect. The point is simply that we react to what happens to others as if it were happening to us. This emotion is not, in fact, warm and woozy, as in welfare-oriented moral concern. It is a mirroring response to whatever the other person is feeling, and it can express itself more imperiously in condemnation of actions that are deemed impure or disgusting. But it is what sets the entire system of preoccupation with *what others do and what happens to them* in motion.

Yet another alternative is an idea suggested by the work of Richard Shweder (Shweder et al. 1997) and Jonathan Haidt (Haidt, Koller, & Dias 1993) and developed by Victoria McGeer (2008). The idea here is that morality is a hodgepodge collection of norms concerned with rather different aspects of human life. Haidt says that morality has certain emotional or cognitive-emotional 'foundations.' If you take one of them away, your resultant morality will have a different, and more limited, shape than that of your fellow men and women. You may have a notion of right and wrong, but it will be abnormal and may lead to divergent intuitions compared to your peers. Note that abnormal does not mean 'bad' or 'wrong' here, just unusual. For instance, people with autism have strangely rigid rules and ideas of moral right and wrong that sometimes seems to bypass sympathy or compassion altogether (McGeer 2008). McGeer suggests that if you take empathy or sympathy out of the equation, you get a distinctive kind of moral agency. And it may be one that can, at times, be hard to recognize as such.

§4.7 Take-home message

In this chapter, we have explored various ways in which Empathy may be central to, or necessary for, morality. Mainly, we have looked at affective empathy, but we saw that Smith talked about affective empathy induced by perspective taking, as does Kauppinen. Others are more partial to sympathy, such as Nichols or Darwall. In addition to there being variety in the forms of Empathy that are thought to be particularly central to morality, there are a lot of different suggestions as to *what* aspects of morality are specifically impacted. It may be the very foundational idea about caring about what happens to others or what others do, as in Hume and Smith, or a particular form of caring, as in Darwall. It may be empathy's role in moral judgment, moral motivation, moral responsibility, moral perception, or moral development that is at issue. There are some weighty considerations that suggest that empathy is sometimes expendable in moral judgment and motivation, but it appears to be an exaggeration to claim, as some do, that empathy is *bad* morally speaking. The evidence strongly suggests otherwise, as does philosophical reflection on the foundational issues in ethics.

To sum up, in this chapter, we have discussed:

- The role Hume and Smith accorded empathy in morality
- Some of the modern views that claim that empathy is central to morality
- What the empirical evidence is concerning the role of empathy in morality
- Some common objections to the role and use of empathy in morality and how to answer (some of) them
- Why affective empathy, perspective taking, or sympathy may be central to, if not required for, ordinary forms of moral responding

Note

1 Darlińska, Szuster, and Winiewski (2018) *claim* that it is cognitive empathy that does the work. However, their cognitive empathy is an empathy induction meant to make the person *identify* with the situation the other person is in, specifically focusing on affect. What we should expect to result from such an instruction is not cognitive but affective empathy.

Further reading

Bloom, P. 2014. Against empathy. *Boston Review*, September 10, 2014. http:// bostonreview.net/forum/paul-bloom-against-empathy. *Bloom's criticism of the idea that empathy has an important role to play in morality, in short form.*

Des Autels, P. 2012. Moral perception and responsiveness. *Journal of Social Philosophy*, 43, 334–346. *A paper on how empathy may be central to perceiving when a situation is morally relevant.*

Hoffman, M. 2014. Empathy, justice, and social change. In: H.L. Maibom (Ed.) *Empathy and Morality*. New York: Oxford University Press, 71–96. *Hoffman explains the developmental significance of empathy when it comes to moral understanding and moral motivation.*

Ilyes, I. 2017. Empathy in Hume and Smith. In: H.L. Maibom (Ed.) *Empathy and Morality*. New York: Oxford University Press, 98–109. *One of the best introductions I have read about the centrality of empathy in Hume's and Smith's moral philosophies.*

Kauppinen, A. 2014. Empathy: Emotion regulation, and moral judgment. In: H.L. Maibom (Ed.) *Empathy and Morality*. New York: Oxford University Press, 97–121. *An exciting new approach to how empathy may be central to morality.*

Maibom, H.L. 2010. Imagining others. *Atelier de l'Ethique*, 5(1), 34–49. *My former self arguing that empathy cannot be necessary for moral judgment or motivation.*

Nichols, S. 2001. Mindreading and the cognitive architecture underlying altruistic motivation. *Mind & Language*, 16, 425–455. *Nichols presents an account of altruistic motivation relying on empathy-related responding.*

Prinz, J. 2011. Is empathy necessary for morality? In: A. Coplan & P. Goldie (Eds.) *Empathy: Philosophical and Psychological Perspectives*. New York: Oxford University Press, *Prinz's classical article against the virtues of empathy as a moral emotion.*

Shoemaker, D. 2017. Empathy and moral responsibility. In: H.L. Maibom (Ed.) *The Routledge Handbook of Philosophy of Empathy*. New York: Routledge, 242–252. *An account of how the ability to empathize may be necessary for certain types of moral responsibility.*

References

Batson, C.D. 1991. *The Altruism Question*. Hillsdale, NJ: Lawrence Erlbaum.

Batson, C.D. 2011. *Altruism in Humans*. New York: Oxford University Press.

Batson, C.D. 2014. Empathy-induced altruism and morality: No necessary connection. In: H.L. Maibom (Ed.) *Empathy and Morality*. New York: Oxford University Press, 41–58.

Batson, C.D., Chao, M.C., & Givens, J.M. 2009. Pursuing moral outrage: Anger at torture. *Journal of Experimental Social Psychology*, 45, 155–160.

Batson, C.D., Kennedy, C.L., Nord, L-A., Stocks, E.L., Fleming, D.A., Marzette, C.M., Lishner, D.A., Hayes, R.E., Kolchinsky, L.M., & Zerger, T. 2007.

Anger at unfairness: Is it moral outrage? *European Journal of Social Psychology*, 37, 1272–1285.

Berndsen, M. & McGarty, C. 2012. Perspective taking and opinions about forms of reparation for victims of historical harm. *Personality and Social Psychology Bulletin*, 38, 1316–1328.

Blair, R.J.R. 1995. A cognitive developmental approach to morality: Investigating the psychopath. *Cognition*, 57, 1–29.

Blair, R.J.R. 2008. Normative theory or theory of mind? A response to Nichols. In: W. Sinnott-Armstrong (Ed.) *Moral Psychology, Vol. 2: The Cognitive Science of Morality: Intuition and Diversity*. Cambridge, MA: MIT Press, 275–278.

Blair, R.J.R., Mitchell, D., & Blair, K. 2005. *The Psychopath: Emotion and the Brain*. Oxford: Blackwell.

Bloom, P. 2016. *Against Empathy: The Case for Rational Compassion*. New York: Ecco.

Carlo, G., Allen, J.B., & Buhman, D.C. 1999. Facilitating and disinhibiting social behaviors: The nonlinear interaction of trait perspective-taking and trait personal distress on volunteering. *Basic and Applied Social Psychology*, 21, 189–197.

Chambers, J.R. & Davis, M.H. 2012. The role of the self in perspective taking and empathy: The ease of self-simulation as a heuristic for inferring empathic feelings. *Social Cognition*, 30, 153–180.

Darwall, S. 1998. Empathy, sympathy, care. *Philosophical Studies*, 89, 261–282.

Davis, M. 1994. *Empathy: A Social Psychological Approach*. Boulder: Westview Press.

Decety, J. & Yoder, K. 2016. Empathy and motivation for justice: Cognitive empathy and concern, but not emotional empathy, predict sensitivity to injustice for others. *Social Neuroscience*, 11, 1–14.

Des Autels, P. 2012. Moral perception and responsiveness. *Journal of Social Philosophy*, 43, 334–346.

Dovidio, J.F., Allen, J.L., & Schroeder, D.A. 1990. Specificity of empathy-induced helping: Evidence for altruistic motivation. *Journal of Personality and Social Psychology*, 59, 249–260.

Eisenberg, N. 2005. The development of empathy-related responding. In: G. Carlo & C.P. Edwards (Eds.) *Nebraska Symposium on Motivation. Volume 51. Moral Motivation Through the Life Span*. Lincoln, NE: University of Nebraska Press, 73–117.

Eisenberg, N., Fabes, R.A., Miller, P.A., Fultz, J., Shell, R., Mathay, R.M., & Reno, R.R. 1989. Relation of personal distress and sympathy to prosocial behavior: A multimethod study. *Journal of Personality and Social Psychology*, 57, 55–66.

Eisenberg, N. & Miller, P.A. 1987. The relation of empathy to prosocial and related behaviors. *Psychological Bulletin*, 101, 91–119.

Eisenberg, N., Zhou, Q., & Koller, S. 2001. Brazilian adolescents' prosocial moral judgment and behavior: Relations to sympathy, perspective taking, gender-role orientation, and demographic characteristics. *Child Development*, 72, 518–534.

Fennis, B.M. 2011. Can't get over me: Ego-depletion attenuates prosocial effects of perspective taking. *European Journal of Social Psychology*, 41, 580–585.

Furlane, K. & Maibom, H.L. 2017. Empathy is a not a thermometer. *Philosophia*, 45, 861–866.

Galinsky, A.D. & Moskowitz, G.B. 2000. Perspective-taking: Decreasing stereotype expression, stereotype accessibility, and in-group favoritism. *Journal of Personality and Social Psychology*, 78, 708–724.

Goldstein, N., Vezich, S., & Shapiro, J.R. 2014. Perceived perspective taking: When others walk in our shoes. *Journal of Personality and Social Psychology*, 106, 941–960.

Haidt, J. 2001. The emotional dog and its rational tail: A social intuitionist approach to moral judgment. *Psychological Review*, 108, 814–834.

Haidt, J., Koller, S.H., & Dias, M.G. 1993. Affect, culture, and morality or is it wrong to eat your dog? *Journal of Personality and Social Psychology*, 65, 613–628.

Hoffman, M. 2000. *Empathy and Moral Development: Implications for Caring and Justice*. New York: Cambridge University Press.

Hume, D. 1739/1978. *A Treatise of Human Nature*. L.A. Selby-Bigge (Ed.) & P. H. Nidditch (2nd Ed.). Oxford: Clarendon Press.

Ickes, W., Stinson, L., Bissonnette, V., & Garcia, S. 1990. Naturalistic social cognition: Empathic accuracy in mixed-sex dyads. *Journal of Personality and Social Psychology*, 59, 730–742.

Kauppinen, A. 2014. Empathy: Emotion regulation, and moral judgment. In: H.L. Maibom (Ed.) *Empathy and Morality*. New York: Oxford University Press, 97–121.

Klein, K.J.K. & Hodges, S.P. 2001. Gender differences, motivation, and empathic accuracy: When it pays to understand. *Personality and Social Psychology Bulletin*, 27, 720–730.

Kokkinos, C.M. & Kipritsi, E. 2017. Bullying, moral disengagement and empathy: Exploring the links among early adolescents. *Educational Psychology*, 38, 535–552.

Konstam, V., Chernoff, M., & Deveney, S. 2001. Toward forgiveness: The role of guilt, shame, anger, and empathy. *Counseling and Values*, 46, 26–39.

Landmann, H. & Hess, U. 2017. What elicits third-party anger? The effects of moral violation and others' outcome on anger and compassion. *Cognition & Emotion*, 31, 1097–1111.

Maibom, H.L. 2009. Feeling for others: Empathy, sympathy, and morality. *Inquiry*, 52, 483–499.

Maibom, H.L. 2010. Imagining others. *Atelier de l'Ethique*, 5, 34–49.

Maibom, H.L. 2014. Everything you ever wanted to know about empathy. In: H.L. Maibom (Ed.) *Empathy and Morality*. New York: Oxford University Press, 1–40.

Maibom, H.L. Forthcoming. Responsibility in the age of neuroscience: Moral understanding and empathy in psychopaths. In: J. Doris & M. Vargas (Eds.) *Oxford Handbook of Moral Psychology*. Oxford: Oxford University Press.

McGeer, V. 2008. Varieties of moral agency. In: W. Sinnott-Armstrong (Ed.) *Moral Psychology: The Neuroscience of Morality: Emotion, Brain Disorders, and Development*. Cambridge, MA: MIT Press, 227–257.

Mohr, P., Howells, K., Gerace, A., Day, A., & Wharton, M. 2007. The role of perspective taking in anger arousal. *Personality and Individual Differences*, 43, 507–517.

Moore, D.A. 2005. Myopic biases in strategic social prediction: Why deadlines put everyone under more pressure than everyone else. *Personality and Social Psychology Bulletin*, 31, 668–679.

Myers, M.W., Laurent, S.M., & Hodges, S.D. 2014. Perspective taking instructions and self-other overlap: Different motives for helping. *Motivation & Emotion*, 38, 224–234.

Nemerovski, R. 2010. Anger in the car—An examination of the role of perspective-taking in the anger response while driving. *Dissertation Abstracts International: Section B: The Sciences and Engineering*, 71 (2-B), 1363.

Nichols, S. 2002. How psychopaths threaten moral rationalism, or is it irrational to be amoral? *The Monist*, 85, 285–303.

Nichols, S. 2004. *Sentimental Rules.* New York: Oxford University Press.

Pahl, S. & Bauer, J. 2013. Overcoming the distance: Perspective taking with future humans improves environmental engagement. *Environment and Behavior,* 45, 155–169.

Pfattheicher, S., Sassenrath, D., & Keller, J. 2019. Compassion magnifies third-party punishment. *Journal of Personality and Social Psychology,* 117, 124–141.

Pohling, R., Bzdok, D., Eigenstetter, M., Stumpf, S., & Strobel, A. 2016. What is ethical competence? The role of empathy, personal values, and the Five-Factor Model of Personality in ethical decision-making. *Journal of Business Ethics,* 137, 449–474.

Prinz, J. 2011. Is empathy necessary for morality? In: A. Coplan & P. Goldie (Eds.) *Empathy: Philosophical and Psychological Perspectives.* New York: Oxford University Press, 211–229.

Raynor, D.R. 1984. Hume's abstract of Adam Smith's Theory of Moral Sentiments. *Journal of the History of Philosophy,* 22, 51–79.

Richardson, D.R.Green, L.R., & Lago, T.S. 1998. The relationship between perspective-taking and non-aggressive responding in the face of an attack. *Journal of Personality,* 66, 235–256.

Sierksma, J., Thijs, J., & Verkuyten, M. 2015. In-group bias in children's intention to help can be overpowered by inducing empathy. *British Journal of Developmental Psychology,* 33, 45–56.

Shih, M.J., Stotzer, R., & Gutiérrez, A.S. 2013. Perspective-taking and empathy: Generalizing the reduction of group-bias towards Asian Americans to general outgroups. *Journal of Abnormal Psychology,* 4, 79–83.

Shih, M., Wang, E., Bucher, A.T., & Stotzer, R. 2009. Perspective taking: Reducing prejudice towards general outgroups and specific individuals. *Group Processes & Intergroup Relations,* 12, 565–577.

Shoemaker, D. 2015. *Responsibility from the Margins.* New York: Oxford University Press.

Shoemaker, D. 2017. Empathy and moral responsibility. In: H.L. Maibom (Ed.) *The Routledge Handbook of Philosophy of Empathy.* New York: Routledge, 242–252.

Shweder, R., Much, N.C., Mahapatra, M., & Park, L. 1997. The 'Big Three' of morality (autonomy, community, and divinity) and the 'Big Three' explanations of suffering. In: A.M. Brandt & P. Rozin (Eds.) *Morality and Health.* New York: Routledge, 119–169.

Sierksma, J., Thijs, J., & Verkuyten, M. 2015. In-group bias in children's intention to help can be overpowered by inducing empathy. *British Journal of Developmental Psychology*, 33, 45–56.

Slote, M. 2009. *Moral Sentimentalism*. New York: Oxford University Press.

Slote, M. 2017. The many faces of empathy. *Philosophia*, 45, 843–855.

Smith, A. 1759/1976. *The Theory of Moral Sentiments*. D.D. Raphael & A.L. Mackie (Eds.). Indianapolis, IN: Liberty Fund.

Smith, M. 1994. *The Moral Problem*. Oxford: Blackwell.

Stavrinides, P., Gergiou, St., & Theofanous, V. 2010. Bullying and empathy: a short-term longitudinal study. *Educational Psychology*, 30, 793–802.

Takaku, S., Weiner, B., & Ohbuchi, K-I. 2001. A cross-cultural examination of the effects of apology and perspective taking on forgiveness. *Journal of Language and Social Psychology*, 20, 144–166.

Todd, A.R., Bodenhausen, G.V., Richeson, J.A., & Galinksy, A.D. 2011. Perspective taking combats automatic expressions of racial bias. *Journal of Personality and Social Psychology*, 100, 1027–1042.

Todd, A.R., Galinsky, A.D., & Bodenhausen, G.V. 2012. Perspective taking undermines perspective taking maintenance processes: Evidence from social memory, behavior explanation, and information solicitation. *Social Cognition*, 30, 94–108.

Vescio, T.K., Sechrist, G.B., & Paolucci, M.P. 2003. Perspective taking and prejudice reduction: The mediational role of empathy arousal and situational attribution. *European Journal of Social Psychology*, 33, 455–472.

Vitaglione, G. & Barnett, M. 2003. Assessing a new dimension of empathy. *Motivation & Emotion*, 27, 301–325.

Walker, L.J. 1980. Cognitive and perspective-taking prerequisites for moral development. *Child Development*, 51, 131–139.

Williams, H.M., Parker, S.K., & Turner, N. 2007. Perceived dissimilarity and perspective taking with work teams. *Group & Organizational Management*, 32, 569–597.

Zechmeister, J.S. & Romero, C. 2002. Victim and offender accounts in interpersonal conflict: Autobiographical narratives of forgiveness and unforgiveness. *Journal of Personality and Social Psychology*, 82, 675–686.

5

EMPATHY AND ART

The word 'empathy' has its roots in the German aesthetic tradition. Although there are earlier uses of the word, Einfühlung began to take off as an important concept in aesthetics with the work of Robert Vischer, who suggested that experiencing it was central to appreciating objects of art. The idea is that when we relate to art, we are 'feeling into' it in some sense. Theodor Lipps picked up the word and explicated it in terms of 'aesthetic imitation.' Later, Edward Titchener translated Einfühlung as 'empathy.' From there on, empathy became a staple of psychological speculation and of phenomenological exploration. But its importance in aesthetics faded relatively quickly. Recent years, however, have seen a revival of the idea that empathy with works of art is central to appreciating them.

In this chapter, I discuss the historical roots of empathy in Einfühlung, the role of 'feeling into' inanimate objects, cognitive empathy and understanding works of art, affective empathy and art appreciation, the variety of artistic characters that can be empathized with, and the potential of art to enhance our empathy and moral attitudes towards others.

§5.1 *Einfühlung*

Einfühlung is German for 'feeling into' or, as some say, 'feeling oneself into.' In principle, one can feel into anything. However, the term was initially used in the context of appreciating art. Robert Vischer (1873/1994) speculated that Einfühlung is an active involvement of the imagination with some object of art. The object embodies a certain harmony that is perceived by the subject, whose inner subjective harmony comes to reflect it. It sounds like a form of introjection, but Vischer also talks of how we project ourselves into the art we admire. This seems fairly close to claiming that it is through identification with art that we come to appreciate it. The basic idea seems to have been this. When we engage with a work of art, say the Pantheon in Rome, we displace ourselves into that object with the aim of exploring what we feel as a result. We might feel majestic, enveloping, or calm as a result.

The idea that we can feel into the world, or parts of the world, was popular in the romantic tradition. Johann Gottfried von Herder and Novalis were both entranced by the idea. Herder thought Einfühlung was central to the interpretation of texts and also to understanding historical agents (Herder 1774/1969). Because there are great differences between people depending on where and when they live, we must take into consideration a range of contextual factors when we interpret them. In particular, we should recapture someone's concepts in their original basis, which is in his or her sensations. To recapture somebody's sensations, it is easy to see, requires some Einfühlung. The spirit of romanticism also involved a degree of pantheism, which went hand in hand with the idea that we can feel ourselves into nature. According to Novalis, we could feel what nature feels (see Stueber 2006).

Einfühlung came to greater prominence with the work of Theodor Lipps, who argued for its use both in aesthetic experience and interpersonal understanding. Aesthetic experiences are experiences that are predicated on our ability to resonate internally with external objects. More precisely, we have certain experiences upon being perceptually presented with an object, and the content of those experiences is projected onto the object and experienced as if it belongs to it. Take, for instance, a Doric column. When we look at such a column, we immediately feel its present activity as one of carrying its own weight and the weight of the ceiling it supports. But this notion of carrying or lifting is taken from our own repertoire of physical activities and used to understand the more mechanical processes of architectural structures. We are, Lipps says, transported *into* the objects of art.

Another way of putting Lipps' idea is to say that in the contemplation of the work of art a fusion is effected. The contrast between the art lover and the art object disappears. In fact, Lipps (1903/1979) goes as far as to say that when he 'feels into' the object, he feels himself to be active *within the perceived figure!* It is an inner imitation of the outer figure. Most commentators agree that Lipps was given to hyperbole, and so we should not suppose that he held that we are *completely* identified with an object of art; we don't lose ourselves in it entirely. We are aware that the object is 'out there' and we are 'here.' What is perhaps most important for Lipps is that Einfühlung stands in contrast to an analytic relation to an object, where one mentally dissects the object, draws inferences about it, and so on. Instead, in one's relation to the object is immediate, much like a perception. Lipps says that Einfühlung "is not the name for any inference; rather it is the name for an original and not further derivable, at the same time most wonderful fact, which is different from an inference, indeed absolutely incompatible" with it (Lipps 1907 as quoted in Stueber 2006, 8–9).

What is special about Lipps' use of Einfühlung compared to many of his predecessors is that he also extends it to our understanding of people, rather than limiting it to objects of art. In fact, he takes Einfühlung to be definitive of how we relate to others. We directly feel into them and see them as other minds. We do not, as some suggest, conclude they have minds by analogy. Looking closer at what Lipps has to say about this process may throw some light on aesthetic Einfühlung. Consider how we are able to recognize what others feel by looking at their faces. Do we first discern certain muscle tensions and *then* infer that the person feels this or that? It doesn't seem so. We see *immediately* that they are angry, afraid, or friendly. The way this process typically works is by our imitating the facial expressions of others when we encounter them. But we do so below the threshold of consciousness. The same can be said about movements generally. Whether movements are imitated in muscle tensions or in 'the mind's muscles' is not quite clear. However, Lipps evidently thought that his Einfühlung involved not only imitating the other's bodily movements but also experiencing the associated feelings, so that the empathizer can truly be said to feel what the other person feels. We should note that Lipps thought this is the only way we can discern affective states in other people (Lipps 1907). Were we incapable of experiencing emotions for ourselves, we would not be able to perceive them in others. Our own selves are the necessary sounding board for the feelings of others.

Lipps's view enjoyed some success but was criticized by both aestheticians and phenomenologists. Edith Stein, for instance, argues that one must first be able to understand what another is feeling or thinking in order to see similarities to one's own feelings and thoughts. There is no breaking down the barriers between self and other in empathy, then. She also disagrees that we need the bodily expressions of the other to be able to discern that she is a minded fellow human being (Stein 1917/1989). Despite such criticisms, a modified version of empathy or Einfühlung came to play an important role in the phenomenological tradition.

In his translation of some of Lipps's work, Titchener chose the term 'empathy' for Einfühlung. According to Gustav Jahoda (2005), it is in Titchener that we find the distinctive sense of 'empathy,' since Lipps himself often used Einfühlung and sympathiziere (German for 'to sympathize') interchangeably. A number of people took up Lipps's idea, but it quickly fell out of favor. This may be because the idea is somewhat obscure and metaphorical, or because other views were thought to be more satisfactory. However that might be, the idea that empathy is central to aesthetic experiences and art appreciation has seen a revival since simulation theory was first introduced in the 1980s. And a range of different philosophers of art have proposed various ways in which empathy plays a role in art. This is what we turn to now.

§5.2 Re-enactment of the inorganic

The idea of empathy in art as Einfühlung finds a contemporary expression in the idea that the appreciation of certain forms of art involves a kind of re-enactment on the part of the art lover. Adopting Vischer's and Lipp's aesthetics, Vernon Lee suggests that as we feel into a building, we feel in our bodies the upwards striving of the columns or the weary calm of the lower buildings stretching out before it (Lee 1913). For modern readers, it is not entirely straightforward to figure out how to interpret this somewhat fanciful description of architectural enjoyment. It seems to involve full-on projection of one's own ideas in a way that almost obliterates the being of the building itself. But there are other ways of making good on the idea that some form of empathy is involved in appreciating the objects of art themselves.

Reviving a suggestion by Herbert Langfeld, Gregory Currie (2011) presents a case for the more traditional idea that we can live ourselves into *objects* of art. Langfeld (1920) suggested that when we observe the curve on a statue, we may experience, very briefly, our hands moving along that curve. The idea here is that motor mimicry is often involved in our making sense of objects. Currie explicates this in terms of simulation theory, which we discussed in Chapter 2. He follows Goldman (2006, 2011) in distinguishing between two forms: low-level simulation (or mirroring empathy) and high-level simulation (or reconstructive empathy) (see also Chapter 2). Low-level simulation takes place relatively automatically at the level of mirroring or mimicking of expressions, by activating mirror neurons, or by generating motor images. High-level simulation can build on low-level simulation but also involves conscious efforts to change one's perspective, to quarantine one's own beliefs and attitudes, and to take on some of the thoughts, dispositions, and feelings one supposes the other has, within the context of the simulation. As we shall see, aestheticians appeal to both forms.

Currie thinks low-level or, as he dubs it, 'sub-personal' simulation makes sense of certain ways of engaging with objects of art. When we look at an object, motor images are activated which help us interpret or recognize it. This is not pure speculation; a body of psychological research supports this idea (for an overview, see Goldman 2006). Low-level simulative processes, Currie says,

> may be activated by artworks, and by other kinds of objects, in ways that conform to, and sometimes extend, the claims of the Empathists. There is a sense of having your body disposed in a way which resembles (perhaps minimally) the geometry of the object viewed and its dynamical relations to other things, as one imagines standing upright supporting a heavy load, in response to the sight of a load-bearing column.
>
> (2011, 86)

We find another development of the idea of re-enactment, or simulation, but this time high-level simulation, in the work of Jenefer Robinson on architecture. Robinson argues that aesthetics research on architecture is too focused on *understanding* or *seeing*. Buildings are conceived of as feasts for the eyes, or as involving elaborate plans and structural features that are epistemologically titillating. What is ignored, she says, is the role of the body *moving through* architectural space. After all, a building is not a picture for us to behold visually as we remain relatively stationary in space. Rather, a building is for *occupation*. As she says:

> To appreciate a work of architecture fully requires not only grasping the structure of a building with the eyes and the mind, but also *interacting* with it, moving through and around it, feeling what it is like to live or work or act in it, to follow its paths, enter its doors, move over its thresholds, pass along its corridors, look out of its windows, and work or play or walk about in its rooms. It is not enough to *see* or *figure out* what the building exemplifies or expresses; one has to engage one's whole body in the process of understanding and appreciation.
>
> (Robinson 2012, 340)

Robinson does not think the process she describes is properly called 'empathy.' Instead, it is a form of (high-level) re-enactment. A building invites us to step inside it, and to move around in it, so as to experience it *in our own bodies*. It is presumably this form of internalizing of the space that is empathic in nature. Compare it to empathizing with a person. Here, we replay in our own bodies what we assume is going on in his or her body. We feel the space of the building much like we feel other people.

Feeling the space of a building is still something we do on our terms, for sure. *We* feel small, constricted, liberated, claustrophobic, or pleasantly enveloped. But these feelings are not only our own projections. To establish this point, Robinson refers to the embodied cognition literature, inspired by James Gibson (1979), with its emphasis on *affordances*. Her idea is that any building *affords* certain movements and certain types of engagements with it. Affordances, however, are not subjective or objective. They are neither, or they are both. There is no affordance without the contribution of the objective world that the organism interacts with, or the subjective structure of the organism (its body, its movement potentials, its plans and goals). Affordances describe the intersection of organisms and their worlds. When we move around a building, Robinson maintains, we *experience* its affordances. And we do so by means of feelings in our bodies. This is, then, not pure projection.

Why, you might ask, is this re-enactment, or even enactment? Isn't it just directly experiencing? Well, it is and it isn't. Recall that one experiences a building over time, not at any one moment of sensory experience. It takes time to move around it and through it, to feel its surfaces, and so on. And so the unified sensation one takes away must rely in part on the imaginary re-enactment of what it was like to move through the parts that are no longer perceptually available. We can also rely on motor memories. This brings us much closer to the sort of simulation that is intimately involved in empathy.

It would be remiss of me if I did not briefly trace the preoccupation with re-enactment back to Robin George Collingwood's philosophy of history (1946/1993). According to Collingwood, understanding historical events requires us to engage in re-enactment. We must adopt the point of view of main actors to see the world as they saw it. To do so, we suspend our own attitudes and our knowledge so that we can understand the thoughts and motivations of someone radically different from ourselves. Failing to do this leads to bad historical narratives, of little interest to a person who wants to *understand* history and not simply cast it in his or her own light. The whole point of doing history is to make it intelligible, but in order to do so we have to engage with the characters *on their own terms*. At a minimum, we must re-enact *their reasons for action*. It is unclear how closely Collingwood meant to cleave to actual psychological re-enactment, as opposed to a more public act of meaning making. Modern takes on this idea, however, have pretty clearly gone the route of psychologizing re-enactment, at least in the realm of aesthetics. Re-enactment accounts are very similar to emotional contagion accounts, which we discuss next.

§5.3 Emotional contagion of expression

Another account of how understanding or appreciating art relies on our empathic repertoire comes from Stephen Davies (1994). Reflecting on why it is that certain types of music reliably make us feel certain things, such as happy or sad, he suggests that it does so because it expresses the affect we come to feel as a result of listening to it. This is an important added element. It is one thing to claim that certain works of art *evoke* emotions, and another to maintain that they *themselves* express emotions. On Davies' account, music *evokes* empathic emotion by means of itself *expressing* such emotion. How, more precisely, does this process work?

According to Davies, I 'catch' sadness from sad music by a process of emotional contagion. In effect, music appreciation piggybacks on a pre-existing capacity to catch emotions *from other people*. Here things get a bit tricky. We relate to music as we relate to other things, most notably human agents. And so we expect, he says, that we will be able to understand one moment in musical space in terms of what came before it, that the piece will present a coherent whole, and so on (2011, 141). Moreover, we are designed by Mother Nature to pick up on affective cues in our environment. Musical expression resembles such cues. Of course, music is not a person, nor should we suppose it must imply a person or a persona in order to move us. For Davies, music can express emotions without there being any person who experiences, or expresses, them. Certain configurations—in people's faces, in musical space, and so on—are capable of expressing affect without being caused by that affect. A basset hound looks sad even if it is not sad, and my friend can exude cheerfulness even if he is sad. Music is no different. Or so the story goes. It is important to note that Davies is not claiming that music's emotional expressiveness *depends* on an emotional response. Music is capable of expressing emotion purely in virtue of bearing a close resemblance to people expressing emotion, whether or not we happen to pick up on it. But when we do, we can empathize with it through mirroring.

When we 'catch' sadness from a sad tune, the music is the *cause* of our sadness, but it is not the intentional of object of it. I'm not sad *about* the music, in other words. My sadness may not have a particular object. This is no different, in principle, from the contagious sadness I might experience as a result of being in the presence of a sad person. Our emotions mimic the emotional tenor of the music. To catch the emotions the music expresses, I must recognize the emotional expression in some sense, but that does not require that I recognize the process of transmission.

Davies does not want to commit to a particular form of transmission, but like Robinson, he likens it to bodily motion. "If contagion operates through mimicry, we might then expect the listener to adopt bodily posture and attitudes (or posturally relevant muscular proprioceptions) like those apparent in the music's progress," he says (2011, 147). He also mentions facial and vocal mimicry. Emotion recognition research has long focused on photographs of faces, but people are also very proficient at recognizing affect in voices (Blair et al. 2002, Grosbras, Ross, & Belin 2018). Moreover, the acoustic cues that convey emotion are similar to speech prosody, and recognition of both appears to develop in parallel (Vidas, Dingle, & Nelson 2018). It is not so farfetched to suppose, then, that music makes us feel emotion by a process of emotional contagion (Juslin & Västfjäll 2008).

Robinson disagrees with Davies. She doesn't think it is necessary for us to recognize the emotional expression in music in order for us to be infected by it. Just as we saw in the case of architecture, listening to music engages our motor system. Musical gestures activate these systems. The

result is that the listener mimics the *movement* of the music. When those
movements are the same as those that are characteristic of particular
emotions, the listener can come to experience those emotions. This is
what Robinson calls the Jazzercise effect (Robinson 2005, 391–395).
Here she relies on William James' insight that "adopting the facial
expression, posture, gaze, autonomic responses, and/or actions characteristic of a particular type of emotion can induce that same emotion"
(Robinson 2017c, 298).

Charles Nussbaum (2007) is another philosopher of art who supports a
re-enactment account of musical appreciation. Like Robinson, he thinks
that when we listen carefully to a piece of music, we enact the plan of the
music in our imagination. How can one enact a *musical plan*? By virtually
moving through the space created by the music: "slow/fast, labored/easy,
expansive/contracted, smooth/angular, and so on" (Nussbaum 2007, 47).
Music creates its own tonal space within which we must move in order to
understand it. We enact the melodies in our imagination, keeping in mind
what has passed, and perhaps anticipating what is to come. This may seem
rather counterintuitive, since as a music lover I don't get the sense of
having had a good workout, virtual or otherwise, when I have listened to a
concerto. Instead, I typically feel *emotionally moved*.

Nussbaum dissolves this apparent difficulty by connecting emotions
with affordances. Just as architecture affords certain types of motion, and
not others, so music too affords particular kinds of movement through its
virtual landscape. The idea fits nicely with Nico Frijda's theory of emotions. According to Frijda, emotions are perceptions of affordances. Those
affordances might be impediments, threats, triumphs, and so on. Because
we associate certain bodily movements with emotional reactions to those
very same affordances, music evokes emotions in us. I may feel exhila-
rated having overcome certain obstacles in musical space, defeated
because I haven't, or alienated by troublesome movements. As we saw in
Robinson's account of architecture, the way we appreciate this form of art
is through bodily enactment, or re-enactment, of moving through the
space of music. According to Nussbaum, the musical space is virtual and
so almost a simulation itself.

One might wonder whether music *expresses* emotion on this account, or
whether it merely *evokes* affect. The answer is that if we are talking about
affordances, there is no good yes/no answer. Suppose you wonder whether
a piece of music expresses emotion all on its own, as it were, and independently of the way a listener responds to it. On Nussbaum's account, the

answer would be no. Why? Because the expressiveness of music is highly response dependent. Nonetheless, the music *affords* certain movements through it, which is why the listener responds the way she does. The expressiveness of music is due *neither* to the music *nor* to the listener on their own but to *both*.

In pictures, too, we might talk of emotional contagion but of a sort that is not strictly tied to catching the affect of any of the characters portrayed. For Dominic McIver Lopes, non-figural representation can, like music, take advantage of *the contour* of the work of art. He calls this 'design expression' (Lopes 2005). How does it work? Well, things can have what he calls 'expression-looks.' These are physical features of a picture that have the function of indicating a certain emotion. Look at it this way. We can all agree that figures express emotions in pictures. How? By their faces and bodies assuming certain configurations: a pinched brow, a tight jaw, or a contracted posture. These are relatively universal features that have the function of signaling that the person experiences a certain emotion. Design expression is just like that, except the person is missing. It is, if you like, *pure* expression.

Often the expressive elements of pictures work together with the characters portrayed to either heighten, or complete, the emotional expression of the characters. For instance, in Edvard Munch's *The Scream*, nature itself appears to experience profound anxiety, expressed by the violent streaks of yellow and red behind the screaming figure. Dominic Lopes (2011) describes this as *scene expression*. Scene expression is "an expression that is attributable to a depicted scene and that is not wholly attributable to any depicted persons" (2011, 129). Scene expression contrasts with figure expression, described above, since the expression in the latter pertains fully to the depicted persons.

According to Lopes, there are many versions of scene expression. A scene can *reflect* what the characters in it feel but without these characters expressing those feelings. A scene can also *express* a reaction to what is conveyed in the picture. For instance, in Théodore Géricault's *The Raft of Medusa*, we see despair in the shipwrecked passengers as they look towards a vessel sailing away from them on the stormy sea. It is these two forms of scene expression that are special to pictorial experiences. They are both instances in which pictures use bits of inanimate nature to express emotions. This is quite different from ordinary life because we don't usually think inanimate nature expresses emotions.

Let us move on to the more obvious ways in which empathy is central to our appreciating art, namely by our responding emotionally to the *people* or animate objects portrayed in it.

§5.4 Empathizing with characters

Pictures, plays, movies, drama, poetry, literature, and music all express emotions of human or human-like characters, mostly fictional ones, but not always. When they do, it is easier to explain how empathy can play a role in enjoying them. Almost everybody responds emotionally to characters portrayed in art, and many think their responses are empathic or, at the very least, the result of identification. Philosophers, however, have argued that there is something fishy about our emotional responses to fictional characters. Since we do not actually believe such characters exist, can we really have *genuine* emotional responses to them? It has often been argued that we cannot. This has led some philosophers of art to claim that emotional reactions to fictions are *quasi-emotions*. Kendall Walton, for instance, argues that the affective reactions we experience in fictional contexts are of a different kind from the ones we experience in real contexts. Why? The former rely on make-believe and the latter rely on belief or knowledge (Walton 1990). Both, however, can have the same phenomenology. Quasi-fear won't differ from its real-life cousin, fear, in terms of what it feels like. It does differ, however, in the epistemic attitude the subject holds towards its object. We are not afraid *of the slime* that rushes through the countryside in the movie we are watching. Why? Because we know the slime is not real. We do not actually believe that the slime is coming towards us.

Robinson targets the underlying assumption of this idea, namely that belief is centrally involved in our emotional responses. She follows James in insisting that emotions are not cognitive (James 1884). Both maintain that our emotions do not ensue upon a judgment concerning the real or fictional nature of a character we are presented with. Instead, affective responses occur relatively automatically in "certain types of situations—dangers, losses, offenses and other 'core relational themes'—so that whether the object of empathic sorrow and pity is real or fictional, our responses can be equally empathic in both cases" (Robinson 2017c, 300). A different way of making the same point is to say that emotions are not sufficiently discerning to distinguish between real and vivid but fictional scenarios. In both cases, we can have exactly the same emotional reaction. It is easy to see how this idea would extend to empathic phenomena.

Setting aside the issue of feeling with fictions, we now turn to the particular form of empathic affect that is common in works of art that represent human or human-like characters. Let us begin with fiction. It seems fairly intuitive that emotional engagement with fictional characters is part of what draws people to literature. Such affective engagement is likely to be central, despite Peter Lamarque's contention that emotional responses to literature are too relative to culture and reader to play an important role in literature criticism (Lamarque 2009, 247). It does rather seem that "[s]ome works of litera-ture—especially realist novels by the likes of Tolstoy and James—needs to be experienced emotionally if they are to be properly understood," to use the words of Robinson (2005, 101). It is also plausible that this involves empathic engagement. Indeed, this is almost too obvious to bear mentioning. But there is a surprising amount of debate among aestheticians about the degree to which empathy with fictional characters is central to our affective responses to literature, and the form such responses take.

According to Noël Carroll, many emotional responses to fiction are mischaracterized as empathic because not enough effort is put into distin-guishing the reader's empathic responses from her directly experienced emotions, which simply happen to *align* with the emotions experienced by the characters (Carroll 2011). Reading *Candide*, I might be horrified when learning about the Lisbon earthquake, as is Candide. Our emotions align, but my being horrified is not an empathic response to his being horrified but a direct response to the earthquake. Carroll calls this a *congruent* state and suggests that many instances of what commonly goes for empathy are nothing but congruent states.

Of course, this does not rule out that *some* of our emotional responses to fictional characters are empathic. Carroll is skeptical, however. He argues that empathic responses are not typically states of what we might call 'infectious identification,' where we feel just what the character feels. Car-roll gives an example of being happy for a couple of reunited lovers. To say that we are empathizing with them seems wrong and right at the same time. We are clearly not experiencing the passion of being in love. It is not even clear that we can empathize with being in love. But we *are* happy for the happy couple. In this case, Carroll says, "[o]ur emotive states converge vectorially—they both belong on the positively charged side of the scale of the emotions" (2011, 171). More precisely, the kind of empathy that Carroll thinks we experience with fictional characters is more like 'com-muning' with them. "We do not replicate the emotional state of others exactly, but instead approximate its general drift" (2011, 172).

Sympathy, not empathy, is the central emotional response to fictional characters, according to Carroll. As he says:

> In the course of a popular fiction we may undergo a gamut of emotional reactions to the relevant characters. But it is the sympathy we feel with regard to these characters that generally plays the major structuring role vis à vis whatever accompanying feelings may emerge. For, we are proud of the hero's success because his well-being is an object of our concern and we are angry at the heroine for sneaking off with the city slicker because we do not think that it is in her best interests. Sympathy is the primary glue that binds us emotively to the protagonists and their fates in popular fictions.
>
> (2011, 175)

This general skepticism is widespread. Aestheticians worry that it is not really affective empathy, understood as emotional mirroring of the experience of a character, which is central to engaging with fiction. Eileen John (2017) points out that the variation in emotional responses to fictional characters is sufficient proof that it is problematic to assume that they are 'matching responses.' If we leave accuracy aside, though, we may still suppose that the process is empathic in nature. The person takes herself to be responding to the other person's affect and does not realize when the two differ. It obviously gets harder to support this response the greater the variance in emotional responses.

An additional problem is that it is unrealistic to construe a reader's empathic reactivity to fiction purely as a passive ability. The reader has quite an active role, and this needs to be considered in any analysis of our responses. Something like that idea is also exemplified in the work of Keith Oatley, who maintains that: "when we understand an action as we read about it in a novel, our understanding depends on making a version of the action ourselves, inwardly" (2011, 19). Instead of our passively receiving the affect of the characters there portrayed, we "create our own version of the piece of fiction, our own dream, our own enactment" (2011, 18). This is a different form of the high-level simulation reading of empathy in art, namely one that stresses enactment in fiction as much as in music. What makes this an imaginative, as well as an empathic, enterprise is that it involves two steps. We put aside our own beliefs and desires and insert those (indicated by the author) of the fictional characters and feed them to our "planning processor" (2011, 116). We are then able to "experience our own fresh emotions in the circumstances of the character's action and their effects" (2011, 116). Of course, not everyone thinks that empathy for characters involves simulation (see Kieran 2003).

In the same vein as Oatley, Robinson stresses the active involvement of the reader in the enjoyment of fiction. But for her, the *emotional* involvement is central. Our own emotional responses actually work to fill in some of the many gaps that we find in a piece of literature. They can do so because "emotion processes actually work just the same way when we respond to characters and events in novels, plays, and movies, as they do when we respond to people and events in real life" (2005, 105). So, for instance, instead of describing Anna Karenina's sorrow at her separation from her darling boy, Tolstoy sets up an emotionally poignant scene, which fills us with compassion and, quite possibly, some of the same sad longing we might feel for a loved one. Our feeling stands in for the character's feeling. This can, of course, be empathic, since we often respond to the *situation* someone is in and not simply to his or her clearly expressed affect. And because emotions aren't simply feelings but also focus our attention and involve cognitive appraisals, they make a significant contribution to understanding literature.

Literature evokes empathy in ways that other art forms cannot. Because the innermost thoughts and feelings of characters can be described, it gives us unprecedented access to what seems to be genuinely other minds. A medium like film sometimes uses voice over to express the private thoughts of a main character. But we are typically left to figure out what's on people's minds, even though we are greatly helped by what the director chooses to show us. What is perhaps the most distinctive feature of film, and of portraiture of any kind, is its *visual* nature, which is liable to produce the same reactions we would have if what we are watching were real (Stadler 2017). Movies can engage our bodily mimicry responses—discussed in Section 5.2 and 5.3—to a much greater extent than many other forms of art. Notice also that movies often include music, which helps guide our interpretation and our experiences of the scenes (is it languorous, frenetic, or calm?). Watching *Rosemary's Baby* with the sound turned off is a very different experience, emotionally, than is watching it with the creepy music in the background.

Pictures featuring human beings and animals are obvious candidates for empathic engagement. For instance, Leonardo da Vinci's *Madonna of the Rocks* portrays the Virgin Mary expressing serene maternal love. Looking closely at that picture—assuming it is a quiet day at the Louvre—one is filled with a feeling recognizable as love or loving-kindness. Pablo Picasso's *Nude Woman Seated in front of a Curtain*, on the other hand, expresses melancholy by means of the woman's melancholy expression. It is worth noting a couple of things. First, we experience the empathy-like emotions we do in response to the characters *because* our affective reactions are related in the right way to *theirs*. This idea should be distinguished from the related thought that pictures *evoke* emotions, even empathic ones, but not because the work of art *itself* expresses the relevant emotions. Second, the two pictures differ in terms of the object of their respective emotions. In the *Madonna* picture, we see the child Jesus with John the Baptist, and it is immediately clear who are the objects of Mary's affection. If we share her affection as we gaze upon the canvas, then we feel that sweet love and affection for little Jesus and John, at least in part. We cannot say the same for Picasso's nude, however. All we know is that she feels melancholy, but the content or quality of her affect remains obscure. In such cases, someone like Carroll argues, we can only 'catch' the affect, but it cannot grow into full empathy in the absence of further information (Carroll 2017). Portraiture often gives rise only to emotional contagion, he says.

One of the things that is special about relating to characters in pictures *via* empathic responses is that it can give us a sense of what it is like for the person in the picture. According to Currie,

> part of an aesthetically aware response to *Descent from the Cross* is a vivid sense of the bodily strain experienced by the mourners, as they lower the dead Christ. And my capacity to think, of one of the figures, 'He feels thusly', where 'thusly' picks out a feeling of bodily contortion and strain which I am currently simulating, gives my thought about the figures a specificity and a vividness that they would not have if I had to rely on using a descriptive concept such as 'feels some unspecific tension in his arms and shoulders.'
>
> (2011, 93)

Music is full of characters also. And here, too, we can expect to experience the gamut of empathic responses (for an overview, see Robinson 2017c). We can empathize with—affectively empathize with, sympathize with, or take up the perspective of—performers, composers or other *personae* in instrumental music. Jerrold Levinson (1996), for instance, argues that music's expressiveness consists in our experiencing it as a sort of narrative. A person, albeit a rather indefinite one, inhabits this narrative, and our emotional responses are due to this imagined character in the music. Alternatively, we can empathize with the implied protagonist when the music includes lyrics. For instance, when listening to 'Someone like you,' you are likely to empathize with the sentiment expressed by Adele because you implicitly assume that she speaks from her own private experience. The music determines the shape your emotions take, while the lyrics seem to give them content.

§5.5 Empathy with the artist

There is another way empathy may be exercised in the comprehension of, or engagement with, works of art. We can empathize with the artist. This view is sometimes called the Romantic theory of artistic expression. In *Deeper Than Reason*, Robinson defends the theory for literature, pictures, and music (Robinson 2005, also 2017a and 2017b). If an artwork is an expression, Robinson says, it is evidence of *a persona*. The persona's emotion is manifested in the character of the work of art and is done so *intentionally*. It is through the "articulation and elucidation of the emotion in the work" (2005, 271) that the audience (the reader, viewer, etc.) understands the emotion. Expression in art is primarily the result of "intentional activity by *artists*" (2005, 272). The emotion does not have to be the artist's own but can be whatever ends up being expressed in the artwork through the intentional manipulation of the medium.

Let us look at the idea specifically in the context of pictures, as we don't have time to go into all art forms here. To get the point that Robinson is pressing, think back to Lopes' work on pictures. Recall that he thought pictures could express emotion in the absence of even an implied character who experiences it. The emotion is simply there, expressed in the various elements of the picture. We also have emotion expression in people, of course, and the two combined. Robinson is skeptical about such a view. The problem, she says, is that Lopes leaves out an important person, whose emotions are expressed in pictures. Who? The artist. A picture expresses the psychological states and emotional attitudes of the artist, or the *implied* artist, who made it. What is an implied artist? It is the maker of the picture, as she appears from the evidence available to the viewer, taking into consideration the historical and cultural context. As she says, "it is the way a painter *designs* or structures a picture which is largely responsible for the emotional attitude expressed by the picture as a whole" (2017b, 355). Pictures "come with a perspective that has been carefully constructed by the artist" and "give us practice in what is perhaps the most important empathic skill: to see the world from the perspective of another person" (ibid.).

The problem with views of expression that leave out of consideration the artist, or implied artist, is not simply that they are incomplete. It is that they fail to account for the expression in many pictures. If we zoom out, as it were, and consider a picture *as a whole*, it is often the case that what ties all the various expressive elements together is the emotion that the artist intends to express with the picture. Sure, there is expression in figures, colors, or movements, much as someone like Lopes argues, but, as Robinson puts it (2017b, 361),

> a successful work of 'Romantic' expression not only depicts a subject-matter but takes an emotional attitude towards it, which the spectator is invited to share. We do not have to be given supplemental directions [...] the subject-matter of the picture *as designed* by the artist encourages the viewer to take the emotional point of view on the subject-matter which is implicit in the picture.

Because the artist painted the picture the way she did, we feel what we feel. In fact, we often *empathize with the artist's emotion* as expressed in the picture as a whole. This way of tying expression to the artist's emotion towards the content of his work is closely connected with what Robinson thinks is a distinctive value of art. As a result of feeling with the artist's emotional perspective, as it is expressed in the picture, we acquire knowledge by acquaintance of what the artist is expressing. This is different from the kind of understanding we can achieve from learning that it is possible to view the world in the way that the artist portrays it. Artworks educate our emotions, often through our empathizing with how the artist feels or with the emotional attitudes he expresses in his art. It teaches us to feel in "new and imaginative ways" (Robinson 2017b, 367).

This brings us to the next, and last, section, where we explore the idea that experiencing empathy with fictions or fictional characters plays an important role in developing our empathy with people in real life.

§5.6 Sentimental education

Art is believed to do more than simply provide aesthetic pleasure or entertainment. It can bring us closer to the truth, widen our horizons, and teach us to be better people. It does so by showing us new ways of thinking, feeling, acting, and living. Because art exercises our empathy, it may be that it makes us better at empathizing with people, and other living beings, in real life in addition to fiction. It could help us grasp genuinely different perspectives, understand what it is like to experience certain things, feel things we have never felt before, and so on. Moreover, given the central role empathy appears to play in morality, aesthetically evoked empathy may even improve our moral agency. This is a rather strong argument for engaging with art.

Why should we believe it? One reason would be that empathy is a capacity, and capacities are typically enhanced by being exercised. If I don't exercise my playing piano or singing, I get rusty. But practice helps. If, then, one practices empathizing with others, one becomes better at it. If we also suppose that empathy for fictional characters is really no different from empathy with real people, as Robinson does, then engaging with fiction is a way of exercising one's empathy. In fact, Robinson's solution to the paradox of fiction—i.e. how we can *genuinely* feel for or with fictional characters—is that we temporarily "[s]top *paying attention* to the fact that characters are fictional" (2005, 150). We can exercise empathy by engaging with fiction as well as we can by engaging with *real* people.

Martha Nussbaum (1990) has famously argued that good literature helps us expand our empathy, thereby developing our moral imagination. It does so by exposing us to how people think and feel in situations where we think and feel differently; by acquainting us with the complexity of lived moral situations and not simply the cardboard cut-outs of moral situations philosophers tend to trade in; and by our feeling with characters of all kinds. Moral imagination is important because without seeing what the situation is like for all members of society, we cannot create a just society. We need to be able to take in not only the individuality of people—as opposed to simply boxing them in with terms such as 'women,' 'Blacks,' or 'gays'—but also what it is like to operate within radically different circumstances. This is exactly what good fiction helps us do, by exposing us to people in all their individuality navigating the situations they find themselves in. And it presents the world *from their point of view*, whether or not it is written in the first person voice. As we saw in Chapter 2, points of view can vary greatly, and gaining the facility with taking up other points of view is important, as is being able to imagine different reactions to certain events. We might add a point here from Robinson: "Novels are not just illustrations of principles of folk psychology. They introduce both characters and readers to emotional states for which there are no one-word descriptions in folk psychology" (Robinson 2005, 159). In other words, good literature affects our psychology and moral decisions in an extremely nuanced and differentiated way. It is therefore likely to teach us lessons about others that we might not otherwise learn. The same could be said about many movies (for more, see Sinnerbink 2016).

The notion that art can *extend* our empathy is echoed in the work of Murray Smith (1995, 2011). Smith's main focus is the *imagination*, which he thinks is necessarily involved in any act of empathizing. Imagining others is fleshed out in terms of a kind of perspective taking, which he calls "'in his shoes' imagining" (1995, 104). This involves projecting ourselves into counterfactual situations to see how *we* would feel in them. He takes seriously the idea that the project of many artists is to give the consumer of their art an understanding of what it is like to be a person like this or that, to have such-and-such feelings, etc. This understanding can only be reached through empathic and imaginative engagement. For instance, we tend to think of depression (assuming we have not ourselves suffered from its clinical version) in stereotypic, abstract ways. When a piece of literature features a depressed person, it can transport us beyond such narrow understandings and into the details of what it might be like. My own favorite personal account is from Sylvia's Plath's *The Bell Jar* when she describes seeing the days stretching out in front of her one after the other in a dull endless row. As Smith says,

> [w]e may come not only to see, but to feel, how an agent in a given situation comes to feel that there are only a particular set of 'live options'—viable choices—open to them, a much narrower range than we might believe them to possess if we assess their situation from the outside—that is, in narrowly rational terms and without an attempt to model or simulate their state of mind.
>
> (Smith 2011, 111–112)

Robinson has a more unwavering focus on how our *emotional* responses to literature are central to what we learn from it. We learn about emotions by how they are described, of course, but also, and more importantly, by *experiencing* them ourselves as we feel with fictional characters. We participate, as it were, in their emotional journey. Of course, not all affect evoked by fiction is empathic, but certainly some of it is. Our emotional responses to literature include emotional contagion, affective empathy, and sympathy (Robinson manuscript). Emotional experiences teach us by "*focusing attention* on certain aspects of situations, [by] *making affective appraisals* of them that appeal to our *wants and interests* and affect us *physiologically,* and [by] *formulating thoughts* about them from a partial point of view" (Robinson 2005, 156). This happens no less in the empathic experience than in the direct emotional one.

Oatley also maintains that reading good narrative fiction improves our empathy noticeably: in the areas of theory of mind, perspective taking, and understanding of relationships. He finds some support for that, such as improved performance on reading the mind in the eyes test (Mar et al. 2006). David Kidd and Emanuele Castano have conducted several studies, which they argue show that reading fiction can improve our theory of mind (Kidd & Castano 2013, Kidd, Ongis, & Castano 2016). Assuming that some type of empathy is being used when we read fiction, it would follow that when we 'practice' empathy with fictional characters, we develop our ability to understand and predict the behavior of other people. Replication studies, however, have mixed results (e.g. van Kuijk et al. 2018 (positive) and Samur, Tops, & Koole 2018 (negative)). A recent meta-analysis suggests that there is a positive, albeit somewhat small, correlation between literary reading and socio-cognitive abilities (Mumper & Gerrig 2017). Additionally, reading fiction correlates with reduced bias (Johnson et al. 2013), improved empathy (Bal & Veltkamp 2013), and increased helping behavior (Johnson 2012).

There are, of course, objections to this way of viewing things. One is that fiction has many negative effects also. The portrayal of physical and sexual violence can have grave effects, particularly on developing minds (Boxer at al. 2009). Fiction can easily cause people to have false beliefs, creating entrenched attitudes that even the best supported science has problems overcoming (Prentice, Garrig, & Bailis 1997; for more of a discussion, see Friend 2014). Moreover, many violent movies induce empathy with the aggressor, as is marvelously displayed in the many Hollywood blockbuster movies that riff on 'us versus them.' Does fiction do more good than harm, or is it the other way around?

Suzanne Keen (2007) expresses doubt that narrative empathy leads to real-life helping behavior. Her point is not necessarily that reading fiction cannot make us better empathizers. Rather, she is curious about *what* drives this effect. It could be the social scaffolding around consuming literature, such as fellow readers, that does the job. Or it might be the effect of feeling a sense of belonging with the fictional characters in their universe (Keen 2014).

One might object that it is implausible to think that we engage with works of art and with fictional characters like we interact with real people: in a fully empathic and emotionally engaged way. After all, we are only partly transported by works of art. Even if we are fully absorbed in them, it is only for a short period of time. This seems right. As Smith says, the fact that I empathize with characters in fiction or film does not imply that such empathy "dominates my consciousness at any point" (2011, 116). Our minds are engaged in a host of other activities at the same time as we consume fiction. This does not mean we don't empathize, though. It is just that the empathic engagement is less complete and more fitful. This could be a problem. But maybe it's not. And, at the end of the day, how involved or complete is real-life empathy anyway?

§5.7 Take-home message

There is a good case to be made that empathy is involved in understanding works of art of all forms: architecture, music, literature, film, and pictures. The list is not complete, of course. Among other things, I have left out drama and dance, the appreciation of which plausibly involves empathy also. But since space is limited, you will have to explore these issues on your own. Some art forms lend themselves to exercising certain forms of empathy over others. As we saw, low-level bodily mimicry may be central to enjoying architecture, for instance, and more high-level empathic engagement seems more central to literature. Understanding how we are moved by these various art forms is central to understanding their power, and their potential in educating our emotional range, our understanding of others, and our affective openness to other people. But more research is needed before we can conclude much about the positive moral effects of engaging with art empathically.

In this chapter, we have explored:

- The concept of Einfühlung and its centrality to debates in aesthetics
- The role of 'feeling into' inanimate objects
- Cognitive empathy and appreciating works of art
- Affective empathy and appreciating works of art
- The many artistic characters that can be empathized with
- The potential of art to enhance our empathy and moral attitudes towards others

Further reading

Lipps, T. 1903/1979. Empathy, inner imitation, and sense-feelings. In: M. Rader (Ed.) *A Modern Book of Esthetics*. New York: Holt, Rinehart, and Winston, 374–382. *A classical paper on Einfühlung and art appreciation in the German aesthetic tradition.*

Matravers, D. 2017. Empathy in the aesthetic tradition. In: H.L. Maibom (Ed.) *The Routledge Handbook of Philosophy of Empathy*. New York: Routledge, 77–85. *An authoritative essay on empathy and aesthetics with a historical emphasis.*

Nussbaum, M. 1990. *Love's Knowledge: Essays on Philosophy and Literature*. New York: Oxford University Press. *On how reading literature will make us better people through empathy.*

Oatley, K. 2011. *Such Stuff as Dreams: The Psychology of Fiction*. Malden: Wiley Blackwell. *A fun and insightful book about the psychology of the imagination within the context of fiction.*

Robinson, J. 2005. *Deeper than Reason: Emotion and its Role in Literature, Music, and Art*. Oxford: Oxford University Press. *A very readable defense of the romantic theory of expression covering a range of different art forms.*

References

Bal, P.M. & Veltkamp, M. 2013. How does fiction reading influence empathy? An experimental investigation on the role of emotional transportation. *PLoS ONE*, 8, e55341.

Blair, R.J.R., Mitchell, D.G., Richell, R.A., Kelly, S., Leonard, A., Newman, C., & Scott, S.K. 2002. Turning a blind eye to fear. *Journal of Abnormal Psychology*, 111, 682–686.

Boxer, P., Huesmann, L.R., Bushman, B.J., O'Brien, M., & Moceri, D. 2009. The role of violent media preference in cumulative developmental risk for violence and general aggression. *Journal of Youth and Adolescence*, 38, 417–428.

Carroll, N. 2011. On some affective relations between audiences and the characters in popular fictions. In: A. Coplan & P. Goldie (Eds.) *Empathy: Philosophical and Psychological Perspectives*. New York: Oxford University Press, 162–182.

Carroll, N. 2017. Empathy and painting. In: H.L. Maibom (Ed.) *The Routledge Handbook of Philosophy of Empathy*. New York: Routledge, 285–292.

Collingwood, R.G. 1946/1993. *The Idea of History.* Oxford: Clarendon Press.

Currie, G. 2011. Empathy for objects. In: A. Coplan & P. Goldie (Eds.) *Empathy: Philosophical and Psychological Perspectives.* New York: Oxford University Press, 82–95.

Davies, S. 1994. *Musical Meaning and Expression.* Ithaca, NY: Cornell University Press.

Davies, S. 2011. Infectious music: Music-listener emotional contagion. In: A. Coplan & P. Goldie (Eds.) *Empathy: Philosophical and Psychological Perspectives.* New York: Oxford University Press, 134–148.

Fisher, D.A., Hill, D.L., Grube, J.W., Bersamin, M.M., Walker, S., & Gruber, E.L. 2009. Televised sexual content and parental mediation: Influences on adolescent sexuality. *Media Psychology,* 12, 121–147.

Friend, S. 2014. Believing in stories. In: G. Currie, M. Kieran, A. Meskin, & J. Robson (Eds.) *Aesthetics and the Sciences of the Mind.* Oxford: Oxford University Press, 227–248.

Frijda, N.H. 2009. Emotion experience and its varieties. *Emotion Review,* 1, 264–271.

Gibson, J.J. 1979. *The Ecological Approach to Visual Perception.* Boston: Houghton Mifflin.

Goldman, A.I. 2006. *Simulating Minds.* New York: Oxford University Press.

Goldman, A.I. 2011. Two routes to empathy: Insights from cognitive neuroscience. In: A. Coplan & P. Goldie (Eds.) *Empathy: Philosophical and Psychological Perspectives.* New York: Oxford University Press, 31–44.

Grosbras, M-H., Ross, P.D., & Belin, P. 2018. Categorical emotion recognition from voice improves during childhood and adolescence. *Scientific Reports,* 8, Article no. 414791.

Herder, J.G. 1774/1969. This too a philosophy of history for the formation of humanity. In: F.M. Bernard (Ed.) *J.G. Herder on Social and Political Culture.* Cambridge: Cambridge University Press.

Jahoda, G. 2005. Theodor Lipps and the shift from 'sympathy' to 'empathy'. *Journal of the History of the Behavioral Sciences,* 4, 151–163.

James, W. 1884. What is an emotion? *Mind,* 9, 188–205.

John, E. 2017. Empathy in literature. In: H.L. Maibom (Ed.) *The Routledge Handbook of Philosophy of Empathy.* New York: Routledge, 306–316.

Johnson, D.R. 2012. Transportation into a story increases empathy, prosocial behavior, and perceptual bias toward fearful expressions. *Personality and Individual Differences,* 52, 150–155.

Johnson, D.R., Jasper, D.M., Griffin S., & Huffman B.L. 2013. Reading narrative fiction reduces Arab-Muslim prejudice and offers a safe haven from intergroup anxiety. *Social Cognition*, 31, 578–598.

Juslin, P.N. & Västfjäll, D. 2008. Emotional responses to music: The need to consider underlying mechanisms. *Behavioral and Brain Sciences*, 31, 559–575.

Keen, S. 2007. *Empathy and the Novel*. New York: Oxford University Press.

Keen, S. 2014. Novel readers and the empathetic angel of our nature. In: M. M. Hammond & J.S. Kim (Eds.) *Rethinking Empathy through Literature*. New York: Routledge, 35–47.

Kidd, D.C. & Castano, E. 2013. Reading literary fiction improves theory of mind. *Science*, 342, 377–380.

Kidd, D., Ongis, M., & Castano, E. 2016. On literary fiction and its effects on theory of mind. *Scientific Study of Literature*, 6, 42–58.

Kieran, M. 2003. In search of a narrative. In: M. Kieran & D.M. Lopes (Eds.) *Imagination, Philosophy, and the Arts*. London: Routledge, 69–87.

Lamarque, P. 2009. *The Philosophy of Literature*. Malden: Blackwell.

Langfeld, H. 1920. *The Aesthetic Attitude*. New York: Harcourt, Brace, and Company.

Lee, V. 1913. *The Beautiful*. Cambridge: Cambridge University Press.

Levinson, J. 1996. Musical expressiveness. In: *The Pleasures of Aesthetics*. Ithaca, NY: Cornell University Press, 90–125.

Lipps, T. 1903/1979. Empathy, inner imitation, and sense-feelings. In: M. Rader (Ed.) *A Modern Book of Esthetics*. New York: Holt, Rinehart, and Winston, 374–382.

Lipps, T. 1907. Das Wissen von Fremden Ichen. *Psychologische Untersuchungen*, 1, 694–722.

Lopes, D.M. 2005. *Sight and Sensibility: Evaluating Pictures*. New York: Oxford University Press.

Lopes, D.M. 2011. An empathic eye. In: A. Coplan & P. Goldie (Eds.) *Empathy: Philosophical and Psychological Perspectives*. New York: Oxford University Press, 118–133.

Mar, R.A., Oatley, K., Hirsh, J., Dela Paz, J., & Peterson, J.B. 2006. Bookworms versus nerds: Exposure to fiction versus non-fiction, divergent associations with social ability, and the simulation of fictional social worlds. *Journal of Research in Personality*, 40, 694–712.

Mumper, M. & Gerrig, R. 2017. Leisure reading and social cognition: A meta-analysis. *Psychology of Aesthetics, Creativity, and the Arts*, 11, 109–120.

Nussbaum, C. 2007. *The Musical Representation: Meaning, Ontology, and Emotion*. Cambridge, MA: MIT Press.

Nussbaum, M. 1990. *Love's Knowledge: Essays on Philosophy and Literature*. New York: Oxford University Press.

Oatley, K. 2011. *Such Stuff as Dreams: The Psychology of Fiction*. Malden: Wiley Blackwell.

Prentice, D., Gerrig, R.J., & Bailis, D.S. 1997. What readers bring to the processing of fictional texts. *Psychonomic Bulletin and Review*, 4, 416–420.

Robinson, J. 2005. *Deeper than Reason: Emotion and its Role in Literature, Music, and Art*. Oxford: Oxford University Press.

Robinson, J. 2012. On being moved by architecture. *The Journal of Aesthetics and Art Criticism*, 70, 337–353.

Robinson, J. 2017a. The missing person found. Part I: Expressing emotions in pictures. *British Journal of Aesthetics*, 57, 249–267.

Robinson, J. 2017b. The missing person found. Part II: Feelings for pictures. *British Journal of Aesthetics*, 57, 349–367.

Robinson, J. 2017c. Empathy in music. In: H.L. Maibom (Ed.) *The Routledge Handbook of Philosophy of Empathy*. New York: Routledge, 293–305.

Robinson, J. Manuscript. *Emotion and Value in Literature*.

Samur, D., Tops, M., & Koole, S.L. 2018. Does a single session of reading literary fiction prime enhanced mentalising performance? Four replication experiments of Kidd and Castano (2013). *Cognition and Emotion*, 32, 130–144.

Sinnerbink, R. 2016. *Cinematic Ethics: Exploring Ethical Experiences through Film*. New York: Routledge.

Smith, M. 1995. *Engaging Characters: Fiction, Emotion, and the Cinema*. Oxford: Clarendon Press.

Smith, M. 2011. Empathy, expansionism, and the extended mind. In: A. Coplan & P. Goldie (Eds.) *Empathy: Philosophical and Psychological Perspectives*. New York: Oxford University Press, 99–117.

Stadler, J. 2017. Empathy in film. In: H.L. Maibom (Ed.) *The Routledge Handbook of Philosophy of Empathy*. New York: Routledge, 317–326.

Stein, E. 1917/1989. *On the Problem of Empathy*. W. Stein (Trans.). Washington, DC: ICS Publication.

Stueber, K. 2006. *Rediscovering Empathy*. Cambridge, MA: MIT Press.

van Kuijk, I., Verkoeijen, P., Dijkstra, K., & Zwaan R.A. 2018. The effect of reading a short passage of literary fiction on theory of mind: A replication of Kidd and Castano (2013). *Collabra: Psychology*, 4, 7.

Vidas, D., Dingle, G.A., & Nelson, N.L. 2018. Children's recognition of emotion in music and speech. *Music & Science*, 1, March 12. doi.org/10.1177/2059204318762650.

Vischer, R. 1873/1994. On the optical sense of form: A contribution to aesthetics. In: H.F. Mallgrave (Ed.) *Empathy, Form, and Space*. Los Angeles: Getty Center for the History of the Arts and Humanities, 89–123.

Walton, K. 1990. *Mimesis as Make-Believe: On the Foundations of the Representational Arts*. Cambridge, MA: Harvard University Press.

6

EMPATHY AND MENTAL DISORDER

It is sometimes argued that certain people are incapable of empathizing with others. The main suspects are usually people with psychopathy and people with autism spectrum disorder. If that is true, we can look at such populations for clues about what role empathy plays in ordinary mental functioning. And there is something of a cottage industry in this, particularly when it comes to psychopathy. The evidence for deficient empathy in both groups of people tends to be somewhat mixed. Nonetheless, we can draw a rough sketch of what is impaired in either group. I emphasize 'impaired,' because we have no evidence of a complete lack of empathy in either group. Moreover, there are big individual differences in empathic ability, and other mental disorders are also characterized by deficient empathy, such as narcissism and borderline personality disorder.

Nonetheless, research in psychopathy and autism gives us tantalizing evidence concerning the machinery of empathic responding to others in distress or need, which may come to affect how we think of empathy and its role in morality.

In this chapter, I discuss how we might learn about ordinary abilities from impaired ones (pros and cons), what evidence we have of empathy impairments in psychopathy, the type of empathic response that is particularly deficient in psychopathy, the empathy impairments in autism spectrum disorder (ASD), the consequences of empathy impairments in ASD for social functioning, and what deficient empathy in psychopathy and ASD can teach us about empathy and the connection between empathy and morality.

§6.1 Mental disorder and learning from it

There are two populations of people suffering from mental disorders that are particularly interesting to researchers of empathy: people with psychopathy and people with autism. There are, of course, other disorders of empathy. These include people with narcissism, people who are depressed, people who suffer from borderline personality disorder, and people with dementia and Alzheimer's. But for various reasons, these disorders do not receive a lot of attention in the philosophical literature.

Why are mental disorders interesting when we are studying ordinary human capacities? The idea is simple. Suppose we have a disorder that consists in the lack of (at least) one ability. We can now explore and see what other capacities are affected in that individual. This can teach us about what wider effects that ability has on an individual. If someone cannot empathize, it is pretty obvious that they won't feel sad along with you when you are sad. But what does this mean for their interpersonal relationships, their sense of self, or their moral sense? Suppose someone lacks *both* empathy and a moral sense. One might suspect that it is lack of empathy that causes that person's deficient moral outlook. This is particularly true if we have pre-existing reasons for thinking that empathy plays an integral role in someone's moral capacity.

The conditions that are easiest to use in this way are a) those that start early in development, and b) are the result of sudden and specific trauma to the brain. In both these cases, the route to showing the interdependency of abilities is more straightforward than in cases of late onset of bipolar disorder or schizophrenia, say. It is worth noting that trying to understand ordinary capacities by means of deficient ones is a method that can be applied to *all* capacities, not simply to empathy.

Many, but not all, mental disorders appear in the *Diagnostic and Statistical Manual of Mental Disorders* (DSM), published by the American Psychiatric Association, and now available in its fifth edition (DSM-5). Another popular manual is *The International Classification of Diseases* (ICD), by the World Health Organization, and now in its tenth edition (ICD-10). Autism spectrum disorder is a DSM classification, collapsing into one what was previously classified as two different disorders: autism and Asperger's syndrome. Psychopathy only appeared in DSM-III, after which it was replaced with antisocial personality disorder, much to the dismay of many psychopathy researchers. The problem is that the condition only overlaps partially with psychopathy as otherwise diagnosed. As a result, Hare's (2004) *Psychopathy Checklist-Revised* is the more commonly used classification tool for this disorder. Conditions that are unlikely to have any reality outside classification manuals also appear in the DSM-5, such as tobacco use disorder or frotteuristic disorder. It is worth keeping in mind that the DSM is used for insurance purposes, which appears to have driven a number of the choices made in what to include and what not to include.

Autism is classified as a developmental disorder but psychopathy is not. This is not because psychopathy is not thought to be a developmental disorder but for more technical reasons. The diagnosis itself can be stigmatizing, and early signs of psychopathy may resolve with development. In general, conduct disorder is supposed to precede any later, adult, diagnosis of psychopathy. Nobody with a normal developmental history suddenly becomes psychopathic *unless* they suffer very specific brain damage. But although papers have been published under the title 'acquired sociopathy,' the extent to which later brain damage mirrors what we find in psychopathy is highly disputed (Blair & Cipolotti 2000). Nonetheless, 'acquired sociopathy' promises to show something about the neural architecture of cognitive capacities. One must be careful not to draw strong conclusions from localized neural damage, however, as much work has shown that human neuroplasticity is quite impressive. The most impressive example I know of are the various reports of people living quite well with only half a brain (Gibbon 2015, Marshall & Marapodi 2009).

Mental disorders that are acquired later, such as schizophrenia or dementia, or that come and go, such as anxiety or depression, present a much messier picture. These are people who, although they may temporarily lack some ability or other, have been shaped by the normal operation of said ability. It is therefore much harder to disentangle the contribution that ability makes to ordinary mental functioning.

A big problem using mental disorders to learn about ordinary cognitive or affective capacities is that there is a real question whether mental disorders exist as discrete categories. If we simply stay with our main targets, psychopathy and autism, both are diagnosed using the following method. A range of criteria is listed, points are assigned to each criterion, and once a certain number of points is reached, the person can be classified as either autistic or psychopathic. The cut-off point has seemed somewhat arbitrary to many. For instance, if you score 29 on the PCL-R you are 'normal,' but once you accumulate over 30 points, you are a psychopath.

A more serious concern is that two people can meet the diagnostic criteria for a disorder and have relatively little in common. Take schizophrenia, for instance, as diagnosed using DSM-5. Person A can suffer from delusions and hallucinations, whereas person B can suffer from disorganized speech and diminished emotional expression. What is required is that they experience these symptoms for a significant amount of time during a one-month period, that this affects their work, interpersonal relationships, or self-care, and that continuous signs of the disturbance lasts for at least six months (plus that other diagnoses are ruled out). If we are interested in delusions, say, and their effects on other aspects of mental functioning, we cannot simply use evidence from people diagnosed with schizophrenia. We must, in addition, make sure that they exhibit this particular symptom. The same is true of people with psychopathy and autism, who differ widely from one another, person to person, within the same diagnostic category. This should come as no surprise. After all, even if they suffer from mental disorder, these are still people, and people, as a rule, differ significantly from one other. But there is often a tendency to forget this in our eagerness to look for supporting empirical data. Some people with autism resist the term 'disorder' and prefer the term 'difference' to describe their diagnosis. Without going into this thorny debate, we can simply note that 'disorder' is not an entirely innocent term but includes a fair amount of social normativity. Thomas Szasz famously argued that the idea of mental illness was a myth and expressed societal oppression of unacceptable differences (Szasz 1961).

One last caveat is that we usually don't find people who simply lack empathy, language, mathematical ability, etc. Typically, a range of different abilities is affected in each disorder. We must therefore do careful work to disentangle the contribution of each deficit to the capacity we are interested in studying. This issue will become clearer when we think about psychopaths and moral ability. Moreover, abilities are usually not absent altogether. Usually, we are dealing with *deficits*. Deficits can still give rise to considerable issues with functioning normally in various contexts, but they are more subtle than simple inabilities, and studying them takes more fancy footwork. To learn from mental disorders, then, requires some detective work. And it is difficult to carry out without some pretty firm theoretical assumptions about how human psychology works.

Keeping these issues in mind, we can proceed. For although there are many pitfalls using psychiatric research to understand human capacities, there is no question that it is an extremely useful source of information. We can learn a lot from it. But, as we shall see, we don't always learn what we thought we would.

§6.2 Psychopaths and affective responses

Psychopaths are the most popular target when lack of empathy is discussed. People with autism are a close second. Why? Well, psychopaths are notorious for taking advantage of the weak and lonely, for threatening, blackmailing or harming other people, and exploiting even those closest to them. They have little moral fiber and tend to engage in a wide range of criminal activities. According to a recent estimate, over ninety percent of male psychopaths in the US are involved with the criminal justice system (Kiehl & Lushing 2014). Moreover, they express little guilt or remorse over their actions, or concern for their victims. They don't sound empathic, do they? And, indeed, we find that lack of empathy is part of the diagnostic criteria for the disorder. It should therefore be an open and shut case. But what, exactly, is meant by 'lack of empathy' in *The Psychopathy Checklist-Revised*, the major diagnostic manual of the disorder? It appears to describe morbid self-absorption combined with a purely instrumental valuing of others. Psychopaths show little regard for the feelings or welfare of others for their own sake (Hare 2004). Should this be described as lack of empathy or lack of sympathy?

One reason to doubt that what is described is lack of empathy is that there is no evidence that psychopaths lack the ability to empathize with people *generally*. Psychopaths are unlikely to empathize with victims' distress, particularly their own victims. But here they may not differ greatly from other violent offenders. What throws doubt on them lacking empathy *tout court* is that they are consistently described as quite charming. People are readily taken in by them. Now ask yourself, have you ever spent any time with someone who appeared to experience no affective empathy, who did not resonate with your mood or your expressions, and nonetheless felt that they were charming? Not likely. At the very least, one would expect their emotional contagion and mimicry to be relatively intact. David Lishner and colleagues (2015) found exactly that. People scoring high on psychopathy showed as much contagion or empathy for happiness, sadness, fear, anger, and sympathy as did people scoring low on this measure. It is therefore tempting to think that psychopaths have intact emotional empathy but do not experience much, if any, sympathy for people. And such a suspicion would be reinforced by the fact that a range of studies show that psychopaths report feeling personally distressed at others' distress or need (Domes 2013, Shamay-Tsoory 2010, von Borries et al. 2012 using IRI).

The problem is that psychopaths are notoriously mendacious. Whether this is because they are manipulative—they will tell you what you want to hear to get what they want—or because they have a poor grasp of truth and falsity is unclear. Whatever the reason, their self-reports are to be taken with a grain, or a rock, of salt. And, indeed, physiological tests of contagious or empathic distress in psychopaths paint a different picture than do their self-reports. Psychopaths often show depressed palmar sweating compared to controls in response to people experiencing distress, pain, or fear (Birbaumer et al. 2005, Gao, Raine, & Schug 2012, Herpertz et al. 2001). Translated into the language of affect, they often do not experience much fear, stress, anxiety, or pain in response to such states in others (Moulton & Spence 1992, Rimm & Litvak 1969). If we move to their startle response, again in the context of being exposed to people in distress or distressing situations, we also find that it is reduced (Herpertz et al. 2001, Levenston et al. 2000). Startle measures defensive reactivity, such as anxiety or fear. According to Levenston et al. (2000), psychopaths' deficient startle response is a failure to respond appropriately to a potential threat, not because the threat is not detected but because the threat-response is impaired. Psychopaths fail to react normally to potential threats emotionally and behaviorally (Aniskiewicz 1979, Budhani, Richell, & Blair 2006, Newman & Kosson 1986, Newman, Patterson, & Kosson 1987). In layman's terms, they experience little fear. Quite likely, what is measured by these studies, and studies like them, is emotional contagion or a more generalized stress (personal distress?) response to human suffering or death. However we interpret it, it has a significant fear component. The upshot is that psychopaths are less upset, stressed, or threatened by others' misfortune or suffering.

The problem with physiological responses as a measurement is that they are often a sign of a range of different affective states. They do not measure precisely the types of affective states we distinguish in philosophy and psychology. Moreover, at least some of these studies do not show impairments. And so if we want to know *precisely* what is wrong with psychopaths vis-à-vis their interpersonal affective responses, we need to dig deeper. Results from neuroscience offer some, often intriguing, insights into what is going on. Neuroscientists sometimes talk of 'the empathy network,' which encompasses the anterior insula (AI), the anterior cingulate cortex (ACC), the inferior frontal gyrus (IFG), and probably the amygdala (e.g. Singer & Tusche 2014). Here's the thing, though. Psychopaths do not show *general* malfunction of the amygdala, AI, or ACC in empathy-related tests (Decety et al. 2014). According to Decety and colleagues (2014), psychopaths have robust activation in the AI in response to pictures of people experiencing pain, fear, and sadness, and a relatively intact response to viewing pictures of body parts in painful situations if asked to imagine this happening to themselves (Decety et al. 2013). What psychopaths are asked to do, in essence, is to empathize or sympathize with their counterfactual selves. And they seem able to do so. However, when asked to imagine *others* in pain, activation in AI is significantly below that of controls. So perhaps psychopaths are not *incapable* of experiencing empathy for people in pain or distress! This suspicion is further supported by Meffert et al.'s (2013) study, which found pretty normal neural activation in ACC and AI in response to explicit instructions to feel with another (pain, exclusion, love, neutral) but abnormal activation when simply observing the (emotional) interaction between two people.

It is too early to draw firm conclusions at this point, but it would appear that psychopaths are not *incapable* of experiencing empathy, even with people in pain. They simply do not seem to be very interested in, or concerned by, others' suffering. By contrast, they are quite concerned about their own. But how should we conceptualize the response that they are lacking, or at least deficient, in? It would appear that the normal response to people in pain, distress, etc. or to situations likely to cause these emotions is as to a threat. It involves activation of defense systems. First, attention is captured by the noxious stimulus. Then, the brain initiates withdrawal or escape mechanisms (de Gelder et al. 2004, Decety 2011, Eccleston & Crombez 1999, Simon et al. 2006). It is this latter part of the defensive response that is not activated to the same extent in psychopaths. This interpretation is consistent with the fact that psychopaths are known to have fear deficits of various kinds (Birbaumer et al. 2005, Lykken 1957). Moreover, it fits with recent evidence that psychopaths experience reduced fear contagion or empathy with fear (Marsh 2014).

Okay, you might say. But what does this teach us about empathy? Quite a lot, actually. If the analyses I have just presented are correct, then the ordinary person's response to another person in distress is more like a fear response than anything else. It involves high sympathetic nervous system activation, with mobilization of defensive reactions. We can put it like this: others being in distressing, painful, or dangerous situations, or expressing pain, distress, or fear is more or less automatically interpreted by us as a threat to us. It motivates us to escape that situation, or otherwise defend ourselves against it. This sounds like our old friend personal, or empathic, distress. Except now we know more about it. It may be more of a blanket defensive response to others in distress than a finely tuned reaction to the particular affective quality of their emotion in the problematic situation. It is the *absence* of this response that psychopathy researchers suspect is the core reason psychopaths are able to be so violent, so uncaring towards others, and so generally impervious to moral prohibitions. It is not the warm, softhearted response that Batson calls empathic concern, or that Darwall calls sympathy. It is a sort of fellow feeling. But in this case, it is a raw state of heightened anxiety and fear.

We can now see how research on empathic responses in mental disorders can throw valuable light on the nature of an ability. But when it comes to empathy research in psychopathy, there are much wider implications. For psychopaths' deficient empathy is often blamed for their frequent immoral or illegal activities. This is often taken for granted in the psychopathy literature. But philosophers have also taken on this idea, arguing that lack of affective empathy causes lack of deep moral understanding, moral motivation, or moral responsibility. We looked at Blair's theory of the Violence Inhibition Mechanism in Chapter 4. We were also introduced to Nichols's concept of a Concern Mechanism. In both cases, the malfunctioning of these mechanisms creates problems on the moral front. Take Nichols's account. A moral judgment that some *harmful* action is wrong consists of, on the one hand, the acceptance of a rule or norm proscribing the act and, on the other hand, *concern*. Take away the latter and you take away a central component of a judgment that something is wrong. This component is also what makes such judgments motivating. Affects drive motivation. If the research I have examined is right, then Nichols is wrong to call this response 'concern.' Blair is probably also wrong about the etiology of the response, which is in the typical primate response to submission in others. If fear is our best descriptor of what is lacking in psychopaths' response to suffering in others, its evolutionary roots probably lie in our social tendency—shared by many other animals—of responding to suffering in others as to a common threat (much as I suggested in Chapter 3).

It should be clear that *any* of the accounts that were presented in Chapter 4 predict that psychopaths have moral deficits, although they often overstate their case. For instance, Kauppinen (2014) says that his neo-classical explanatory sentimentalism "predicts that people who are wholly deficient in empathy (as are psychopaths) will only be capable of making interpersonally acceptable moral judgments parasitically on others" (2014, 112). The data does not support such a sweeping characterization. We know that at least a sizeable number of psychopaths experience less empathy for suffering others than ordinary people do. But we also know that many people diagnosed with psychopathy have intact empathic *ability*.

An additional difficulty with drawing quick conclusions about moral abilities from the psychopathy literature is that there is broad agreement that psychopathy encompasses two significantly different subclasses: primary and secondary psychopaths. One way to classify the two types is in terms of who scores high on facets of psychopathy such as: deficient affect, disordered interpersonal relations, irresponsible lifestyle, or antisociality (Hare 2004). Primary psychopaths—sometimes known as low-anxious or callous-unemotional psychopaths—score high on the first two items; secondary psychopaths score high on the last two. More specifically, primary psychopaths are *affectively cold*, particularly when it comes to remorse, guilt, shame, and empathy (Cleckley 1982, Hare 2004). They believe themselves to be superior to everybody else and put their own needs and desires before anyone else's. They manipulate, lie, and con. Secondary psychopaths are more likely to be irresponsible, impulsive, and parasitic. They have unrealistic goals and are often addicted to drugs and alcohol. They engage in harmful acts, such as torturing defenseless animal, and often frame others for their own misconduct. They are criminally versatile, and they are more likely to reoffend, to violate conditional release, or to escape from prison compared to other criminals. These different profiles, particularly on the affective front, suggests that although both groups tend to engage in a great amount of immoral and illegal behavior, the sources of this are different. Primary psychopaths may have little compunction about using others to serve their own selfish needs because they are 'cold-hearted,' whereas secondary psychopaths may engage in harmful actions because of an overabundance of anxiety and distress.[1]

As we saw, Shoemaker argues that we cannot hold psychopaths accountable for their actions because they lack the ability to affectively empathize with others. By contrast, I have argued that we can indeed hold psychopaths responsible because a) they do not seem to lack the ability to empathize with others altogether, b) there are other ways to comprehend right and wrong than through empathy, and c) mad simply is bad in psychopathy (Maibom 2008). The evidence I presented above about psychopaths being able to empathize under certain circumstances supports a), but also the idea that what might be wrong with psychopaths is not that they do not comprehend the harm they do to others; it is that they do not *care*.

§6.3 Psychopaths and cognitive empathy

It is sometimes said that psychopaths have intact *cognitive empathy*, which is why they are so good at manipulating people. Psychopaths obviously do not have any major generalized inability to understand the mental episodes of others. They do not have a theory of mind deficit *per se*. However, psychopaths appear to have specific difficulties recognizing fear and possibly sadness and anger too (Blair 2005, Blair et al. 2002, Guo et al. 2017, Iria & Barbosa 2009, Pera-Guardiola et al. 2016). Moreover, it is quite unclear whether they are able to see the world from another person's perspective. And here is why. Although they are able to manipulate others, and often act in unconscionable ways towards them, they seem to have little idea what effect that has on others and on how others view them. Hervey Cleckley describes the situation this way:

> He has absolutely no capacity to see himself as others see him. It is perhaps more accurate to say that he has no ability to know how others feel when they see him or to experience subjectively anything comparable about the situation. All of the values, all of the major affect concerning his status, are underappreciated by him.
>
> There is also indication of inability in his fundamental reactions to size up normally what he has done, *what he is*, and *what he has been*. (my emphases)

(1982, 214 and 216)

This sounds very much like Cleckley is describing an inability to take a third-person perspective on oneself. As I suggested in Chapter 2, without the ability to see oneself as from another point of view, one can appreciate neither *who* one is nor the significance of one's actions. So perhaps the psychopath's ability to deceive and manipulate relies on a certain blindness or lack of insight. Otherwise, why would he be shocked by the prospect of going to jail for crimes that he knows people go to jail for? If Cleckley is right, a psychopath may not see himself *as* a criminal, *as* someone who has stolen, raped, cheated, etc. These actions may be recognized as having been performed in some superficial sense, but their true significance and what they say about who he is escapes him. This idea can be pushed even further. For instance, it may not be because a psychopath has double standards that he insists on getting special treatment. Perhaps he just fails to see himself as just another person; or he doesn't see his own actions the way others do. Perhaps he can only ever see their significance in terms of their significance *to him*. He always sees himself and his actions from 'the inside.' His view of his actions can therefore be utterly insensitive to their effects on others. The failure to see himself as from the outside results in a larger failure to appreciate that he is just like everybody else and that his actions have no special status (see also Maibom 2017).

Do we have empirical evidence that psychopaths cannot take another person's perspective? Not much. Psychopaths typically fare well on theory of mind tasks (Dolan & Fullam 2004, Jones et al. 2010), on facial recognition of emotion (Dolan & Fullam 2004, Richell et al. 2003), and on the perspective-taking component of the *Interpersonal Reactivity Index* (van Borries et al. 2012). But they also score well on empathic concern, and we know that their empathic concern is *not* intact. So there is little to go on here. Some recent studies, however, suggest that psychopaths do not automatically adopt the visual perspective of others, although they are able to when instructed to do so (Drayton, Santos, & Baskins-Sommers 2018), and that people high in callous-unemotional traits (typical of psychopathy) are impaired in imagine-other but not imagine-self perspective taking (under instruction, Beussink, Hackney, & Vitacco 2017). To get evidence to support Cleckley's idea and my own, we need more targeted studies of perspective-taking ability.

Should psychopaths turn out to have a significant deficit in the ability to take other people's perspective, this would mitigate their moral and legal responsibility to the extent that we think this ability is involved in understanding one's actions, as was suggested in Chapter 4. However, it is interesting to note that just as we find that psychopaths have an intact ability to affectively empathize with others but are unlikely to do so in the general run of things, so too do they appear to have an intact capacity to take other points of view but do not do so automatically or spontaneously. This makes absolving them of responsibility a more complex matter.

§6.4 Autism and empathic responses

Autism spectrum disorder, or ASD for short, is another psychological condition characterized by impaired empathy. According to the current DSM-5, autism spectrum disorder involves "deficits in social communication and social interaction across multiple contexts" and "[r]estricted, repetitive patterns of behavior, interests, or activities" that have been present from an early age and that cause noticeable impairment in social and occupational functioning (American Psychiatric Association 2013, 50). Because the disorder is so closely related to difficulties understanding and engaging with others, Simon Baron-Cohen called it 'mindblindness' in an early book (Baron-Cohen 1995). He now leans towards describing it as the extreme male brain, much to the chagrin of feminist philosophers (Baron-Cohen 2003, Grossi & Fine 2012).

Most of the literature in philosophy focuses on people with ASD that are high performing, which is to say people who do not have notable physical, intelligence, or speech impairments. This constitutes a significantly smaller group than ASD more generally, which is frequently associated with aforementioned deficits. High-performing persons with ASD have deficits in all the major areas of empathy we have discussed: theory of mind, perspective taking, emotional contagion, and affective empathy. But their socio-emotional profile is quite distinct from that of people with psychopathy. And this is not simply because psychopaths' empathy deficit is more circumscribed. It seems like the two impairments affect different aspects of empathy.

People with ASD experience major delays in certain basic theory of mind capacities, such as understanding that others can have false beliefs (Happé 1995). Children with autism tend not to follow eye gaze (Leekam, Hunnisett, & Moore 1998). One study shows that they are as likely to visually orient to the direction an arrow is pointed at as they are to follow human gaze direction (Senju et al. 2004). This contrasts with normally developing children, who preferentially orient to eye gaze direction. Children with ASD often do not engage in joint attention either (Baron-Cohen 1995, 2001).

Although some adolescents and adults with ASD learn to pass second-order theory of mind tasks—i.e. tasks that test the individual's ability to discern what one person thinks another person thinks—not all do (Bowler 1992). This contrasts with normally developing children, who pass the test around 6 or 7 years of age.

Other theory of mind tasks commonly used to test performance or ability include Reading the Mind in the Eyes Task. Here, younger individuals with ASD have issues, but older ones typically do not (Back et al. 2007, Baron-Cohen et al. 2001). Some have suggested that this is due, in large part, to the test demanding high verbal skills and good knowledge of social stereotypes (Feder, Ressler, & Germine 2019). A recent metastudy, however, has found that whereas performance on the test requires a certain level of full and verbal IQ when it comes to typically developing individuals, IQ does not correlate with performance for people with ASD, who typically underperform (Peñuela-Calvo et al. 2019). This suggests that people with ASD use a different cognitive strategy for providing answers on this test. Other studies, using dynamic facial expression recognition (movie clips instead of photographs), also show impairments in individuals with ASD (Dziobek et al. 2006, Golan et al. 2008). In tests of empathic accuracy that involve full interactions between people, people with ASD perform pretty well when the conversation is scripted and they have unlimited time to interpret others. When, however, they are required to respond in real time, they are not as good at inferring others' mental states as control subjects (for an overview, see Roeyers & Demurie 2010). They also perform relatively poorly on other advanced theory of mind tests, such as those that test for sarcasm, lies, and deception (Mathersul, McDonald, & Rushby 2013).

In sum, high-performing people with ASD have delays in their ability to ascribe mental states to others. Even as adults, they experience difficulties, particularly with deception, lies, and sarcasm. They also seem to need longer to be able to figure out what others think, which may create significant problems in real-time interactions.

When it comes to performance on empathy tests, such as The Interpersonal Reactivity Index, the results are mixed. Rogers and colleagues (2007), for instance, report normal performance on empathic concern (what we have called 'sympathy') but elevated personal distress. This is not what Danielle Mathersul and colleagues found. Their ASD group reported both lower perspective taking and empathic concern (Mathersul, McDonald, & Rushby 2013). Moreover, when asked to report on their emotional responses to vignettes (affective empathy), children with ASD score lower than do normally developing children (Travis, Sigman, & Ruskin 2001, Yirmaya et al. 1992). They also experience less emotional contagion than normal, but this may depend on the familiarity of the target and whether or not they are instructed to pay attention to the facial expressions of the target (Helt, Fein, & Vargas 2019). By contrast to children with psychopathic tendencies, they appear to care as much as controls about making others feel bad (Jones et al. 2010), and they generally exhibit normal skin conductance responses to others in distress (Blair 1999). However, Emily Trimmer and colleagues (2016) found that although their skin conductance reaction is intact, their subsequent empathy is reduced, probably as a result of the way they interpret others' distress.

Baron-Cohen's somewhat infamous extreme male brain hypothesis uses two different tests, the Empathy Quotient (EQ) and the Systemizing Quotient (SQ) (for an overview see Baron-Cohen 2003). On these tests, people with autism standardly underperform on EQ and overperform on systemizing, compared to people without autism and with normal intelligence. Although Baron-Cohen's experimental results support his theory, it should be noted that there are critical examinations of his work that raise questions about its validity, broadly speaking (Grossi & Fine 2012). First of all, the questionnaire already seems gendered, as systemizing is measured by interest in activities that are typically male—i.e. cars, electrical wiring, computers, machines, sports, and the stock market. Empathizing, by contrast, is measured in terms of interest in personal relationships (Levy 2004). The problem is exacerbated by the fact that self-report questionnaires are notoriously liable to be influenced by self-stereotyping (Sinclair, Hardin, & Lowery 2006). I took the tests myself a couple of years back. It turns out that I have more of a male brain than your typical male and a standard female brain. This is not unusual, you will be happy to know. Recent studies also show that brain types "typical" of males are also typical of females and vice versa (Joel et al. 2018). It is quite plausible that Baron-Cohen's tests do show that people with ASD are less empathic (read: interested in personal relationships) than normally developing individuals, but it is unclear what it says about sex and gender.

It is relatively uncontroversial to maintain that deficient cognitive empathy is at the core of people with ASD's reduced affective empathy. They may not pay attention to the right cues, such as faces, or may experience difficulties recognizing what they see, or even difficulties understanding what they, themselves, experience as a result of observing another's affect. Approximately fifty percent of individuals with ASD suffer from alexithymia, namely poor awareness of one's own emotions (Hill, Berthoz, & Frith

2004). Some researchers argue that affective empathy in autism is the result of comorbid alexithymia, as people with ASD but no alexithymia do not have deficient affective empathy (Cook et al. 2013). In other words, people with autism might catch another's emotions but end up being confused about what they are feeling and what the relation is between that and what the other person is experiencing. It should be noted, however, that a recent study found that autistic traits were a better predictor of deficient affective, cognitive, and overall empathy than were alexithymia, suggesting that alexithymia cannot fully explain the empathy deficit in individuals with ASD (Shah et al. 2019). Moreover, at least one study shows *no* relation between deficient performance on ToM tasks and affective empathy in either normally developing children or children with ASD once age and verbal maturity is controlled for (Peterson 2014). One should note, however, that this study does not distinguish very clearly between sympathy and affective empathy. Holopainen et al. (2019), however, found that empathy for surprise and excitement was improved in people with ASD *after* theory of mind training. This suggests at least *some* association between deficient affective empathy in people with ASD and impaired theory of mind.

Often people with ASD will acquire a better ability to ascribe mental states with time but through what appears to be a long and difficult process. Often they have to reason explicitly about contingencies between certain behavior and movements of the sort that leap out to other people. Oliver Sacks describes Temple Grandin—one of the more famous people with ASD—as having to "'compute' others' intentions and states of mind, to try to make algorithmic, explicit, what for the rest of us is second nature" (Sacks 1995, 258). In the BBC series *The Face*, John Cleese interviews a young man with ASD, who describes how he has learnt to associate certain movements of facial muscles with emotions. Most of us see right through these facial movements to the emotion itself.

Unsurprisingly, these problems with understanding other minds create difficulties in social interaction. Some people with autism, such as Temple Grandin, seem mainly concerned with this because it constitutes a barrier to professional life. She has become very adept at dealing with the people she works with but often notes her frustration at how emotional others seem to be. As she says, "I only understand simple emotions, such as fear, anger, happiness, and sadness" (Grandin 1995, 90–91). She continues to have "difficulty understanding and having a relationship with people whose primary motivation in life is governed by complex emotions, as my [her] actions are guided by intellect" (ibid.). Others with ASD are much more social, and for them acquiring social skills so as to get on better with others is an end in itself. An important part of that is, of course, simply being able to figure out what people think or feel. But another part is becoming more oriented towards the other and less absorbed in the self. As Shaun Barron puts it (Grandin & Barron 2005):

> People with autism can be so wrapped up in their own thinking that they fail to see the effect their words and actions have on the people around them.
>
> (222)

> It was being so caught up in trying to preserve some semblance of order in my life and having little ability to deviate from it. It was also an inability to see something through someone else's eyes.
>
> (225)

> If people failed to respond the way I expected, I assumed I had done something wrong or stupid. It never occurred to me that there were other perspectives than mine, and in fact, many possible, plausible different ways to interpret such an interaction.
>
> (255)

Barron credits his later success in creating relationships with other people to his learning to take their perspectives. This is unsurprising. To get on with others, we need to have some significant ability to understand their thoughts and feelings, to resonate emotionally with them, and to take up their point of view.

A different example of lacking empathy may be taken from John Elder Robison's (2008) memoir. Here he describes with glee how he punished a teacher he was convinced singled him out, by having pornographic magazines sent to his house and then, later, 100,000 pounds of rock. This disproportionate, and aggressive, response to a teacher Robison describes simply as a prank. He was a trickster, he says. At the time of writing, he clearly thought it a perfectly reasonable thing to have done, and he never attempts to see things from the teacher's point of view or consider the impact his actions might have had on him.

The idea that people with ASD experience pervasive issues with perspective taking fits with psychologists Peter and Jessica Hobson's research. They trace the problem back as far as perceptual perspective taking. In an ingenious experiment, Hobson and Lee tested children's ability to imitate the actions of an adult. In one case, the adult demonstrated how to use a makeshift instrument (a pipe-rack and a stick). The adult held the pipe-rack against his shoulder and strummed it with a stick. The children without developmental disabilities imitated by adopting the adult's relation to the instrument—i.e. they put the pipe-rack against their shoulders thereby changing the orientation of the pipe-rack relative to what they observed. Children with autism, by contrast, simply positioned the instrument in front of them and began strumming. This failure to take another's perspective at such a basic level suggests that the problem experienced by people with autism has to do with all kinds of perspective taking, or 'identification' as Hobson and Hobson (2014) put it. Other studies show difficulties with trading places, as in taking up another's perspective (Rehfelt et al. 2007).

A general pattern emerges from this evidence. We observe more severe deficits in theory of mind, affective empathy, and perspective taking in people with ASD early on and then gradual improvement. Performance never quite normalizes, however, particularly not in more naturalistic tests of cognitive and affective empathy. Reports from teachers and others related to people with ASD also reveal persistent deficits in empathy-related responding to others in everyday situations. These deficits tend to be underplayed particularly when people with autism are compared to people with psychopathy. As far as I can tell, the reason is that most individuals with ASD exhibit a basic underlying concern for the wellbeing of others that is not displayed by individuals with psychopathy.

§6.5 Autism and moral outlook

The difficulties experienced in understanding others, empathizing with them, or being able to take up their perspective influences the lives of people with ASD beyond their social relationships. It seems to affect their moral outlook as well. In some respects, it can be more rigorous (lying is always wrong), but it can also betray a startling lack of understanding of someone's situation. For instance, a young man with ASD was presented with the following moral dilemma. A woman steals a small amount of food from a local store. The storeowner knows that she has no income but several small children to feed. The man was asked what he thought the owner should do. He did not hesitate "Everyone has to go through the checkout line. It is illegal not to go through the checkout line. She should be arrested." To many of us, this seems a bit harsh (Keel 1993, 49 as discussed in McGeer 2008).

This pattern of moral responding has led some philosophers to argue that we find a particular variety of moral agency in people with ASD. For instance, McGeer (2008) has argued that there are three big sources of moral consideration: 1) concern or compassion for others, 2) concern with social position and structure, and 3) concern with cosmic structure or position. People with ASD's moral outlook are dominated by 2) and 3), and less so by 1), McGeer claims. The rigid adherence to rules and laws that is often evident in this population reflects these two concerns and can often override concern for others' wellbeing. Someone like Jeanette Kennett has used ASD to argue in favor of the psychological reality of Kantian morality. People with autism have 'reverence for reason,' she says, and it is this that sets them apart from psychopaths despite the fact that they both have deficient empathy (Kennett 2002).

Although there may be differences in the actions that are emphasized as being particularly central to morality, there is little doubt that people with ASD are able to tell right from wrong. James Blair (1996) found that even children who performed poorly on theory of mind tasks made the moral-conventional distinction. The ability to draw a distinction between conventional and moral wrongs on the dimensions of permissibility, seriousness, and authority dependence is sometimes taken as indicative of moral competence. It is a test that Blair has claimed psychopaths do not pass, although the evidence is mixed (see Maibom forthcoming).

On the behavior front, Stål Bjørkly (2009) found no evidence that people with Asperger's syndrome are more likely to be violent than any other person. He did, however, find that misinterpretation of others not responding as wanted or triggering sensory issues were significant pre-dictors of aggression in people with the syndrome. The broader, and less differentiated, category of ASD, however, is associated with aggression in children and adolescents and is often a significant issue for caregivers and clinicians (Kanne & Mazurek 2011, Mazurek, Kanne, & Wodka 2013). Another study reports that inattention, hyperactivity, anxiety, and beha-vioral rigidity are significant predictors of aggression (Sullivan, Gallagher, & Heron 2019). It seems that social anxiety is often a trigger, and such anxiety is associated with poor understanding of others and low IQ. A recent study of helping behavior in people with ASD suggests they tend to help less than people without the disorder (Jameel et al. 2014). However, in the absence of further supporting studies, it is hard to conclude much on this basis. It is also hard to know why. Except for the Sandy Hook shooter, who had Asperger's syndrome (Solomon 2014), there is little to suggest that people with ASD are more likely to be involved with the justice system than are people without this diagnosis. And so although the contrast between psychopathy and autism may not be as great as it is sometimes made out to be, it is certainly still significant. And there are good reasons to think that deficient *affect* affects affective empathy *more* than deficient understanding, particularly when it comes to moral attitudes towards others.

Some people, like McGeer, have based their research more on auto-biographical accounts by people with autism than on large-scale studies of their moral ability. There are excellent reasons for doing so. One may question the ability of current tests to measure moral competence. And personal reports add richness and depth to otherwise disembodied statistical data. However, having read a bunch of autobiographical narratives of people with ASD, it seems to me unclear that we can detect anything more than a general pattern. There is probably a tendency towards more rigid thinking in moral matters just as there is when it comes to norms and regulations. There is often a de-emphasizing of empathically inspired attitudes and motivations, while a genuine concern for the wellbeing of others remains intact. As McGeer stresses, it would be a real mistake to think of people with ASD as lacking moral agency in any deep sense, although there is a case to be made for their having a certain distinctive *type* of moral orientation. Let us keep in mind, at the same time, the rather large individual differences you find between different people with ASD. Reading Temple Grandin gives a very different impression of the disorder than does reading John Elder Robison. I imagine normally developing people paint as complex a picture of their 'condition' as do people with ASD.

§6.6 Degrees of empathy

Although psychopathy and autism spectrum disorder are the most famous empathy-impaired psychiatric diagnoses, narcissism and borderline personality disorder are typically thought of as disorders of empathy also. In *Zero Empathy*, Baron-Cohen includes all these disorders under that heading. The evidence tends to be rather mixed for narcissism and borderline, though. Psychopathy researcher David Lishner and colleagues only found pervasive impairments in emotional contagion and empathic concern (sympathy) in psychopathy (and only for the trait 'callous affect'), whereas the impairments in narcissism and borderline were more specific. Only certain facets of these disorders are associated with low anger and sadness contagion when people are in need (measured by facial emotion expression) but not with contagion of happiness, or with empathic concern/sympathy (Lishner et al. 2015). How to interpret this data is not exactly clear, as division of disorders into facets is about as problematic as are mental disorder categorizations. What it does suggest, however, is that empathy impairments in narcissism and borderline are more circumscribed than in psychopathy and autism.

Before we end this quick exploration of impairments of empathy in psychiatric conditions, it is important to stress that empathic ability varies greatly in the population at large. There is no case to be made that deficient empathy is characteristic of a mental disorder alone. A number of so-called normal people have about as low empathy as do people with autism or psychopathy, for instance. People differ in their ability to experience emotional contagion, affective empathy, cognitive empathy, and sympathy. They also vary in the degree to which their psychological ascriptions are accurate. Unfortunately, people who are particularly good at figuring out what others actually think or feel are not typically aware of it, and most people believe they are far better than they actually are (Ickes et al. 2000).

Probably the best way to think about empathy deficits in people with a mental disorder is that they find themselves on the more extreme end of a spectrum we all find ourselves on.

§6.7 Take-home message

In this chapter, we have explored the two most famous mental disorders that are associated with deficient empathy: psychopathy and autism spectrum disorder. We saw that affective empathy, particularly with people in distress or need, is impaired in psychopathy. Whether their cognitive empathy is as intact as many appear to suppose is less clear, but not many studies are dedicated to this topic. We do know of impairments in recognition of certain types of facial and vocal expressions of emotion (fear in particular). It is interesting to observe that the deficient response to people in distress appears to be defensive in nature—i.e. to concern fear or anxiety. This lack is typically connected with psychopaths' general deficient moral responding to others. Research on empathy in psychopathy may make us rethink the importance of this type of response in moral ability more generally.

Individuals with ASD also have an empathy deficit. Their basic understanding of other minds is developmentally delayed, and they often do not acquire more high-level abilities, such as discernment of irony or deception. There is some evidence of deficient affective empathy but not, it seems, a general of lack of concern for the wellbeing of others. This contrasts with what is found in psychopathy. Many speculate that it is psychological *understanding* rather than *emotional responsiveness* to others that is the problem. Whether this is quite right is not clear. But we can conclude with some certainty that deficient cognitive empathy appears to have less of an impact on moral ability than does deficient affective responding. The particular constellation of capacities and deficits in people with ASD has led some people to speculate about the various components of moral ability and about how autistic morality may be a special kind of moral responsiveness.

To sum up, in this chapter, we have discussed:

• The pros and cons of using abilities in people with a mental disorder to understand the functioning of those same abilities in ordinary people
• What empathy deficits psychopaths actually have
• The specific nature of the most serious empathy deficit in psychopathy
• What psychopathy teaches us about the role of empathic responding in morality
• Empathy and theory of mind impairments in people with ASD
• How empathy deficits in people with ASD affects their moral attitudes

Note

1 Sometimes 'primary psychopathy' refers to individuals who meet PCL-R criteria *and* score low on Wechsler's Anxiety Scale (WAS) *or* meet PPI-I. PPI-I focuses on stress immunity, social potency, fearlessness, and cold-heartedness, whereas PPI-II concerns impulsive nonconformity, blame externalization, Machiavellian egocentricity, and carefree nonplanfulness and is more characteristic of secondary psychopathy (e.g. Mullins-Nelson, Salekin, & Leistico 2006).

Further readings

Blair, R.J.R. 1996. Morality in the autistic child. *Journal of Autism and Developmental Disorders*, 26, 571–576. *A standard interpretation of how moral judgment is impacted in autism, considering the empathy deficit.*

Cleckley, H. 1982. *The Mask of Sanity*. St. Louis, MO: Mosby Co. *The classic book on psychopathy, which includes an overall description of the disorder and a number of case studies.*

Jones, A.P., Happé, F.G.E., Gilbert, F., Burnett, S., & Viding, E. 2010. Feeling, caring, knowing: Different types of empathy deficit in boys with psychopathic tendencies and autistic spectrum disorder. *Journal of Child Psychology and Psychiatry*, 51, 1188–1197. *A classical treatment of the different empathy deficits in children with ASD and children with psychopathic tendencies.*

Kennett, J. 2002. Autism, empathy, and moral agency. *Philosophical Quarterly*, 52, 340–357. *Argues that recent evidence that empathy is at the root of our ability to make moral judgment is not to be trusted because people with autism have impaired empathy but intact moral judgment.*

Maibom, H.L. Forthcoming. Responsibility in the age of neuroscience: Moral understanding and empathy in psychopaths. In: J. Doris & M. Vargas (Eds.) *Oxford Handbook of Moral Psychology*. Oxford: Oxford University Press. *An in-depth analysis of what the recent empirical research teaches us about the moral capacities and empathic abilities of psychopaths.*

McGeer, V. 2008. Varieties of moral agency: Lessons from autism (and psychopathy). In: W. Sinnott-Armstrong (Ed.) *Moral Psychology, Volume 3: The Neuroscience of Morality: Emotion, Brain Disorders, and Development*. Cambridge, MA: MIT Press, 227–257. *This paper draws very different conclusions from Kennett, namely that people with autism have a special form of empathy that only engages two out of three moral foundations.*

References

American Psychiatric Association. 2013. *Diagnostic and Statistical Manual of Mental Disorders, Fifth Edition*. Arlington, VA: American Psychiatric Association.

Aniskiewicz, A.S. 1979. Autonomic components of vicarious conditioning and psychopathy. *Journal of Clinical Psychology*, 35, 60–67.

Back, E., Ropar, D., & Mitchell, P. 2007. Do the eyes have it? Inferring mental states from animated faces in autism. *Child Development*, 2, 397–411.

Baron-Cohen, S. 1995. *Mindblindness*. Cambridge, MA: MIT Press.

Baron-Cohen, S. 2001. Theory of mind in normal development and autism. *Prisme*, 34, 174–169.

Baron-Cohen, S. 2003. *The Essential Difference*. New York: Basic Books.

Baron-Cohen, S. 2011. *The Science of Evil*. New York: Basic Books.

Baron-Cohen, S., Wheelwright, S., Hill, J., Raste, Y., & Plumb, I. 2001. The "reading the mind in the eyes" test revised version: A study with normal adults and adults with Asperger syndrome or high-functioning autism. *Journal of Child Psychology and Psychiatry*, 42, 241–251.

Beussink, C.D., Hackney, A.A., & Vitacco, M.J. 2017. The effects of perspective taking on empathy-related responses for college students higher in callous traits. *Personality and Individual Differences*, 119, 86–91.

Birbaumer, N., Veit, R., Lotze, M., Erb, M., Hermann, C., Grodd, W., & Flor, H. 2005. Deficient fear conditioning in psychopathy. *Archives of General Psychiatry*, 62, 799–805.

Bjørkly, S. 2009. Risks and dynamics of violence in Asperger's syndrome: A systematic review of the literature. *Aggression and Violent Behavior*, doi: 10.1016/j.avb.2009.04.003.

Blair, R.J.R. 1996. Morality in the autistic child. *Journal of Autism and Developmental Disorders*, 26, 571–576.

Blair, R.J.R. 1999. Psychophysiological responsiveness to the distress of others in children with autism. *Personality and Individual Differences*, 26, 477–485.

Blair, R.J.R. 2005. Responding to the emotions of others: Dissociating forms of empathy through the study of typical and psychiatric populations. *Consciousness and Cognition*, 14, 698–718.

Blair, R.J.R. & Cipolotti, L. 2000. Impaired social response reversal: A case of 'acquired psychopathy'. *Brain*, 123, 1122–1141.

Blair, R.J.R., Mitchell, D., Kelly, S., Richell, R., Leonard, A., Newman, C., & Scott, S. 2002. Turning a deaf ear to fear: Impaired recognition of vocal affect in psychopathic individuals. *Journal of Abnormal Psychology*, 111, 682–686.

Bortolotti, L. 2010. *Delusions and Other Irrational Beliefs*. Oxford: Oxford University Press.

Bowler, D.M. 1992. Theory of mind in Asperger Syndrome. *Journal of Child Psychology and Psychiatry*, 33, 877–893.

Budhani, S., Richell, R., & Blair, R.J.R. 2006. Impaired reversal but intact acquisition: Probabilistic response reversal in adult individuals with psychopathy. *Journal of Abnormal Psychology*, 115, 552–558.

Cleckley, H. 1982. *The Mask of Sanity*. St. Louis, MO: Mosby Co.

Cook, R., Brewer, R., Shah, P., & Bird, G. 2013. Alexithymia, not autism, predicts poor recognition of emotional facial expressions. *Psychological Science, 24*, 723–732.

de Gelder, B., Snyder, J., Greve, D., Gerard, G., & Hadjikhani, N. 2004. Fear fosters flight: A mechanism for fear contagion when perceiving emotion expressed by a whole body. *PNAS, 101*, 16701–16706.

Decety, J. 2011. Dissecting the neural mechanisms mediating empathy. *Emotion Review, 3*, 92–108.

Decety, J., Chen, C., Harenski, C., & Kiehl , K. 2013. An fMRI study of affective perspective taking in individuals with psychopathy: Imagining another in pain does not evoke empathy. *Frontiers in Human Neuroscience, 7*, doi: 10.3389/ fnhum.2013.00489.

Decety, J., Skelly, L., Yoder, K., & Kiehl, K. 2014. Neural processing of dynamic emotional facial expressions in psychopaths. *Social Neuroscience, 9*, 36–49.

Dolan, M. & Fullam, R. 2004. Theory of mind and mentalizing ability in antisocial personality disorders with and without psychopathy. *Psychological Medicine, 34*, 1093–1102.

Domes, G., Hollerbach, P., Vohs, K., Mokros, A., & Habermayer, E. 2013. Emotional empathy and psychopathy in offenders: An experimental study. *Journal of Personality Disorders, 27*, 67–84.

Drayton, L.A., Santos, L.R., & Baskin-Sommers, A. 2018. Psychopaths fail to automatically take the perspective of others. *PNAS, 115*, 3302–3307.

Dziobek, I., Fleck, S., Kalbe, E., Rogers, K., Hassenstab, J., Brand, M., Kessler, J., Woike, J.K., Wolf, O.T., & Covit, A. 2006. Introducing MASC: A movie for the assessment of social cognition. *Journal of Autism and Developmental Disorders, 36*, 623–636.

Eccleston, C. & Crombez, G. 1999. Pain demands attention: A cognitive-affective model of the interruptive function of pain. *Psychological Bulletin, 125*, 356–366.

Feder, D., Ressler, K.J., & Germine, L.T. 2019. Social cognition or social class and culture? On the interpretation of differences in social cognitive performance. *Psychological Medicine*, doi:10.1017/S003329171800404X.

Gao, Y., Raine, A., & Schug, R.A. 2012. Somatic aphasia: Mismatch of body sensations with autonomic stress reactivity in psychopathy. *Biological Psychology, 90*, 228–233.

Gibbon, J. 2015. Meeting the extraordinary Cameron. *Behind the Scenes Blog, PBS.* November 16, 2015. http://www.pbs.org/the-brain-with-david-eagleman/ blogs/behind-the-scenes-blog/meeting-the-extraordinary-cameron.

Golan, O., Baron-Cohen, S., Hill, J.J., & Golan, Y. 2008. The reading the eyes in the film task (child version): Complex emotion and mental state recognition in children with and without autism spectrum conditions. *Journal of Autism and Developmental Disorders,* 28, 1534–1541.

Grandin, T. 1995. *Thinking in Pictures and Other Reports from My Life with Autism.* New York: Doubleday.

Grandin, T. & Barron, S. 2005. *The Unwritten Rules of Social Relationships.* Arlington,TX: Future Horizons, Inc.

Grossi, G. & Fine, C. 2012. The role of fetal testosterone in the development of the "essential difference" between the sexes: Some essential issues. In: R. Bluhm, A.J. Jacobson, & H.L. Maibom (Eds.) *Neurofemimism: Issues at the Intersection of Feminist Theory and Cognitive Science.* New York: Palgrave, 73–104.

Guo, X., Song, P., Zhao, H., Zhang, F., Wang, Q.-L., Sun, X.-M., Yin, H.-B., Zhang, Z., & Yang, B. 2017. Fear facial emotion recognition characteristics of psychopathic violent offenders. *Chinese Journal of Clinical Psychology,* 25, 591–596.

Happé, F.G.E. 1995. The role of age and verbal ability in the theory of mind task performance of subjects with autism. *Child Development,* 66, 843–855.

Hare, R. 2004. *The Hare Psychopathy Checklist-Revised* (2nd Ed.). Toronto: Mental Health Services.

Helt, M.S., Fein, D.A., & Vargas, J.E. 2019. Emotional contagion in children with autism spectrum disorder varies with stimulus familiarity and task instructions. *Developmental Psychopathology,* March 29, 2019.

Herpertz, S.C., Werth, U., Lukas, G., Qunaibi, M., Schuerkens, A., Kunert, H. J., Freese, R., Flesch, M., Mueller-Isberner, R., Osterheider, M., & Sass, H. 2001. Emotion in criminal offenders with psychopathy and borderline personality disorder. *Archives of General Psychiatry,* 58, 737–745.

Hill, E., Berthoz, S., & Frith, U. 2004. Brief report: Cognitive processing of own emotions in individuals with autistic spectrum disorder and in their relatives. *Journal of Autism and Developmental Disorders,* 34, 229–235.

Hobson, R.P. & Hobson, J.A. 2014. On empathy: A perspective from developmental psychopathology. In: H.L. Maibom (Ed.) *Empathy and Morality.* New York: Oxford University Press, 172–192.

Holopainen, A., de Veld, D.M.J., Hoddenbach, E., & Begeer, S. 2019. Does theory of mind training enhance empathy in autism? *Journal of Autism and Developmental Disorders*, 49, 3965–3972.

Ickes, W., Buysse, A., Pham, J., Rivers, K., Erickson, J., Hancock, M., Kelleher, J., & Gesn, P. 2000. On the difficulty of distinguishing "good' and "poor" perceivers: A social relationships analysis of empathic accuracy data. *Personal Relationships*, 7, 219–234.

Iria, C. & Barbosa, F. 2009. Perception of facial expressions of fear: Comparative research with criminal and non-criminal psychopaths. *Journal of Forensic Psychiatry & Psychology*, 20, 66–73.

Jameel, L., Vyas, K., Bellesi, G., Roberts, V., & Channon, S. 2014. Going 'above and beyond': Are those high in autistic traits less pro-social? *Journal of Autism and Developmental Disorders*, 44, 1846–1858.

Joel, D., Persico, A., Salhov, M., Berman, Z., Oligschläger, S., Meilijson, I., & Averbuch, A. 2018. Analysis of human brain structure reveals that brain "types" typical of males are also typical of females, and vice versa. *Frontiers of Human Neuroscience*, October 2018. https://doi.org/10.3389/fnhum.2018.00399.

Jones, A.P., Happé, F.G.E., Gilber, F., Burnett, S., & Viding, E. 2010. Feeling, caring, knowing: Different types of empathy deficit in boys with psychopathic tendencies and autistic spectrum disorder. *Journal of Child Psychology and Psychiatry*, 51, 1188–1197.

Kanne, S.M. & Mazurek, M.O. 2011. Aggression in children and adolescents with ASD: Prevalence and risk factors. *Journal of Autism and Developmental Disorders*, 41, 926–937.

Kauppinen, A. 2014. Empathy: Emotion regulation, and moral judgment. In: H.L. Maibom (Ed.) *Empathy and Morality*. New York: Oxford University Press, 97–121.

Kennett, J. 2002. Autism, empathy, and moral agency. *Philosophical Quarterly*, 52, 340–357.

Kiehl, K.A. & Lushing, J. 2014. Psychopathy. *Scholarpedia*, 9, 30835.

Leekam, S.R., Hunnisett, E., & Moore, C. 1998. Targets and cues: Gaze-following in children with autism. *Journal of Child Psychology and Psychiatry and Allied Disciplines*, 39, 951–962.

Levenston, G., Patrick, C., Bradley, M., & Lang, P. 2000. The psychopath as observer: Emotion and attention in picture processing. *Journal of Abnormal Psychology*, 109, 373–385.

Levy, N. 2004. Understanding blindness. *Phenomenology and the Cognitive Sciences*, 3, 315–324.

Lishner, D.A., Hong, P.Y., Jiang, L., Vitacco, M.J., & Neuman, C. 2015. Psychopathy, narcissism and borderline personality: A critical test of the affective empathy-impairment hypothesis. *Personality and Individual Differences*, 257–265.

Lykken, D. 1957. A study of anxiety in the sociopathic personality. *Journal of Abnormal and Social Psychology*, 55, 6–10.

Maibom, H.L. 2008. The mad, the bad, and the psychopath. *Neuroethics*, 1, 167–184.

Maibom, H.L. 2017. Shame and necessity redux. In: K. Bauer, S. Varga, & C. Mieth (Eds.) *Dimensions of Practical Necessity*. New York: Routledge.

Maibom, H.L. Forthcoming. Responsibility in the age of neuroscience: Moral understanding and empathy in psychopaths. In: J. Doris & M. Vargas (Eds.) *Oxford Handbook of Moral Psychology*. Oxford: Oxford University Press.

Marsh, A. 2014. Empathic and moral deficits in psychopathy. In: H.L. Maibom (Ed.) *Empathy and Morality*. New York: Oxford University Press, 138–154.

Marshall, K. & Marapodi, E. 2009. Born with half a brain, woman leading full life. *CNN*, October 12, 2009. http://www.cnn.com/2009/HEALTH/10/12/woman.brain/index.html.

Mathersul, D., McDonald, S., & Rushby, J.A. 2013. Understanding advanced theory of mind and empathy in high-functioning adults with autism spectrum disorder. *Journal of Clinical and Experimental Neuropsychology*, 35, 655–668.

Mazurek, M.O., Kanne, S.M., & Wodka, E.L. 2013. Physical aggression in children and adolescents with autism spectrum disorders. *Research in Autism Spectrum Disorders*, 7, 455–465.

McGeer, V. 2008. Varieties of moral agency: Lessons from autism (and psychopathy). In: W. Sinnott-Armstrong (Ed.) *Moral Psychology, Volume 3: The Neuroscience of Morality: Emotion, Brain Disorders, and Development*. Cambridge, MA: MIT Press, 227–257.

Meffert, H., Gazzola, V., den Boer, J.A., Bartels, A.A.J., & Keysers, C. 2013. Reduced spontaneous but relatively normal deliberate vicarious representations in psychopathy. *Brain*, 136, 2550–2562.

Moulton, B. & Spence, S.H. 1992. Site-specific muscle hyper-reactivity in musicians with occupational upper limb pain. *Behaviour Research and Therapy*, 30, 375–386.

Mul, C-I., Stagg, S.D., Herbelin, B., & Aspell, J.E. 2018. The feeling of me feeling for you: Interoception, alexithymia, and empathy in autism. *Journal of Autism and Developmental Disorders*, 48, 2953–2967.

Mullins-Nelson, J.L., Salekin, R.T., & Leistico, A-M.R. 2006. Psychopathy, empathy, and perspective taking ability in a community sample: Implications for the successful psychopath concept. *Journal of Forensic Mental Health*, 5, 133–149.

Newman, J.P. & Kosson, D.S. 1986. Passive avoidance learning in psychopathic and nonpsychopathic offenders. *Journal of Abnormal Psychology*, 95, 252–256.

Newman, J.P., Patterson, C.M., & Kosson, D.S. 1987. Response perseveration in psychopaths. *Journal of Abnormal Psychology*, 96, 145–148.

Peñuela-Calvo, I., Sareen, A., Sevilla-Llewellyn-Jones, J., & Férnandez-Berrocal, P. 2019. The "Reading the Mind in the Eyes" test in autism-spectrum disorders comparison with healthy controls: A systematic review and meta-analysis. *Journal of Autism and Developmental Disorders*, 49, 1048–1061.

Pera-Guardiola, V., Contreras-Rodríguez, O., Batalla, I., Kosson, D., Menchón, J.M., Pifarré, J., Bosque, J., Cardoner, N., & Soriano-Mas, C. 2016. Brain structural correlates of emotion recognition in psychopaths. *PLoS ONE*, 11, May 13.

Peterson, C. 2014. Theory of mind understanding and empathic behaviour in children with autism spectrum disorders. *International Journal of Developmental Neuroscience*, 39, 16–21.

Rehfelt, R.A., Dillen, J.E., Ziomek, M.M., & Kowalchuk, R.K. 2007. Assessing relational learning deficits in perspective-taking in children with high-functioning autism spectrum disorder. *The Psychological Record*, 57, 23–47.

Richell, R., Mitchell, D., Newman, C., Leonard, A., Baron-Cohen, S., & Blair, R.J.R. 2003. Theory of mind and psychopathy: Can psychopathic individuals read the language of the eyes? *Neuropsychologia*, 41, 523–526.

Rimm, D.C. & Litvak, S.B. 1969. Self-verbalization and emotional arousal. *Journal of Abnormal Psychology*, 74, 181–187.

Robison, J.E. 2008. *Look Me in the Eye: My Life with Asperger's*. New York: Broadway Books.

Roeyers, H. & Demurie, E. 2010. How impaired is mind-reading in high-functioning adolescents and adults with autism. *European Journal of Developmental Psychology*, 7, 123–134.

Rogers, K., Dzobiek, I., Hassenstab, J., Wolf, O.T., & Convit, A. 2007. Who cares? Revisiting empathy in Asperger syndrome. *Journal of Autism and Developmental Disorders*, 37, 709–715.

Sacks, O. 1995. *An Anthropologist on Mars.* New York: Picador.

Senju, A., Tojo, Y., Dairoku, H., & Hashegawa, T. 2004. Reflexive orienting in response to eye gaze and an arrow in children with and without autism. *Journal of Child Psychology and Psychiatry,* 45, 445–458.

Shah, P., Livingston, L.A., Callan, M.J., & Player, L. 2019. Trait autism is a better predictor of empathy than alexithymia. *Journal of Autism and Developmental Disorders,* 49, 3956–3964.

Shamay-Tsoory, S., Harari, H., Aharon-Perez, J., & Levkovich, Y. 2010. The role of orbitofrontal cortex in affective theory of mind deficits in criminal offenders with psychopathic tendencies. *Cortex,* 46, 668–677.

Simon, D., Craig, K.D., Miltner, W.H.R., & Rainville, P. 2006. Brain responses to dynamic facial expressions of pain. *Pain,* 126, 309–318.

Sinclair, S., Hardin, C.D., & Lowery, B.S. 2006. Self-stereotyping in the context of multiple social identities. *Journal of Personality and Social Psychology,* 90, 529–542.

Singer, T. & Tusche, A. 2014. Understanding others: Brain mechanisms of theory of mind and empathy. In: P.W. Glimcher & E. Fehr (Eds.) *Neuroeconomics* (2nd Ed.). Waltham, MA: Academic Press, 513–532.

Solomon, A. 2014. The reckoning: The father of the Sandy Hook killer searches for answers. *The New Yorker,* March 10, 2014.

Sullivan, M.O., Gallagher, L., & Heron, E.A. 2019. Gaining insight into aggressive behavior in autism spectrum disorder using latent profile analysis. *Journal of Autism and Developmental Disorders,* 49, 4209–4218.

Szasz, T. 1961. *The Myth of Mental Illness.* New York: Harper & Row.

Travis, L., Sigman, M., & Ruskin, E. 2001. Links between social understanding and social behavior in verbally able children with autism. *Journal of Autism and Developmental Disorders,* 31, 119–130.

Trimmer, E., McDonald, S., & Rushby, J.A. 2016. Not knowing what I feel: Emotional empathy in autism spectrum disorders. *Autism,* 21, 450–457.

von Borries, A.K.L., Volman, I., de Bruijn, E.R.A., Bulten, B.H., Vertes, R.J., & Roelofs, K. 2012. Psychopaths lack the autonomic avoidance of social threat: Relation to instrumental aggression. *Psychiatry Research,* 200, 761–766.

Yirmaya, N., Sigman, M.D., Kasari, C. & Mundy, P. 1992. Empathy and cognition in high-functioning children with autism. *Child Development,* 63, 150–160.

7

THE FUTURE OF EMPATHY STUDIES

Yes, I know. This is a rather grand title for a chapter. But let's be bold and see where that takes us. We have explored the state of the art of empathy research, with a primary focus on philosophy. Nonetheless, we have kept an eye on empirical work, not only because this is clearly relevant to any speculation on a topic but also because empathy is particularly popular with empirically minded philosophers. It is now time to look ahead. What are fertile areas for research in empathy, and where might such studies take us? In this chapter, I give you my ideas about this, although I have hinted at them in earlier chapters. I'll explain why I think the avenues of thought I suggest are exciting and promising.

§7.1 The empathy process

One of my criticisms of empathy research in previous chapters was that it often seems to regard empathy as a *state*. Of course, I don't actually think that researchers think empathy is a momentary event, exactly. But the way that it is examined and talked about betrays an underlying assumption about it being a relatively distinct state (or set of states) that is well explored without considering other psychological phenomena that co-occur with it, cause it, contribute to it, or are the result of it. Although I have talked about empathy this way too, I think it is better regarded as a process. More precisely, I think we should take seriously the idea that empathy—by which I mean all forms of affectively feeling with or for others—is a process and study it *as such*. Empathy being a process is *why* there is so much confusion about what is, and what is not, empathy 'proper'. The fact is that all the events that I have discussed in this book are closely related and can form part of the very same process. Our understanding of empathy is bound to be impoverished if we don't take a more holistic approach towards studying it.

How are we going to do this, more precisely? If we are going to do experiments, we should focus on exploring the subject's experiences several times *during* an empathic process. Here the studies of Carrera and colleagues serve as a model (Carrera et al. 2013). We need to get a sense of what a subject is feeling *and* thinking at different points during the episode. I'm not saying that's going to be easy as an experimental set-up. But it is possible. One might, for instance, provide the subject with various ways to continue engaging with the target.

From a philosophical perspective, we need to start thinking more in terms of mental *events* rather than mental *states*. Now you might justifiably ask: what do you mean? After all, philosophers are careful to specify the causes and effects of any mental state. What more could you want? What more could there be to it, other than it being stretched out more in time than the term 'state' suggests? That is, indeed, an excellent question.

One might argue that there really is no such thing as a *mental state*. It is pure fiction, perhaps created by our linguistically focused minds. Take something like Jerry Fodor's language of thought hypothesis, according to which thoughts are sentences in a language of thought tokened in the mind. This certainly provides a solution to a number of puzzling issues about the mind. It forms part of a nice logical solution. The only problem is that it is unlikely that anything in reality corresponds to it. Why? Beliefs only make sense against the background of many other beliefs; concepts may differ from person to person; and one's propensity to experience certain emotions depends on one's previous experiences and what other emotions one might feel at the time. In other words, the state of the organism plays a crucial role in determining what thoughts will occur, how they unfold, what is felt, and so on. To put the point more vividly, you cannot take a sentence in a language of thought and put it into someone else's mind and have it mean the very same thing without also holding lots of other things about the two individuals constant. What is needed is a more holistic picture of the workings of the mind.

This type of response attacks the way philosophy of mind has conceived of the mind for many decades. I'm sympathetic to this attack, but the point that I want to make here is more modest. Emotions are events that unfold over time. Whereas a thought can occur pretty suddenly and quickly be displaced by another, emotions linger, and in lingering they often develop. How? In response to thoughts about why one is feeling as one does, for instance. Is there a difference in principle between emotions and other mental events that have little or no affective quality to them, such as thoughts? I don't know. But I will bet on emotions being extended in time in a way that requires special analysis. I'm not alone in thinking this. Robinson (2005) suggests the same. Emotions are not usefully thought of as states.

In Chapter 3, I talked about emotion regulation and its importance to the empathic process. I was relying on some of the work done by Nancy Eisenberg, who has long been interested in thinking about empathy as a process. Her insight is that our empathic experience is partly a function of other, more executive processes. The strength of what we feel can be manipulated, and the way we conceive the emotion, its cause, or our ability to act on it affects how it develops. For instance, if the affect is very strong and we focus on how badly a situation makes us feel, empathic distress may turn personal. But our ability to manage our emotions is only one part of the puzzle. People's characters are also important. To this, we might add moral ideals and experiences. For instance, ultra-conservatives are presumably able to experience empathy, but they don't think welfare is particularly important compared to other moral ideals, such as purity, in-group loyalty, or authority (Graham, Haidt, & Nosek 2009). As a result, they score like psychopaths on harm and fairness considerations, which is to say abnormally low. I will bet good money on their empathic response being modulated accordingly. If that is right, it is another indication that we cannot understand the empathic process in isolation from such factors.

If we look at things this way, it immediately becomes clear that more reductive accounts of empathy's role in morality are problematic. Consider, for instance, the following troubling fact. Psychopaths respond normally to people who suffer initially, then their response dies down. This later response is under conscious control. Decety has compared it to the response doctors have to seeing people undergoing painful injections. But although there are certainly a fair number of callous and insensitive doctors, they do not regard other people as pure instruments to satisfy their own needs and wants, as psychopaths appear to. What explains that? There must be something else that differentiates the two. Now we might say that whereas doctors *care* about other people, psychopaths don't. But psychopaths are supposed to not care about others *because* of their deficient empathy. You see where I'm going with this? We appear to be explaining lack of care in terms of lack of empathy, and lack of empathy in terms of lack of care. The best way out of the circularity, it seems to me, is to identify something about the particular psychological constellation present in psychopathy, which will account for the difference. No matter what it turns out to be, it will be something we only find once we look beyond empathy-as-a-state.

In short, I think much knowledge can be gained from thinking about empathy in terms of an extended process that is capable of significant change over time. The best work, at the moment, on this idea is that of Eisenberg, but the idea has not been taken up much by other researchers in the field.

§7.2 Empathy = fear and avoidance?

For researchers in moral psychology, the fact that psychopaths' lacking empathic distress is based on a deficient defensive response is a juicy piece of information. It encourages a *very* different way of thinking about how empathy contributes to our moral outlook. The response appears to be relatively primitive. It is an immediate orienting towards a person who is suffering or threatened, along with a sudden ramping up of fear and defensiveness. As we saw, psychopaths are good at ramping down this response quickly, but in ordinary people it continues to unfold. They remain focused on the target *and* experience a significant amount of shock and fear. How can a response like this help us develop our moral psychology?

I think there is a real possibility that it is in this defensive response that we find an appreciation of why pain in others is bad. It is not that we refer their pain back to ourselves by some form of analogy. That is, we do not go through the following inferential process. Pain is bad for me; this is another person just like me; that person is in pain; therefore, that pain is bad for her. Rather, we respond immediately to her pain with affect that is not unlike the stressed response we ourselves have to pain. It is as if she were part of our own selves. Our defensive care for ourselves is extended to the other in this particular response. We are on 'code red,' as it were. Put differently, we experience *directly* that others' pain is bad by means of this process.

But if another's pain makes *me* feel bad, is that not simply personal distress? And isn't personal distress *bad*? Recall that Batson thinks personal distress leads to egoistic motivation. In his studies, this emotion often caused people to leave the person in need in the lurch, as it were. Even though this distress is *caused* by another person's affect or situation, Batson calls it 'personal' because: a) we feel about the same amount of distress for ourselves and for the other and b) we are more likely to escape the upsetting situation than we are to help the person in need (if escape is easy). I indicated earlier that I think Batson is wrong to call this affective response 'personal' instead of 'empathic.' It is neither purely *personal*, because it is also felt as for the other person, nor does it invariably cause people who experience it to escape the distressing situation if it is easy to do so. A sizeable number of people who feel significant personal distress help the person in need when escape is easy, and when escape is hard, distressed people help as much as people experiencing a preponderance of empathic concern/sympathy. This type of distress, then, really does seem different from purely personal distress. Otherwise, why would people stay to help the person in need at all?

If this reasoning is correct, we should rethink the category of personal distress in psychology. Briefly put, if you study the empathy literature in psychology, you often find no mention of the category that philosophers call 'empathy.' Instead, empathic concern is conceptualized as sympathy, and the only distress emotion is 'personal.' On my proposal, personal distress is the closest we get to the empathy that is missing in action. Purely personal distress would not count as empathic, but only distress that includes as its object the other person.

Alright, you might say. Let us suppose that psychologists are guilty of giving empathic distress the wrong name, thereby distorting what it is really about. But are they not right that distress experienced when another is in need is counterproductive to helping him or her? Yes and no. Let's start with the 'no.' Personal distress is not *counterproductive*; it is just less productive than sympathy is when it comes to helping another in need. Batson consistently found that when it was hard to escape a situation where people are exposed to another's suffering, those who experienced more distress than sympathy were as likely to help as were those who experienced more sympathy than distress. It is only when it is easy to escape the situation, where one is exposed to the other in distress, that (a preponderance of) distress is less helpful than (a preponderance of) sympathy. This takes us to the 'yes' part. There is no denying this data. Even if the *object* of the distress is mixed between self and other, the motivation to relieve the distress the person feels, when not appropriately counterbalanced by sympathy, tends to tip the scales in favor of the subject relieving *herself* of her distress. When it comes to people's *dispositions*, the picture is even worse, it seems. Because here personal distress, as measured by something like the IRI, is often *negatively* correlated with many of the things that empathy is supposed to be good for. I take this to be the more serious problem. And it is something that merits further investigation.

For now, we can make the following observations. Dispositional measures of empathy are based mainly on self-reports, which are notoriously fallible. More importantly, the way that distress is described on many empathy measures may not capture the normal distress element in being exposed to others in pain or distress. For instance, if we list *all* the items classified as relating to personal distress on the *Interpersonal Reactivity Index* we find that a number of them are quite puzzling (Davis 1980). (Note that 'reverse coded' means that if you score high on this factor, it is a sign that you are *not* liable to being personally distressed.)

1.   In emergency situations, I feel apprehensive and ill-at-ease.
2.   I sometimes feel helpless when I am in the middle of a very emotional situation.
3.   When I see someone get hurt, I tend to remain calm. (Reverse coded)
4.   Being in a tense emotional situation scares me.
5.   I am usually pretty effective in dealing with emergencies. (Reverse coded)
6.   I tend to lose control during emergencies.
7.   When I see someone who badly needs help in an emergency, I go to pieces.

This sort of measures distress. But what kind of distress? Four out of the seven questions have the word 'emergency' in them (6, 19, 24, 27). Needless to say—but I will say it nonetheless—emergencies are extreme situations. Most of the time when we feel distressed with and for others, the situation is less severe; someone has been hurt, is in need, or is upset.

Most of my own empathic distress is felt in those situations. This means that IRI mostly measures reactions to unusual and extreme situations. This may not get you good data about what happens in more ordinary situations.

Even supposing that people are more likely to get flooded by distress in emergency situations, as both Eisenberg and Hoffman believe, it is not exactly clear what the connection is with being unable to deal with it (Eisenberg & Fabes 1992, Hoffman 2000). Perhaps a person who does not know what to do in such a situation is not flooded with distress but just doesn't know how to go about helping. If that is right, what is measured is not distress but knowing how to deal with emergency situations. Moving on to the other items, two simply talk of 'emotional situations,' which may have nothing to do with another's pain or distress (10, 17). And one item concerns being calm when someone gets hurt, but reverse coded, which is surely a weird (non)reaction to have (13). To be honest, I'm not sure what to make of it. My hunch is that whatever IRI-PD measures, it is at best an extreme form of empathic distress and at worst not empathic distress at all. It is certainly not a clean way of testing for a person's tendency to find another's distress distressing.

Adding to this concern is the fact that people with ASD often score high on personal distress on measures like the IRI (e.g. Aaron, Benson, & Park 2015, Senland & Higgins-D'Alessandro 2013). My own view is that this likely has to do with a certain emotional unpreparedness to deal with other people who are in need of help. Given what else we know of ASD, we have reason not to interpret it as their not caring about what happens to other people. In other words, a high score of IRI-PD may not itself be a sign that a person has an egoistic orientation towards others. And the fact that there are some discouraging correlations between personal distress and antisocial tendencies should not make us give up on the suggestion that empathic distress is central to moral functioning. A further exploration of what to make of this component of empathy is in order.

What we learn from contrasting psychopaths' responses to others' distress with that of ordinary people is yet another reason to suspect that distress at another's distress should not simply be understood as being 'personal' or 'egoistic,' and therefore presumably morally irrelevant. Recall that psychopaths appear to suppress their full empathic response to others in pain or distress. The fact that the later part of the response can be suppressed in the first place is what is interesting, and it should lead us to wonder why ordinary people do not do as psychopaths. This would give us an extra clue to help us disentangle this central human response. At this point, we are left with speculation. But here are some avenues worth exploring.

Doctors respond as psychopaths do when shown pictures of people getting painful injections. Presumably, they have been desensitized due to their giving such injections themselves. Their desensitization is manifested by a controlled inhibition of their affective reactions. Now, it is undoubtedly true that many psychopaths have been desensitized to others' pain and distress in much the way doctors have. But not all psychopaths are violent, and so we cannot simply draw a straight parallel here. What else might be going on? Elsewhere, I have suggested that psychopaths may not find others' distress particularly interesting, and so although they find themselves initially riveted by it, they do not continue to be so (Maibom forthcoming). But there are other, just as plausible, interpretations. The empathic response described is clearly unpleasant. Escaping the original cause of that response would therefore seem attractive for the very simple reason that it would reduce the displeasure. And so we should expect anybody who experiences this type of distress at another's distress to be at least partially motivated to escape the upsetting situation. As we know from the PCL-R, psychopaths are *very* selfish. And it may be this that is the real underlying factor. It is not simply that they have no interest in others' pain. But the fact is that paying attention to it is itself a noxious experience, so why go there if you can avoid it? I think spending more time disentangling the overriding response in psychopaths will help us understand much more about ordinary human moral psychology.

If we allow ourselves to speculate for now and suppose that psychopaths don't want to feel bad for no reason, this actually does show something about ordinary human responses to others in need. The fact that it is unpleasant to be faced with another's distress is not sufficient—at least not when they are in the laboratory—to make your average person suppress *his* response. The bad press regarding personal distress notwithstanding, someone so distressed remains engaged with the other person's hurt. This in itself ought to be a sign of the importance that is assigned to others' suffering.

Another point in favor of a more favorable view of the role of distress in morality comes from considering what was likely its original function. As I suggested in Chapter 3, empathy may well have evolved because it is adaptive for group animals to be sensitive to at least certain types of affect in other members of the group. At the top of this list are fear, pain, distress, and anger. If this is right, then the adaptive roots of empathy have little to do with caring about other members of the group per se. But neither does parental concern for offspring. Both tendencies are clearly selfish in an evolutionary sense. Yet, we would be hard-pressed to call a mother's love for her child selfish. Elliott Sober and David Sloan Wilson (1998) rightly distinguish between what they call egoism at the level of evolution and egoism at the level of the individual. Parental love may be selfish in the first sense and yet lead to extraordinary acts of unselfish behavior, motivated by an ultimate desire for the welfare of the child. With this in mind, we can ask ourselves what the significance is of our sensitivity to what (relevant) others feel. What we see, I think, is that our sensitivity signals that the welfare of relevant others is *directly relevant to our own welfare*. As such, our responses to what others are going through is quite like our responses to what we are going through—at least when we empathize. And this is really quite extraordinary, if you think about it. What more could we want from a moral emotion?

These reflections just scratch the surface of what we might make of empathic responding to others' distress in particular. It is something well worth exploring further.

§7.3 Other overlooked features of empathy: perspectives and sharing

There are two other empathy-related issues that I think deserve more attention than they have received. These are the nature of a psychological perspective and what sharing in empathy amounts to. As it is time to wrap up, I just briefly mention what those issues are here, without attempting to offer solutions.

There is a lot of talk about perspective taking, but there are actually precious few studies of what, exactly, it consists of and its precise effects on the way a person thinks. Bertram Malle is one of the few psychologists who has systematically explored what a first-person and a third-person perspective consists of (he calls them 'actor' and 'observer' perspectives). And perspective taking is the topic of my upcoming book (Maibom manuscript). What I do is collect evidence from disparate fields, suggesting that there are well-defined formal differences in the way that one regards things from two different perspectives. But much more work can be done in exploring more complex attributions. As I mentioned in Chapter 2, when Malle did ask someone to take another person's perspective, he did not find that the resultant psychological ascriptions characterized an actor perspective, although they didn't quite characterize an observer perspective either. We need better studies to determine what a psychological perspective is—precisely, what are the effects of changing it? Without this, how do we know that the effects we find perspective taking has—e.g. reduced stereotyping—is not due to something *other* than the shift in perspective?

Last, but not least, we have the issue about sharing in empathy. As discussed in Chapter 3, sharing is a thorny issue in empathy research. On the one hand, almost everybody agrees that empathy involves sharing in some sense. On the other, almost everyone also thinks that empathy involves a clear self-other differentiation. This can easily create tension. Most agree that when I empathize with your joy I experience joy empathically. Moreover, I *share* your joy. But how? By my feeling joy. But if so, am I not just feeling my own joy and you are feeling your joy? I cannot, in any case, feel *your* joy without *feeling it myself*, in which case it is *also* my joy (at the very least). Things seem to get confusing fast.

We could, of course, have one without the other. But nobody seems to like that solution very much. Why not? Suppose we get sharing but no differentiation. In that case, it would seem there would be no empathy. For we would be feeling what we are feeling with no difference between feeling for ourselves, as it were, and feeling it for or with someone else. Suppose, on the other hand, we get self-other differentiation but no sharing. Where, then, is empathy? Scheler (1912/2008) insists that we only ever feel our own emotion and that 'real' empathy, as we have conceived of it in this book, is an illusion. We can never truly share what another feels, he says. But this seems like giving up on empathy altogether. Others, such as Zahavi and Rochat (2015), maintain that sharing requires reciprocal awareness that each is trying to take the other's perspective, or is attempting to feel what the other feels. This activity, however, is itself *based on* self-other differentiation. But Zahavi and Rochat's proposal requires more than we typically think is necessary for empathy. After all, we frequently empathize with people who are unaware that we are doing so. How to solve this conundrum is an important question for anyone working on empathy.

§7.4 Take-home message

It is time to end. I hope you have enjoyed this tour of empathy and empathy-related phenomena. You should now be in a good position to know what the major issues in this research are. You will also have a sense of what some of the main theories are and who some of the people are that work on empathy, particularly in philosophy and psychology. What is left out, you will have to explore on your own. But the many references to further readings should put you on the right track to exploring empathy further.

In this last chapter, I gave you my own ideas about some of the central issues in empathy research that deserve further exploration. I talked about how exploring the empathic *process* will improve our understanding and possibly unify the field. I discussed how to interpret the empathic response to others in need and its relation to the psychological construct of 'personal distress'. Lastly, I raised the issues concerning what a psychological perspective really is and what sharing amounts to, suggesting that these questions are important to answer; you might find that you are inspired to do so. I know I am. So, let's get cracking!

References

Aaron, R.V., Benson, T.L., & Park, S. 2015. Investigating the role of alexithymia on empathy deficits found in schizotypy and autism spectrum traits. *Personality and Individual Differences*, 77, 215–220.

Batson, C.D. 2011. *Altruism in Humans*. Oxford: Oxford University Press.

Carrera, P., Oceja, L., Caballero, A., Muñoz, D., López-Pérez, B., & Ambrona, T. 2013. I feel so sorry! Tapping the joint influence of empathy and personal distress on helping behavior. *Motivation and Emotion*, 37, 335–345.

Davis, M.H. 1980. A multidimensional approach to individual differences in empathy. *JSAS Catalog of Selected Documents in Psychology*, 10, 85.

Eisenberg, N. & Fabes, R.A. 1992. Emotions, regulation, and the development of social competence. *Review of Personality and Social Behavior*, 14, 119–150.

Graham, J., Haidt, J., & Nosek, B.A. 2009. Liberals and conservatives rely on different sets of moral foundations. *Journal of Personality and Social Psychology*, 96, 1029–1046.

Hoffman, M. 2000. *Empathy and Moral Development: Implications for Caring and Justice*. New York: Cambridge University Press.

Maibom, H.L. Forthcoming. Responsibility in the age of neuroscience: Moral understanding and empathy in psychopaths. In: J. Doris & M. Vargas (Eds.) *Oxford Handbook of Moral Psychology*. Oxford: Oxford University Press.

Maibom, H.L. Manuscript. *Knowing Me, Knowing You.*

Robinson, J. 2005. *Deeper than Reason: Emotion and its Role in Literature, Music, and Art*. Oxford: Oxford University Press.

Scheler, M. 1912/2008. *The Nature of Sympathy.* P. Heath (Trans.). New Brunswick, NJ: Transaction Publishers.

Senland, A.K. & Higgins-D'Alessandro, A. 2013. Moral reasoning in adolescents with autism spectrum disorder: Implications for moral education. *Journal of Moral Education,* 42, 209–223.

Sober, E. & Wilson, D.S. 1998. *Unto Others.* Cambridge, MA: Harvard University Press.

Zahavi, D. & Rochat, P. 2015. Empathy ≠ sharing: Perspectives from phenomenology and developmental psychology. *Consciousness and Cognition,* 36, 543–553.

GLOSSARY

ACC see anterior cingulate cortex.

Affective empathy empathy with another that necessarily involves affect. It is typically thought to involve experiencing what the target experiences *because* she experiences what she experiences. It involves at least emotion matching and self-other differentiation. Some think it also involves perspective taking.

AI see anterior insula.

Altruistic motivation motivation to do something for another person's sake, not simply for one's own.

Amygdala an almond-shaped cluster of neurons in the deeper parts of the middle of the temporal lobes. Is associated with the perception and processing of emotions, such as fear, sadness, anxiety, and happiness. Fear conditioning, appetitive learning, and reward are all functions that appear to be carried out by this system. It is one of the oldest parts of the brain.

Anterior cingulate cortex a frontal brain area (of the cingulate cortex) important for autonomic functions (blood pressure, heart rate), attention, reward, decision-making, and moral processing.

Anterior insula the biggest part of the insular cortex, closest to the front of the brain. Its function is associated with emotional awareness and bodily feelings.

Approbation approval. Both Hume and Smith used the term in the context of approving of the character or action of someone, usually in a morally pregnant sense.

Autism see Autism spectrum disorder.

Autism spectrum disorder a developmental disorder characterized by deficient theory of mind, poor interpersonal relating, constrained and repetitive play, impaired empathy, and often associated with severe verbal impairments and sensory abnormalities.

Behaviorism a school of psychology that eschewed the use of internal processes to explain behavior. Instead, attempts were made to provide explanations purely in terms of observable behavior and observable causes.

Bias a way of viewing things that is influenced, often unconsciously, by certain pre-conceived ideas or motivations.

Concern mechanism a psychological mechanism posited to explain why we experience concern when being exposed to need in others.

Cognitive empathy empathy that need not involve emotions and that primarily concerns some form of cognitive understanding of another. The terms is sometimes used broadly, so as to cover theory of mind and perspective taking, and sometimes more narrowly, so as to refer simply to perspective taking.

Diagnostic and Statistical Manual of Mental Disorders a manual published by *The American Psychiatric Association* to aid practitioners in diagnosing mental disorders. It is currently in its 5th edition (DSM-5).

Direct perception the perception of features of the environment which does not require sophisticated cognitive processing. Is often used to describe perception of relatively high-level features of the environment that were traditionally thought to require elaborate processing in order to be represented.

Disapprobation disapproval. Used by Hume and Smith to describe disapproval of another person's character or action, usually in a morally pregnant sense.

Dispositional empathy one's tendency to experience empathy in a variety of different situations.

DSM see Diagnostic and Statistical Manual of Mental Disorders.

Egoism the opposite of altruism; being concerned with or motivated by only what concerns oneself.

Einfühlung directly translated from German, it means 'feeling into.' Titchener translated it as 'empathy.' The idea played an important role in the German aesthetic tradition.

Embodied cognition cognition that involves the body. This contrasts with traditional attitudes to cognition, where this is thought to be mainly a matter of neural processes in the brain.

Emotion matching matching someone else's emotion with an emotion of one's own of the same kind.. An example is feeling sad when someone else is sad.

Empathic concern a term typically used in the psychology literature to mean what philosophers call 'sympathy.' It is a concerned reaction to a person in need. For someone like Batson, it is a cover term, which includes a number of more specific reactions, such as feeling concerned, compassionate, or warm-hearted.

Empathic overarousal arousal caused by exposure to another in need. It is very strong and, as a result, causes the person who experiences it to become overwhelmed.

Empathy sometimes used broadly to include a whole swath of different psychological reactions and processes, such as emotional contagion, affective empathy, cognitive empathy, sympathy, and perspective taking. When used more narrowly, it refers to either affective empathy or cognitive empathy.

Emotion regulation the regulating of one's emotions, typically in terms of strength. Most commonly used to describe a process whereby an emotional reaction is dampened.

Emotional contagion catching an emotion from another person by a process that is typically unconscious and yet is a response to perceptual cues (possibly also imaginative ones).

First-person perspective actor perspective, immersed perspective. It is the perspective that all sentient creatures occupy intuitively and naturally.

Folk psychology common sense psychology—i.e. the everyday practice of ascribing psychological states to oneself and others.

High-level simulation simulation that takes place at a conscious level. It involves imagining that one is in someone else's situation (perhaps: as them).

Imagine-other perspective taking imagining what it is like for another person to be in the situation that they are in. It may not actually involve switching one's perspective but just careful consideration of the other's situation using the standard tools of folk psychology (e.g. those of theory theory).

Imagine-self perspective taking imagining yourself in another person's situation with almost exclusive focus on how *you* would think and feel as a result. It is often thought of as a sort of elaborate projection. Nonetheless, it involves real perspective shifting.

Impartial spectator a fully informed observer who is not partisan to any one perspective. Most famously associated with the moral philosophy of Adam Smith.

INF see inferior frontal gyrus.

Inferior frontal gyrus the lower part of the gyrus, which is located at the front part of the brain. It is a central language processing area; e.g. Broca's area is located here. The right INF is also associated with impulse control and risk aversion.

Interpersonal Reactivity Index a famous psychological measure of dispositional empathy with four subscales: empathic concern, perspective taking, personal distress, and fantasy.

Introspection literally 'looking in.' It describes the act of gaining information about one's own mental states or processes more or less directly and not by means of thinking about oneself as one would about others.

IRI see Interpersonal Reactivity Index.

Low-level simulation simulation below the level of consciousness. Is sometimes thought to include such processes as the activation of mirror neurons.

Mental state attribution the act of attributing mental states to others, such as saying or thinking "he thinks the cat has eaten the fish," "she wants a beer," "they are quite angry" or "he went to the supermarket intending to buy food."

Mimicry intentionally mirroring someone.

Mirroring experiencing or expressing a psychological state in response to observing it in another. For example, smiling in response to someone smiling. It can also refer to bodily mirroring, such as the placement of one's arms or legs.

Mirror neurons neurons that fire *both* when the agent himself performs an action of a certain type, such as 'grasping,' *and* when someone else does.

Moral judgment a statement, belief, or affective reaction that may be described as judging something to be right or wrong, good or bad. For instance, "it was wrong for her to lie" or "he's a bad person."

Moral motivation motivation fueled by moral considerations or with moral content, such as motivation to act in accordance with one's moral principles, or to punish someone who has done moral wrong.

Moral perception direct perception of morally relevant facts.

PCL-R see Psychopathy Checklist-Revised.

Personal distress distress experienced directly and *for* the self, even if it is ultimately caused by the distress of others.

Perspective taking taking up a perspective other than the one that one currently inhabits. Typically, one can take a third-person perspective on oneself, or a first-person perspective on others.

Phenomenological tradition a philosophical school originating with Edmund Husserl, whose response to skeptical concerns about whether we can have real knowledge of the world was to bracket this concern and instead explore subjective experience.

Prosocial emotion similar to prosocial motivation, only it refers to emotion. These are emotions where others' wellbeing is part of their cause or their object. Examples include empathy and sympathy.

Prosocial motivation motivation that is social in nature, such as helping others. People tend to use this term to refer to motivation whose aim is to help others, without taking a stand on whether it is ultimately egoistic or altruistic.

Psychological state attribution see mental state attribution.

Psychopathy Checklist-Revised the most important psychiatric test of psychopathy.

Rationalism in ethics the position that morality rests in reason, not in emotion. This may mean that our moral judgments are purely cognitive, that our motivation derives directly from understanding that something is wrong, or something along those lines.

Reactive emotions emotions that are experienced in reaction to another person's emotions. Although empathic emotions are technically speaking reactive in this sense, reactive emotions are typically used to describe personally felt emotions, such as personal distress or anger.

Re-enactment an enactment of some thought, feeling, or other psychological state that has already been had or that might be had under certain circumstances either by the person herself or another person. It is most often used to describe the act of simulation.

Self-other differentiation in the empathy literature, it refers specifically to the understanding that although a person feels what she supposes the other feels, she is in no doubt as to who the target of the emotion is, namely the other.

Sentimentalism in ethics the position that morality rests in emotion, not reason. Typically, this means that moral judgments are emotional reactions, such as approving or disapproving emotions for Hume and Smith.

Simulation the simulating of a process. For instance, a computer simulation of a weather pattern, a flight simulation, or imagining how one would feel in a certain situation. The important part of a simulation is that it is a process that models a real-life process in a medium that is more contained, easier to control, and yet close enough to the other process to get good results.

Simulation theory a theory of the psychological underpinnings of our folk psychological practice. According to this theory, we simulate others so as to ascribe psychological states to them. More precisely, we imagine having certain beliefs and desires, imagine being in their situation, or imagine having acted as they did, and then 'see' how we would think, feel, or intend to act as a result. We then ascribe the result to them. To do well, we might sometimes have to imagine other things too, like being an alcoholic or liking bitter beers.

Situational empathy the empathy one actually feels in a particular situation. To be contrasted with dispositional empathy.

Sympathy feeling bad or sad for someone who is in a bad situation or is in need, or feeling happy for someone who is in a good situation.

Theory of mind folk psychology. It is the term most commonly used by psychologists and covers *both* theory theory and simulation.

Theory theory a theory of the psychological underpinnings of our folk psychological practice. According to this theory, we all have knowledge of generalizations or models of what people usually think, feel, want, and intend under different circumstances, how psychological states typically interact, and so on. We apply this theory when we ascribe psychological states to others.

Third-person perspective our immediate, nonreflective way of conceiving of people other than ourselves (perhaps also: and the ones we most closely identify with). Also: observer perspective. When we take a third-person perspective on ourselves, we regard ourselves as we would another, as 'from the outside.'

Violence inhibition mechanism a mechanism posited by Blair, according to which displays of fear and sadness cause an aggressor to desist from, or modify, their attack.

INDEX